BANNOCKBURN

Bannockburn

The Scottish War and the British Isles, 1307–1323

————

Michael Brown

EDINBURGH UNIVERSITY PRESS

Edinburgh University Press Ltd
22 George Square, Edinburgh

Typeset in Minion
by Servis Filmsetting Ltd, Stockport, Cheshire, and
printed and bound in Great Britain by
MPG Books Ltd, Bodmin, Cornwall

A CIP record for this book is available from the British Library

ISBN 978 0 7486 3332 6 (hardback)
ISBN 978 0 7486 3333 3 (paperback)

Michael Brown is supported by

 Arts & Humanities
Research Council

The AHRC funds postgraduate training and research in the arts and
humanities, from archaeology and English literature to design and
dance. The quality and range of research supported not only provides
social and cultural benefits but also contributes to the economic
success of the UK. For futher information on the AHRC, please see
www.ahrc.ac.uk

Contents

Illustrations

PLATES

Abbreviations

A.P.S.	*Acts of the Parliaments of Scotland*
B.B.C.S.	*Bulletin of the Board Celtic Studies*
C.C.R.	*Calendar of Close Rolls*
C.Ch.R.	*Calendar of Charter Rolls*
C.D.S.	*Calendar of Documents relating to Scotland*
Chrons. Edw. I and Edw. II	*Chronicles of the Reigns of Edward I and Edward II*, ed. W. Stubbs, 2 vols (Rolls Series, 1882–3)
C.P.L.	*Calendar of Papal Letters*
C.P.R.	*Calendar of Patent Rolls*
E.H.R.	*English Historical Review*
E.R.	*The Exchequer Rolls of Scotland*
Foedera	*Foedera, Conventiones, Litterae et Cuiuscunque Generis Acta Publica*, ed. T. Rymer, revised edition (London, 1816–69)
H.M.C.	*Historic Manuscripts Commission: Reports of the Commission on Historical Manuscripts*
I.H.S.	*Irish Historical Studies*
N.A.S.	National Archives of Scotland
R.M.S.	*Registrum Magni Sigilli Regum Scottorum*
R.R.S.	*Regesta Regum Scottorum, vol. v, The Acts of Robert I*
Rot. Scot.	*Rotuli Scotiae in Turri Londonensis et in Domo Capitulari Westmonasteriensi asservati*
S.H.R.	*Scottish Historical Review*
T.R.H.S.	*Transactions of the Royal Historical Society*
W.H.R.	*Welsh History Review*

Acknowledgements

The completion of this book has been greatly helped by a number of institutions and individuals. The University of St Andrews provided me with a period of leave which allowed me to undertake much of the writing. The completion of the book was made possible by the grant of funding for an additional semester of leave by the Arts and Humanities Research Council. The presentation of this volume has also benefited from the financial help of the Carnegie Trust for the Universities of Scotland and from the Strathmartine Trust, both of which provided generous assistance towards the illustrations included in the book. Production of this book has also been greatly helped by the efforts of Edinburgh University Press and, in particular, Vivian Bone and Esmé Watson, whose encouragement and patience have been of the highest order. Last but not least, I would like to thank Margaret, Robert and Isabelle, who have had to put up with a distracted and (occasionally) grumpy husband and father in their midst during the final stages of this book.

'The Most Victorious Battle of Bannockburn'

At Midsummer 1314 on the fields to the south-east of Stirling Castle the army of Edward II king of England faced a smaller host led by Robert Bruce king of Scots. This direct confrontation between the two kings marked the culmination of warfare waged by them and their supporters over the previous eight years. This fighting had seen Bruce win control of much of Scotland from his enemies. Now his claim to be king would be tested in open battle with his royal opponent, seen by contemporaries as a divine as well as earthly judgement of rights. At the head of a host of spearmen, fighting on foot, Robert's force inflicted a total defeat on an army which was not simply larger, but also contained two thousand armoured horsemen. This victory against the odds has been seen, from the fourteenth century onwards, as a central landmark in the history of Scotland. The victory of the Scottish army has often been presented as securing the independence of Scotland and has cemented Robert Bruce's place as the heroic leader of his people and has long been regarded as the climax of the Scottish wars of independence.

Bannockburn was both more and less than this popular view. Despite the scale of the Scottish victory and of the disaster that engulfed the English, Bannockburn did not decide the conflict between Bruce and Plantagenet. For all the drama of the great clash of armies and the praise and horror it drew from each side, Bannockburn was only one episode in an almost unbroken period of warfare which ran from 1307 to 1323. Its effect on this war was considerable. The battle ended the hard struggle between Robert and his enemies inside Scotland but, in the years which followed, the fighting would escalate and spread. These 'wars of the Bruces' would themselves only form part of a longer struggle, which had begun with Robert's seizure of the Scottish throne in 1306 and would ultimately outlast both Bruce and his English rival. It would be decades after Bannockburn before Scotland would be free from the threat of English conquest or absorption.

However, Bannockburn was a battle whose significance went well beyond Scotland. It is one of a group of later medieval battles whose reality and subsequent mythology acquired a special place in the identity of a nation. Bannockburn represented a victory against the odds for a small community facing defeat, subjection and loss of sovereignty at the hands of a more

1

powerful neighbouring realm. It had parallels with similar struggles in the thirteenth and fourteenth centuries in Flanders, Switzerland, Portugal, Brittany and elsewhere, and in the way in which battles involving these and greater realms were hailed as national triumphs by rulers and peoples. It was also a battle which resonated through the dominions of the English kings. The Scottish wars waged by these rulers from 1296 until the 1350s marked a major shift in the relationships between the peoples of the British Isles, and the road to, and from, Bannockburn had major implications for England, Ireland and Wales. The campaign of 1314 and the battle in which it resulted involved lords and men from not just Scotland and England, but from Wales, Ireland, the Western Isles and from the continent. The results of Edward's defeat had an impact on all these lands and played a part in both short- and long-term changes in the British Isles.

It is not surprising that, given its long-recognised importance, Bannockburn has been the subject of many detailed studies. Over the past century a plethora of works on the battle has been published. However, the focus of these books has been overwhelmingly on the military events of 1314, the location of the various phases of the battle on the modern landscape south of Stirling and the tactical successes and failures on the field.[1] Bannockburn has received much attention as an example of fourteenth-century warfare but to understand the battle and its consequences a wider examination of the warfare and politics of which it formed a part is essential. Attempts to consider this broader, political context of the battle are much more limited in number. Though Bannockburn has formed a set piece of Scottish historical writing since the days of Walter Scott and commands space and attention in both general accounts of Scottish history and in works which focused on the Scottish wars of the late thirteenth and early fourteenth centuries, full considerations of its place in broader developments remain relatively rare.[2] The best detailed account of Bannockburn which appreciates these political dimensions remains that of G. W. S. Barrow in his seminal and frequently reprinted study of *Robert Bruce and the Community of the Realm of Scotland*.[3] The most original new insights into the wars from 1306 to 1323 and into the events before Bannockburn have been provided by A. A. M. Duncan, especially in his notes to Barbour's *The Bruce* and his article 'The War of the Scots'.[4]

These studies are, however, from a Scottish perspective and, along with the predominantly military accounts, have encouraged a limited appreciation of Bannockburn's context and importance in the wider audience of students and interested general readers. The wars as a whole have also tended to be viewed as a largely Scottish affair. The extent to which they impinged on other lands has traditionally received only limited attention. Recent decades have witnessed the erosion of such nationally orientated perspectives. The works which integrate such perspectives most effectively are the ground-breaking overviews of the high medieval British Isles provided by Professors Rees Davies and Robin Frame.[5] The only detailed and sustained discussion of the

Scottish wars from a broad geographical perspective is the excellent *The Wars of the Bruces: Scotland, England and Ireland, 1306–1328* by Colm McNamee.[6] McNamee's work provides a fresh appreciation of the war and its impact on society, focusing especially on northern England and Ireland in the period after Bannockburn and demonstrating the impact of the conflict on a wide geographical region.

It is the intention of this book to examine the full significance of the battle of Bannockburn and the Scottish wars of the early fourteenth century in the history of the British Isles. Attention will be paid to the direct and indirect involvement of the peoples of these islands in the sustained conflict between Robert Bruce and Edward II and how the wars, and Bannockburn in particular, affected politics and society in Ireland, Wales and England, as well as Scotland. In particular, the link between the Scottish wars and the workings of politics and national identity in the realms of Britain and Ireland will be examined. Bannockburn was a critical moment in the history of these islands. Its roots and significance were political as much as military. The events which led to the battle are charted in an examination of the war in Scotland from 1307 and its connections with events in England and beyond. The battle was a virtually unique clash between two royal-led armies which met in response to a prior agreement. The readiness of the two sides to fight, unusual in medieval warfare, requires a full explanation of the battle's context. This context raises questions about the attitudes of Scots to Bruce's kingship and the parts played by the English, Welsh and Irish communities in the war and battle. The aftermath of the battle and its legacy also receive full attention. Did Bannockburn mark the end of ambitions for an English empire covering the whole island group and represent a decisive point in a process which saw the emergence and expression of new senses of nationhood and political consciousness among both nobles and common folk? The overall intention is to assess the interplay of warfare, politics and diplomacy across the British Isles during the critical years between 1300 and 1330. Centring on the two days of fighting at Bannockburn, it will demonstrate the importance of the battle in the formation of the British Isles as a diverse and multi-centred region in the late Middle Ages. Just as Bannockburn remains a symbol of distinct identity, so the legacy of this divergent experience remains potent today.

NOTES

1. W. M. Mackenzie, *The Battle of Bannockburn* (Glasgow, 1913); J. E. Morris, *Bannockburn* (Cambridge, 1914); P. Christison, *Bannockburn: A Soldier's Appreciation of the Battle* (Edinburgh, 1960); P. Reese, *Bannockburn* (Edinburgh, 2000); W. W. S. Scott, *Bannockburn Revealed* (Rothesay, 2000); A. Nusbacher, *The Battle of Bannockburn, 1314* (Stroud, 2000); P. Armstrong, *Bannockburn 1314* (Oxford, 2002).
2. W. Scott, *Tales of a Grandfather: Being the History of Scotland from the Earliest Period to the close of the rebellion of 1745–6* (London, 1898), 91–8.

3. G. W. S. Barrow, *Robert Bruce and the Community of the Realm of Scotland* (Edinburgh, 1988).
4. John Barbour, *The Bruce*, ed. A. A. M. Duncan (Edinburgh, 1997); A. A. M. Duncan, 'The War of the Scots, 1306–1323', *Transactions of the Royal Historical Society*, 6th series, ii (1992), 125–51.
5. R. R. Davies, *The First English Empire: Power and Identities in the British Isles, 1093–1343* (Oxford, 1999); R. Frame, *The Political Development of the British Isles, 1100–1400* (Oxford, 1990); R. R. Davies, *Domination and Conquest: The Experience of Ireland, Scotland and Wales, 1100–1300* (Cambridge, 1990).
6. C. McNamee, *The Wars of the Bruces: Scotland, England and Ireland, 1306–28* (East Linton, 1997).

CHAPTER 1

The Battle and its Story

Bannockburn and the Scottish cause

At dawn on 24 June 1314 two armies numbering in total tens of thousands of men were encamped in the lands south of Stirling in central Scotland. The smaller force moved first. It left the woods of the New Park where it had been based and formed up. The leader of this host was Robert Bruce king of Scots. His army had been raised from those parts of Scotland which recognised his claims to be king. Though Robert and his leading nobles were heavily armed and armoured, the vast majority of the host wore coats of leather or padded cloth and carried long spears. Nobles and commoners alike formed up in close order and prepared to fight on foot. Despite the lack of cavalry and archers and the limited equipment most of the army possessed, this was no amateur levy. Since 1307 a growing number of Scots must have become used to carrying weapons in the service of King Robert. The almost incessant campaigning of these years, and the run of successes won by Robert and his men, left their mark on this host. Led by King Robert, his brother, Edward Bruce, and nephew, Thomas Randolph, the army had shown its skill and confidence in two clashes on the previous day. They now made ready for the test of battle by kneeling in prayer.

Seeing the advance of Bruce's army, the second host began their preparations. This army was much larger and visually much more impressive than its enemy. Accounts speak of bright banners and flashing armour and of the comforts of their camp and the beauty of their horses. This too was a royal army. At its head was Edward Plantagenet, king of England, lord of Ireland, duke of Aquitaine and ruler of Wales. Edward also claimed to be the sovereign lord of Scotland and had come to the fields of Stirling to defend and recover this inheritance from Bruce, in his eyes a rebel and usurper. The army he had raised was one of the largest and strongest assembled by an English king up to that point. It had been raised from across and beyond the Plantagenet dominions and included many of Edward's leading subjects like the veteran Aymer Valence earl of Pembroke and the young and gallant Gilbert Clare earl of Gloucester. The key to the army's strength rested in the two thousand armoured horsemen recruited for the host. The social standing, lavish equipment and military skill of these cavalry caught the eye, but the bulk of the force was composed of footmen levied from the English shires and from the lands and lordships of Wales. Far from home and after long journeys, these men too prepared for the coming fight.

The battle that was about to break was the first full-scale clash between the armies of King Robert and King Edward in seven years of warfare. It would be the first major battle for fourteen years in the Scottish wars which had raged since 1296. These wars were fought over the survival of Scotland as a realm free from the rule of the English king. Twice, in 1296 and again in 1304, Edward I, father of the king at Bannockburn, had forced the submission of his Scottish enemies. In 1296, Edward had stripped the Scottish king, John Balliol, of his royal insignia, and imposed his rule, but the war had been renewed by new leaders and gathered support from Scots who refused to accept the English king's rule. Though never enjoying united support from Scotland, these leaders waged a determined struggle against Edward I from 1297 to 1304, forcing him to grind down their resistance in a series of expensive and exhausting campaigns. The victory apparently achieved by the elderly English king proved to be short-lived. In 1306 Robert Bruce started a new war, not in defence of Balliol's kingship, but in pursuit of his own family's claim to rule Scotland. After desperate beginnings, and against the hostility of many Scots, by 1314 Robert was on the point of winning his realm. The war he had waged had led to the fields beside the Bannockburn and made him ready to risk a battle for control of Scotland.

The outcome of the battle was sudden and decisive. Edward's larger army and its much-vaunted cavalry of knights and men-at-arms were swept from the field. Thousands of the defeated host were killed, mostly in the horrific crush to escape the enemy. The English king himself was forced to flee and was pursued some sixty miles before he escaped. King Robert and his men were left in control of the battlefield, masters of many prisoners and a vast quantity of loot. The victory also made Bruce the ruler of the whole of Scotland. Bannockburn has been accorded a place as the crowning achievement of King Robert's heroic career, as the decisive moment in the Scottish wars of independence and as a key event, and perhaps the best-known date, in the history of Scotland.

The special importance accorded to Bannockburn by the Scots seems to have developed in the immediate aftermath of the battle. In the mid-fifteenth century the chronicler Walter Bower included in his great history of the Scottish nation, *Scotichronicon*, three verses written about the battle within a decade or so of 1314. One of these works was composed by the English friar Robert Baston, 'the most famous poet in the whole of England', who had been included in King Edward's entourage 'so that he might compose to the shame of the Scots some verses about the triumph he [Edward] had gained over them'. Baston was captured in the English defeat and 'in return for his release he was compelled to compose . . . verses' recording the Scottish victory.[1] The other verses were Scottish in origin. One was part of a contemporary verse chronicle about the period, while the other was an extract attributed to Bruce's chancellor, Abbot Bernard of Arbroath. None of these works was intended as a detailed record of the events of 23 and 24 June 1314. Instead all treat the battle as an event of great moral and symbolic importance. The Scottish verses also represent the genesis of the sense that Bannockburn was the climax of the Scottish wars and marked the victory of King Robert's cause. The verse chronicle stated that:

> Thus the Scottish people praise the Lord of Lords.
> Between the stony stream and the obstruction of their camp
> The treacherous English people come to grief as a result of their own
>   dishonest conduct.
> O infinite God how just the sword with which you strike,
> Trampling on the necks of the proud and fulfilling the prayers of
> your people.

And ended with the words:

> May the assembly of the Scots flourish, abounding in valour:
> And may the king rejoice turning tears into joy,
> Now that the English have been cast down in all directions and
>   routed
> And made prisoner. May the king be praised for his goodness.[2]

Bernard's verse similarly linked the victory to King Robert and to divine favour and represents the reputed words of Bruce to his men before the battle. The king begins by saying:

> 'My lords, my people, who lay great weight on freedom,
> For which the kings of Scotland have suffered many trials, dying for
>   the Lord
> Now all of you take note of the many hardships we have undergone
> While struggling now certainly for eight years
> For our right to the kingdom, for honour and liberty.'

The king also appeals for divine aid:

> 'Happy is this day! John the Baptist was born on it;
> And St Andrew and St Thomas who shed his blood
> Along with the saints of the Scottish fatherland will fight today
> For the honour of the people, with Christ the Lord in the van.
> Under this leader you will conquer and make an end to war.'[3]

This language of freedom, of the struggle in defences of liberties and of an appeal to Christ and his Apostles, so prominent in the centrepiece of the Bruce Cause, the Declaration of Arbroath, were also linked by contemporaries to the victory at Bannockburn.[4] As a physical demonstration of the justice of Robert's claim to kingship and of Scotland's rights as a sovereign realm, the battle was at once accorded a place at the heart of defences of these rights.

This symbolic significance was not obscured by the continued, and largely successful, warfare of Robert's own reign which lasted until a peace was agreed with England in 1328. Nor was the importance of Bannockburn for the Scots dimmed by the renewal of war from 1332, which brought with it the fresh possibility of defeat for the Bruce dynasty and loss of sovereignty for Scotland. The survival of the dynasty and realm during the 1330s and 1340s created new heroes alongside Bruce and his captains but produced no great military victory to match Bannockburn. As a result of this, and because of its own unique significance, the battle clearly retained its glamour and importance when the key accounts of Scotland's past began to be composed from the later fourteenth century. The first of these was the *Gesta Annalia* composed at St Andrews (and later incorporated into John of Fordun's *Chronica Gentis Scottorum*). It gave no special place to Bannockburn in its tale of recent warfare but observed that King Edward trusted in 'the glory of man's might', while 'King Robert' put 'his trust, not in a host of men but in the Lord God', adding that 'the whole land . . . always rejoiced in victory over the English'.[5]

It was in the 1370s that the status accorded to the battle in Scottish historical writing was cemented by John Barbour's composition of *The Bruce*. This epic poem was a celebration of the martial deeds of King Robert and his leading captains, James Douglas, Thomas Randolph and Edward Bruce. It dealt with the lives and exploits of these men from Bruce's seizure of the throne in 1306 until Randolph's death in 1332.[6] However, though far from the end of the narrative, Bannockburn is the key event in *The Bruce*. The battle occurs about halfway through the story but is represented as the climax of the tale of Bruce's struggle to claim his rightful place as king of Scots. After telling the tale from 1307 to summer 1314 in just over 7,000 lines, Barbour's account of Bannockburn runs to nearly 2,000 lines, about a seventh of the total poem. Barbour's concern to give the battle a central place in his epic was probably born of mixed motives. The battle was to show the working out of some of *The Bruce*'s key themes. Like earlier works, Bannockburn was given a clear moral message. The English king had treasure to buy mercenaries and could draw on his lands and friends across Europe to bring to Scotland an army which was both powerful and lavishly equipped. But, says Barbour, 'na mannys mycht may stand agayn the Grace of God'.[7] When Bruce addresses his men he makes Scottish motivation clear. First, 'we have the rycht and for the rycht ay God will fycht'. Second, the enemy have brought their riches into 'our awne land', which, if the Scots win, will fall into their hands. Third, the Scots are ready to fight 'for our lyvis, and for our childer and for our wyvis and for our fredome and for our land'.[8] Victory is presented as a test of justice and of personal qualities, a test which the Scots pass and the English fail. The battle is also proof of the turn of Fortune's wheel, the image beloved of medieval writers. 'This mychty king off Ingland' had been 'set on hyr quheill on hycht' when he entered Scotland with his great host. In one night and a day Edward had been tipped from the summit and the 'quhelys turnyng' had carried Robert 'on hycht'.[9] For Bruce, whose early defeats and dangers as king Barbour narrates at length, the rise to the top of the wheel marks the culmination of the tale of his reign through the first two-thirds of the poem.

As well as God and the lady Fortune, Barbour develops his account of the battle as a set piece of warfare and chivalric prowess. The two days of fighting are portrayed as a series of episodes, described in generic but dramatic language with horses brought down, weapons thrust and thrown, blows struck, armour burst and men knocked to the ground and unable to rise again. Rather than record numerous participants and their deeds, Barbour is concerned to convey the excitement and danger of the fight as a competition between worthy adversaries. Some displays of personal prowess are recounted. King Robert's famous encounter with Henry Bohun is one set piece reminding the audience of Bruce's skill at arms, while another is the return to the battle by the 'third best knight' of his day, Giles Argentan, who made a suicidal lone charge against the Scots to preserve his honour.[10] However, the focus of the poem's description of Bannockburn is on the skill of Bruce and his lieutenants as leaders of men in battle. Bruce's speech, already identified by Abbot Bernard as a key element in the battle story, is given a key role in the portrayal of the king as a great captain, encouraging his followers to victory. The leadership of King Robert and the other Scottish commanders is shown in the account of the fighting as division after division of the army enters the fray.[11] This is great storytelling and it highlights the place of Bannockburn as a moral and martial test for Bruce, which he and his supporters pass with flying colours.

Whether it is great history remains to be seen, but it seems clear that the prominence and place given to the battle by Barbour reflected its significance for the Scottish ruling class in the 1370s. The roles given to lords whose heirs were in Barbour's audience and episodes such as the knighting of Walter Stewart, the father of Barbour's royal patron, Robert II, reflect the desire to be associated with the battle and its central place in the defence of the Scottish Cause. The account of Bannockburn in *The Bruce* provided the basis for all later Scottish accounts of the combat. Chroniclers in the next generation, like Andrew Wyntoun and Walter Bower, directly referred their readers to Barbour's account of the battle.[12] As we have seen, Bower also collected additional early verses and stories about Bannockburn, including a mysterious tale of two men-at-arms on white horses who appeared at Glastonbury Abbey in Somerset on the night before the battle. They were given food but refused lodging 'saying, that on the very same night before sunrise they must . . . take part in a certain battle at Bannockburn . . . and give help on the side of the

Scots, so as to bring revenge for the deaths of Simon de Montfort and his followers, so cruelly inflicted at the battle of Evesham'.[13] The meaning and
purpose of this story is unclear, but it may be the genesis of the, much later
and unsupported, myth of support given by the Knights Templar to Bruce in
the battle.[14] It also illustrates the way new stories and legends continued to be
attached to the story of the battle to explain its remarkable outcome and associate individuals and groups in the victory.

From the 1370s, and perhaps much earlier, the victory of Bruce and his supporters at Bannockburn had secured a place as a vital element in the story of the
defence of Scotland as a separate realm. This was a vital element in all the narratives of the Scottish past produced in the later Middle Ages and the role of
Bannockburn in these accounts was not simply as another episode in the struggle. The battle assumed a significance as a moment of national salvation for the
Scottish people, proving their right to exist and God's blessing on their rights
and liberties as a people. The Scots were far from being alone in regarding
victory in a single battle in terms of the destiny of kingdom and community.
Almost exactly a century before Bannockburn on 27 July 1214, the army of the
French king, Philip II, defeated a coalition of enemies including the German
king and the count of Flanders at Bouvines. To Philip's many admirers, this
victory set the seal on his achievements and within a decade an epic poem, the
Philippiad, was composed which made Bouvines its climax and devoted almost
a third of its length to the battle. Philip, like Robert, exhorts his men to fight
well, leads from the front and puts his cause to the test. The 'sons of France' are
victorious against their more powerful and treacherous enemy. Later writers
added to the legend claiming odds of one against ten, and including stories
which emphasised their message, for example, having Philip lay down his crown
until his people promise to defend the kingdom. The myth was developed
during the century after Bouvines that the battle had united king and nation, a
message not dissimilar in tone to the significance accorded to Bannockburn.
Though in the later Middle Ages Bouvines' importance declined, its early sym-
bolism provides a valid comparison with Bannockburn.[15]

The centuries before and after Bannockburn produced numerous other
battles which were accorded considerable symbolic importance in the formation or preservation of national communities and identities. The great victory
of the Christian Spanish rulers over the Islamic Almohads at Las Navas de
Tolosa in 1212 attracted the attention of many chroniclers and poets who
embellished the battle with numerous miraculous events. In subsequent centuries, many noble families claimed descent from participants in the battle to
prove their own status. The same was true in Portugal following the defeat of
the Castillians at Aljubarotta in 1385, a victory celebrated as the salvation of
the small realm from conquest by its larger neighbour. Like the Stewart and
Douglas families in Scotland, certain Portuguese families took pride in the
knighting of their ancestors before the crucial battle.[16] Battles of symbolic
importance from this period were not all victories. The rapid generation

of a mythology around the defeat of the Serbs at Kosovo, the reverse of Bannockburn, gave an elevated importance to the battle as the end of a people's liberties. Equally, such battles were not always fought in defence of native soil. It is striking and revealing that the English equivalents of Bannockburn, producing rapid celebrations of nation and the judgement of battle, were Crécy, Poitiers and, above all, Agincourt. All were waged against an enemy claimed to be more powerful and more arrogant, but all also took place in pursuit of English royal lordship in France.[17]

The most obvious parallel for Bannockburn, however, is provided by the battle of Courtrai which was fought in Flanders in July 1302. The victory of an army of Flemish burgesses and nobles fighting on foot against the mounted chivalry of France was cited by several near contemporaries as the precursor and model for Bannockburn.[18] While this has excited numerous military historians to seek parallels on the battlefield, the real comparison was one of symbolic and historical importance. Like Bannockburn, the legend of Courtrai is centred on the defence of the existence and rights of a small community threatened with conquest and absorption by a larger and more powerful neighbour. Sources written in the years after the battle, like the *Annales Gandenses* and the *Spiegel historiael*, depict the French as sacreligious and arrogant but also, as with Bannockburn, divided in their approach to the battle. The victory was won 'by the disposition of God' but also by the 'foot soldiers of Flanders, . . . strong, manly, well-armed and under expert leaders'. Against them were the French, 'the flower of knighthood' and 'the beauty and strength of that great army was turned into a dung-pit, and the glory of the French made into dung and worms'.[19] Like Bannockburn too, this display of Divine favour and their skill in arms had to sustain the Flemings through continued long and frequently unsuccessful warfare against France in the later Middle Ages. The value of both victories to their communities was probably the greater for their relative rarity.

The great significance accorded to Bannockburn by the Scots did not necessarily carry to other lands. While Courtrai and Bouvines were events which reached a European audience, drawing judgements and conclusions from chroniclers in many realms, Bannockburn's impact was more localised. Even in France and the Low Countries, lands which were caught up in the Scottish wars, coverage of the battle was limited. The official history of the French monarchy, *Les Grandes Chroniques de France*, makes no mention of Bannockburn, though it included other events in Scotland, such as Edward I's campaigns of 1296 and 1303–4 and Bruce's defeat in 1306 and gives considerable attention to Edward II's disastrous invasion of Scotland in 1322. The chronicle shows an interest in Edward as the son-in-law of the French king but it, and presumably the French government, was distracted from Scotland in 1314. A campaign against Flanders which caused a domestic crisis and the death of Philip IV took attention away from distant events.[20] Other continental writers show a similar lack of awareness of the battle. The exception is the

Paris burgher Geoffroy de Paris, who wrote at the time and included a passage on the battle which stated that of Edward's '*grant chevalerie*' almost all were killed or captured in 'marsh and mire, as were the French at Courtrai'. The French chronicler clearly took a degree of pleasure in English defeat, speaking of the profit and honour won by the Scots and the shame of the English.[21]

However, Bannockburn was clearly not an event which captured the imagination of European chroniclers in the manner of Courtrai. Instead its impact was more confined. While Scots composed verses about the victory in the following decade, writers elsewhere in the British Isles lamented the defeat at length. All the main chronicles produced in England during Edward II's reign dwelt long and remorsefully on the humiliating and bloody defeat. Probably the best account of the period, the *Vita Edwardi Secundi*, captured the mood when it said, 'Perhaps someone will enquire and ask why the Lord smote us this day, why we succumbed to the Scots, when for the last twenty years we have always been victorious.'[22] Both the *Vita* and the chronicle of the great abbey of St Albans blamed divisions within the English host for the defeat, while the northern English chronicle associated with Lanercost Priory near Carlisle contrasted the piety of the Scots with King Edward's plundering of great churches to pay for his army.[23] The *Lanercost Chronicle* included English verses lamenting the defeat and spoke of 'Bannockburn' being 'spoken about for many years in English throats'.[24] This northern English perspective hints at a negative significance for the battle in the regions which would come to be the seat of warfare. Its tone is echoed in other lands. In Wales 'the battle in the Pools' was remembered for the death of the lord of Glamorgan, Gilbert Clare, and the flight of King Edward, while in Ireland both Gaelic and English annalists recorded the battle as a bloody defeat.[25]

This widespread concern across the British Isles from western Ireland to Cardiganshire to St Albans is not a matter of surprise. The Scottish wars which had been raging for eighteen years before Bannockburn were not just a matter for the English king and his Scottish enemies. They involved all the lands and peoples of the British Isles. For chroniclers writing in these lands, news from Scotland had an immediacy which was lacking on the continent. They were aware of the context of the battle and were much more shocked by the ability of Robert Bruce, hitherto known for his skill in avoiding the English in battle, to win such a crushing victory. These writers and their communities also had reason to recognise the battle's consequences, not just in Scotland, but on their own doorsteps. To them, writing in the decades which immediately followed the battle, Bannockburn assumed an increased significance as a turning point in the history of the archipelago. For the Scots it symbolised the survival of their realm. For the subjects of the Plantagenet king it would have more mixed and less positive importance. However, to understand the battle is also to understand its place in the war for Scotland and the way that war, and particularly the struggle of Bruce to secure the Scottish crown, altered the shape of the British Isles.

THE OPENING OF THE BANNOCKBURN WAR

In late March 1306 Robert Bruce earl of Carrick was crowned king of Scots at Scone. His crowning was the culmination of six weeks of local fighting and political uncertainty which had followed Bruce's murder of his political and personal enemy, John Comyn lord of Badenoch, in Greyfriars Kirk in Dumfries. In these weeks Robert may have acted not in fulfilment of a planned seizure of power, but only as the implications of his deed became apparent.[26] However, by taking the throne he had committed himself to a position which would end in his violent death, the utter humiliation of his family or, perhaps least likely, his victory. Robert Bruce had made himself the central figure in a crisis which had already been running for twenty years. The immediate effect of his actions was to divide the Scottish community and turn simmering rivalries into open civil war. While Bruce could count on the support of many of his family's tenants and friends and his claims to be king resonated with the wider population, most of the leaders of the kingdom stayed well away from Scone and many were actively hostile.[27] During the previous decade many Scots had fought hard and risked much in defence of their rights as a kingdom and of John Balliol as their king. Though the war had ended in defeat in 1304, Balliol still lived as an exile in France. For nobles and soldiers who had supported the rights of the Balliol family, Bruce was an illegal usurper as well as a shedder of blood on holy ground.[28]

As well as facing war with the kinsmen of John Comyn and former Balliol partisans, by becoming king of Scots Robert had made himself a rebel in the eyes of the English king, Edward I. In 1302 Bruce had sworn an oath of allegiance to Edward, promising loyal service to the English king. He had now utterly broken his faith. More than that, he had broken the peace which King Edward had fought so hard and spent so heavily to force on Scotland. Eight years of warfare, from 1296 to 1304, had been required to make the Scots recognise Edward as their sovereign lord. Only five months before Bruce's killing of Comyn, the English king had issued his 'Ordinance for the good order of Scotland', the blueprint for Edwardian rule in his new dominion.[29] By his personal act of rebellion, Bruce threatened the whole settlement of the Scottish question. Edward, now in his late sixties, was determined not to let this last, crowning, achievement of his reign slip away.

By April 1306 an English army was already gathering at Berwick under the able Aymer Valence earl of Pembroke, Edward's lieutenant.[30] With him were other captains who would play a leading role in the coming war, like the north country nobles and veterans of the Scottish wars, Robert Clifford and Henry Percy, and the French lord, Henry Beaumont. As the army advanced through southern Scotland, burning the estates of Bruce and his supporters, it was joined by numerous Scottish opponents of the rebel king.[31] Among them were John Comyn earl of Buchan, cousin of Robert's victim, the brothers John and Philip Mowbray and Ingeram Umfraville, all enemies of Edward I in the

previous war who now sided with him against their common enemy.[32] The
army of about 300 cavalry and 2,000 foot reached Perth in early June.[33] Robert
gathered his own force, which included the earls of Atholl and Lennox, and
marched to Perth. Arranging with Valence to fight on the next day, Bruce withdrew six miles to Methven where his army began to make camp. Anticipating
this, Valence led his force in pursuit and, though Robert's army was able to
form up, his foot soldiers were routed. Robert himself narrowly escaped
capture by Philip Mowbray and was forced to flee, leaving many of his knights
behind as prisoners.[34]

King Edward received news of Valence's victory at Methven as he was himself
en route to join a second army mustering at Carlisle. He was clearly determined
to ensure that the rising was crushed completely and ordered Valence to
execute all 'enemies and rebels' he captured, an order which the latter did not
carry out to the full.[35] The only rebels excepted from immediate execution were
Bruce, John earl of Atholl and Simon Fraser, who were to be sent to Edward for
punishment.[36] Fraser and Atholl were captured, tried and brutally executed but
Bruce remained elusive. In the weeks after Methven, Robert was pursued with
vigour by both English and Scottish forces. His escort was defeated on the
shores of Loch Tay by some of Valence's cavalry and again at Dalry by men from
Argyll led by John of Lorn.[37] Both times Bruce escaped capture and by late
August was in the Lennox, the province of his ally, Earl Malcolm. Even here
Robert was vulnerable. The nearby stronghold of Dumbarton was held by John
Menteith, who had refused to join Bruce in March. Menteith now led the
pursuit of the king, who fled by galley to Dunaverty Castle at the Mull of
Kintyre.[38] Even at this western extremity of the Scottish mainland, Robert was
hunted. By 22 September John Menteith and an Anglo-Scottish force had
arrived at the castle equipped with siege engines. Though Dunaverty quickly
fell, Robert had gone. Taking to their ships, the king and his remaining followers crossed the narrow sea to Ulster and the Isles.[39]

Though Robert had escaped, his cause in Scotland seemed completely lost.
While he had fled westwards, his supporters and strongholds had largely been
taken. In September, his brother, Neil, was captured when Kildrummy Castle
in Aberdeenshire fell to Edward prince of Wales. His wife, Elizabeth de Burgh,
and his daughter, Marjorie, were surrendered to Edward by William earl
of Ross. The fugitive king's chief advisers, the bishop of Glasgow, Robert
Wishart, and the bishop of St Andrews, William Lamberton, had already fallen
into Edward I's hands.[40] While the women and clergy were imprisoned, Neil
and a number of other nobles were savagely put to death. The executions, the
treatment of noble ladies and prelates and the burning of the lands of rebels
marked a greater ruthlessness in Edward's prosecution of the war. This was
inspired by his determination to stamp out this new outbreak of Scottish
defiance and demonstrate the price of any future opposition.

These objectives were displayed not just by the harsh treatment of captive
bodies, but by Edward's treatment of the property held by Bruce's main

backers. Land and the legal rights which were attached to it concerned not just individual income but the identity and status of noble dynasties. The removal of land from its hereditary lord was, therefore, a highly sensitive action for a king to take. If it was done too frequently it would arouse anxieties and suspicion throughout the king's dominions. During the Scottish wars Edward I had used the power to deprive enemy landowners of their lands sparingly and had shown a readiness to restore forfeited estates to nobles who later did homage. The peace settlement of 1304–5 restored to Edward's former enemies in Scotland the lands which they had forfeited in Scotland, but also the extensive estates of many in England.[41] In 1306, however, Edward showed no restraint. Even before Methven, sentences of forfeiture had been passed on Robert Bruce and his leading adherents, the earls of Atholl, Lennox and Menteith, while the lukewarm James Stewart was also deprived of his lordships in south-west Scotland after his heir was implicated in the rising.[42] On 16 June the temporalities, the lands and revenues of the bishoprics of St Andrews and Glasgow had been assigned to keepers, and by September Edward had begun to lobby the pope to have the rebel bishops removed from office.[43] By the end of the year over a hundred of Bruce's supporters had suffered, or been threatened with, forfeiture. While some of these had been executed, others, like Neil Campbell, Gilbert Hay and Reginald Crawford, were in exile with King Robert.[44] However, the majority of those punished had probably surrendered to King Edward or his men. These had suffered imprisonment but some were released on bail over the winter and during 1307. Among this group were influential local barons like Alexander Fraser, Robert Boyd, Alexander Lindsay and Bruce's nephew and future right-hand man, Thomas Randolph.[45] Either threatened with, or punished by, forfeiture, these men were given a final chance to serve the Edwardian administration or meet the fate meted out to others. However, their treatment in 1306 also meant that a group of locally important nobles remained disenchanted with the regime. Faced with a renewed choice of loyalties, such men might not respond to threats but gamble on further rebellion.

Edward surely also appreciated the advantages of depriving a significant group of Scottish landowners of their estates. His relative restraint up to 1305 was influenced by a desire to avoid antagonising those Scots in his allegiance and to encourage his enemies to seek terms. In 1306, with a significant group of Scottish barons bound to him by their hostility to Bruce, the permanent disinheritance of 'rebels and enemies' had clear attractions.[46] It brought with it the prospect of creating a new balance within the Scottish nobility. Edward did show some generosity towards his Scottish liegemen. John Menteith was rewarded for refusing to join Bruce with a grant of the earldom of Lennox, while two long-standing adherents of Edward, Alexander Balliol of Cavers and Alexander Abernethy, were among those who sought lands forfeited by Bruce and his followers. In September the English king asked the pope to provide William Comyn, brother of the earl of Buchan, to the bishopric of

St Andrews, and Geoffrey Mowbray to the see of Glasgow.[47] Though the pope did not respond to this request, Edward's plans indicate a desire to establish friendly leaders of the Scottish church who would not articulate resistance to his lordship.

However, the main beneficiaries of royal patronage in 1306 were English magnates. Not usually lavish in his bestowal of rewards on his leading subjects, during 1306 Edward was quicker to distribute rewards to a small group of barons than to respond to the petitions of a larger body of lesser figures seeking to claim property forfeited by Bruce partisans. This may have been partly because the settlement of 1304–5 had meant that several English barons had to relinquish estates which they had previously been granted both in England and Scotland. Henry Percy, for example, had resigned any claim on the earldom of Buchan when its earl made his peace.[48] Now his long service in the Scottish wars could be recognised again and Percy was granted Robert Bruce's earldom of Carrick. The other new Scottish earls were Ralph Monthermer who received Atholl and John Hastings who was granted Menteith, while the forfeited Bruce lordship of Annandale was given to Humphrey de Bohun earl of Hereford and Essex. Bruce's principal English estate of Hart and Hartlepool was given to Robert Clifford, who already held the lordship of Douglas in Scotland. Valence was rewarded for his victory at Methven with a grant of the royal forest of Selkirk to go with his castle of Bothwell in Clydesdale. The final and, as it proved, shortest-lived grant was made to Henry de Lacy earl of Lincoln who received the lands of James steward of Scotland.[49] This was a select group of barons. Hereford and Monthermer were King Edward's sons-in-law and Pembroke his cousin. Lincoln was described as the king's 'chief councillor', while Hastings had been one of the principal claimants for the Scottish crown in 1291. Clifford and Percy had been among the most active and able English leaders in the Scottish wars.[50]

By giving extensive interests in Scotland and the defeat of Bruce to such men, Edward was concerned with more than just dispensing rewards for service and favouring his chief lords. His actions were related to his objectives in Scotland. The grant of major Scottish interests to several leading English barons, like the restoration of English estates to Scots landowners in 1305, was intended to strengthen links between the two realms and draw Scotland into closer contact with Edward's dominions. Marriages, like that between Robert Bruce and Elizabeth Burgh, the daughter of Richard de Burgh earl of Ulster, or between John Comyn and Aymer Valence's sister, had similarly been encouraged by Edward to create cross-border social networks.[51] As Bruce's marriage showed, such networks were not confined to England. His father-in-law, the so-called Red Earl of Ulster, was the greatest English magnate in Ireland, exercising lordship over English tenants and Irish dependants in Connacht and Ulster. He was closely involved in Edward I's Scottish wars, leading armies and fleets across the North Channel. With his son-in-law seeking refuge on the fringes of his province, Earl Richard would remain a central figure in the renewed conflict. The English king's recent patronage had also created links between Edwardian Scotland and his first conquest, Wales. Five of the barons who received major Scottish estates in 1306 were also lords in the Welsh march. The earls of Pembroke, Hereford and Lincoln, Monthermer and Hastings were the semi-independent rulers of blocs of territory in south and east Wales.[52] Edward may have calculated that they would be more ready to raise the large contingents of Welsh foot soldiers on which the king relied if they had Scottish interests of their own to defend. In general, by giving his great barons a stake in Plantagenet control of Scotland, Edward was copying his successful conquest of Wales two decades earlier when, as well as creating a royal principality, Edward bestowed new marcher lordships on key baronial supporters.[53]

Such calculations were natural to King Edward. The submission of his remaining Scottish enemies in 1304 had led to English writers hailing their monarch as 'the king and lord of two kingdoms' who, like a second King Arthur, had united all the islanders under his rule. The rising of Bruce had shaken Edward's 'triumphant peace' but with the defeat of the rebels and the exile of their 'King Hobbe', or King Fool, as the English called Robert, this threat may have been regarded as a final spasm of resistance.[54] With Scotland's castles once again in his hands, Edward's achievement of the previous two years probably seemed secure to most observers. As king of England, lord of Ireland, duke of Aquitaine and master of Wales, this fresh and easy suppression of Scottish opposition confirmed Edward as sole royal ruler in the British Isles. Though England was by far his most important dominion, Edward recognised the importance of all of the realms and lands he held or claimed, both for the prestige they conferred upon him and for their resources. The wars he fought, in Flanders, Wales and Scotland, were never simply 'English'. Rather they were Edward's wars, aimed at defending or extending his dynasty's rights and employing the men and money of all his lands.[55]

In his conquest of Wales and during the Scottish wars of the previous decade the king had drawn heavily on the nobles and resources of all his dominions. Welsh soldiers formed a major component in all the armies Edward had led to Scotland during the previous decade, and in the Falkirk campaign of 1298 over 10,000 archers and spearmen from the principality and marcher lordships had served under the king's banner.[56] Edward's lordship of Ireland also contributed to the wars. The king's authority in Ireland extended over a large area of the east and south where, since the late twelfth century, English nobles, townsmen and peasants had acquired land and settled. In a far more limited fashion, the English king also claimed to rule the native Irish lords who remained in the mountains and bogs of the east and those who still dominated the west and north of the island.[57] Forces of several thousand soldiers, mostly English, had been shipped from Ireland to campaign in Scotland in 1296, 1301 and 1303, and seem to have been particularly brutal in their approach to warfare. Fleets raised from the towns of English Ireland had been sent to extend Edward's authority in the Firth of Clyde and up the western coasts and isles.[58] In the last months of 1306, with 'Robert Bruce and his accomplices lurking' in the Western Isles, the value of Ireland, and especially Ulster, as a source of ships and men became even more important to the English king, who, from early October, was based at Lanercost Priory near Carlisle, in easy communication with Ireland down the Solway Firth.[59]

In late January 1307 Edward I issued orders for a fleet to be raised in Ireland to bring about Robert's final defeat.[60] The king was taking nothing for granted. His anxieties about the future were not simply due to his age and possible signs that his impressive physique was beginning to fail. Edward probably also recognised that his enemy had taken refuge in those parts of the British Isles which were furthest from his reach and rule. Though later writers were confused about Robert's whereabouts between his flight from Dunaverty in September 1306 and his landing in Carrick the following February, Edward I seemed aware of his general location in 'the isles between Scotland and Ireland'. The near contemporary accounts of Walter of Guisborough and the *Lanercost Chronicle* clearly identified Robert's location as in 'the outer isles of Scotland'. The king may have made initial landfall on Rathlin Island off the Ulster coast, but this was too exposed and lacking in possible friends to be more than a brief visit.[61] Instead the real refuge sought by Bruce and his surviving friends was further north in the tangle of isles and sea lochs which stretched up the coast of the Scottish realm from Islay to Skye and Lewis.

These Western Isles and adjacent coasts formed a region which had long possessed a distinct character and identity. Because of Scandinavian settlement in the ninth century they were known in Gaelic as *Inse Gall*, the Isles of the Foreigners, and, along with the Isle of Man further south, they had been recognised as the kingdom of the Isles. Though this political entity had lost much of its significance when the region came under the lordship of the Scottish king in the 1260s, the magnates of the Isles were no ordinary royal vassals but retained their ancestors' character as sea-kings. These lords could call up fleets of galleys and bands of mail-armoured axemen in their private enterprises. In an economically poor region like the Isles, there was a long tradition of such leaders seeking rewards as traders, pirates and mercenaries.[62] Ireland had proved a fertile ground for such activities and the galloglass, as the Islesmen were known, had become a key element in the armies and retinues of Gaelic Irish kings. The military character of the Isles was produced by the frequent warfare between the leading men of the region. During the two decades before 1306 this had merged with the rivalries and wars which had beset the Scottish kingdom. Though the leading Islesmen had all submitted to Edward I by 1304, the events of these years had also shown that the Isles were hard to police and a ready source of ships and soldiers.[63]

Robert Bruce was no stranger to the lords and men of the Western Isles. As earl of Carrick, on the Ayrshire coast, he inherited contacts and interests in

Kintyre, the Isles and Ulster which all lay nearby. Robert would have been well aware of the military potential of these regions and, as early as March 1306, he may have secured Dunaverty Castle as a point of contact access with the Isles and Ireland. His actions in 1306 had won him the enmity of one of the great families of the Isles. Alexander mac Dougall of Argyll and his son, John of Lorn, were kinsmen of the murdered John Comyn. John's hostility had already been demonstrated in his attack on Bruce at Dalry. As lords over Lorn, Mull and Morvern, Alexander and John were powerful enemies in the west, but their hostility also worked in Bruce's favour. Later Scottish writers identified Robert's protectors and allies in the Isles as Angus Og of Islay and Christina of the Isles. These were leading members of the other main Hebridean kindreds. Angus was one of the heads of Clan Donald, whose lands were centred on Islay, while Christina was from the mac Ruairi kindred. Robert's links with these nobles and their kindreds were distant and tenuous and Barbour's later account of Angus Og paying Bruce homage may not capture the relationship between exile and host in late 1306.[64] However, both Angus, Christina and their kindreds had poor relations with the mac Dougalls, and they may have offered Bruce galleys and men in expectation that his success would damage their rivals.

Robert also looked beyond the Isles for military aid. Over the winter he sent his brothers Thomas and Alexander to Ireland. They probably made the short journey from Islay to Ulster in search of allies. Their audience would have been the leaders of the Irish in western Ulster and Connacht. Though they often employed the title of king, these men were really nobles, many of whom had shed blood to win control of their kindreds.[65] In 1306 many of these Irish chiefs were under the dominion of Richard Burgh earl of Ulster and lord of Connacht. Since 1286 the Red Earl had imposed his authority on the Irish of the north, installing friendly chiefs and removing enemies. His power over the Irish did fluctuate but the earl frequently intervened in disputes within powerful kindreds like the O'Neill of Tir Eoghain and the O'Domnhaill of Tir Connaill and drew lesser families like the O'Cathain directly under his lordship.[66]

Thomas and Alexander Bruce may have come from the earl's son-in-law but they did not seek aid from Earl Richard or the English colonists of eastern Ulster. They carried letters addressed to 'all the kings of Ireland, . . . the prelates and clergy and inhabitants of all Ireland'. Their language clearly indicated a native Irish audience. They spoke of 'our people and yours . . . arising from one branch of a nation' which shared a 'common language' and 'customs'. Should the Irish aid him, Robert hoped that 'God willing, our nation may be able to recover her ancient liberty'.[67] In speaking of the Scots and Irish as 'one nation', Bruce was referring to ideas that were well-understood in both realms. However, in suggesting that the Gaelic Irish and the Scots were engaged in a single struggle for their 'ancient liberty', Robert was pursuing an approach which was new to the Scots and, given his own background and connections within the Anglo-French nobility of Britain, Ireland and beyond, marked a political departure. The letter was, of course, propaganda, shaped by Robert's needs and circumstances and designed to appeal to Irish leaders, like Donal O'Neill, who had clashed with the Red Earl since the 1280s.[68] However, the alignment between the Gaels of Scotland and Ireland against the English was a development of earlier efforts to articulate the rights of the Scots alone. It represented a widening of the Anglo-Scottish propaganda conflict to encompass Ireland for the first time. The implications of this would last well beyond the winter of 1306–7. In real terms, the provision of ships and men led by one Irish 'kinglet' was more likely to have been secured by more pragmatic means than an appeal to a war of liberation. Bruce's hosts from Clan Donald had connections with Donal O'Neill and other lords from Ulster which may have been the real source of this Irish contingent.[69] Like the Islesmen who agreed to follow Bruce, these Irish were probably serving in the hope of plunder and pay rather than any wider ideals.

When the war was renewed in early 1307 it would stretch beyond the heartlands of the Scottish kingdom where the earlier fighting had taken place. The centre of military preparations for both sides lay on either side of the narrow seas separating Scotland and Ireland. In using the Western Isles and Ulster as a springboard for his forcible re-entry into Scotland, Bruce was following the precedents of several claimants to royal or provincial power during the previous century and a half.[70] However, all such attempts had ended in defeat and, despite his success in retaining a body of supporters and securing the support of some new allies, Robert must have been aware of the difficulties he faced. In Scotland, where his coup of the spring and summer seemed only to have achieved the death or disinheritance of his leading friends and partisans, Bruce could hardly look for rapid or enthusiastic backing for a further bid for the kingdom.

However, King Edward too had worries. During the later months of 1306 he sent letters to William earl of Ross and to Lachlan and Ruairi, the half-brothers of Christina of the Isles, perhaps encouraging these magnates to use their power in the Isles against Robert. Other letters announcing the excommunication of Bruce for Comyn's murder were sent to the Irish bishops in a possible attempt to counter any efforts to raise support in Ulster.[71] Edward knew of Bruce's location and his search for allies. He could probably guess that the target of any new venture by his enemy would be the south-west of Scotland and, in particular, Carrick, Bruce's own earldom. However, the letters which the king sprayed out to his adherents during the autumn and winter and the tone of impatience they displayed suggests Edward was an old man in a hurry to remove this latest challenge.[72] In the opening weeks of 1307 both kings, Robert and Edward, were keen for war to be renewed.

NOTES

1. W. Bower, *Scotichronicon*, ed. D. E. R. Watt, 9 vols (Aberdeen, 1987–98), vi, 366–7.
2. *Scotichronicon*, ed. Watt, vi, 356–61.

3. *Scotichronicon*, ed. Watt, vi, 362–5.

4. For the text of the Declaration of Arbroath, see *The Bruce*, ed. Duncan, 779–82.

5. *John of Fordun's Chronicle of the Scottish Nation*, ed. W. F. Skene, 2 vols, ii, 339–40.

6. *The Bruce*, ed. Duncan; *Barbour's Bruce*, ed. M. P. McDiarmid and J. A. C. Stevenson, 3 vols (Scottish Texts Society, 1980–5).

7. *The Bruce*, ed. Duncan, 415.

8. *The Bruce*, ed. Duncan, 460–1.

9. *The Bruce*, ed. Duncan, 512–17.

10. *The Bruce*, ed. Duncan, 448–51, 494–7.

11. *The Bruce*, ed. Duncan, 472–93.

12. *Scotichronicon*, ed. Watt, vi, 352–3; Andrew de Wyntoun, *The Original Chronicle*, ed. F. Amours, 6 vols (Scottish Texts Society, 1908), v, 367.

13. *Scotichronicon*, ed. Watt, vi, 354–5.

14. A. Coutts, 'The Knights Templars in Scotland', *Records of the Scottish Church History Society*, 7 (1938), 126–40; J. Edwards, 'The Templars in Scotland in the Thirteenth Century', *S.H.R.*, 5 (1908), 13–25.

15. G. Duby, *The Legend of Bouvines*, trans. C. Tihanyi (Berkeley, 1990), 141–66.

16. D. W. Lomax, *The Reconquest of Spain* (London, 1978), 124–8; R. Costa Gomes, *The Making of a Court Society: Kings and Nobles in Late Medieval Portugal* (Cambridge, 2003), 180, 206, 225.

17. N. Malcolm, *Kosovo: A short history* (London, 1998), 58–80; A. Curry, *The Battle of Agincourt: Sources and Interpretations* (Woodbridge, 2000).

18. *Vita Edwardi Secundi*, ed. W. Childs (Oxford, 2005), 97; *Scalachronica*, ed. A. King, 75. For Courtrai, see J. F. Verbruggen, *The Battle of the Golden Spurs: Courtrai, 11 July 1302*, ed. K. Devries (Woodbridge, 2002).

19. *Annales Gandenses*, ed. H. Johnstone (Oxford, 1951), 30–1; Verbruggen, *Battle of the Golden Spurs*, 83–110.

20. *Les Grandes Chroniques de France*, ed. J. Viard (Société de l'histoire de France, 1935), viii, 223–4, 250–5, 295–317; ix, 101–5.

21. Geoffroy de Paris, *Chronique Rimée*, ed. N. de Wailly and L. Delisle (Receuil des historiens de la Gaule et de la France), xxii, 148.

22. *Vita Edwardi*, 95.

23. *Johannes de Trokelowe and Henrici de Blandeford, Chronica et Annales*, ed. H. T. Riley (Rolls series, 1866), 83–7; *Vita Edwardi*, 87–95.

24. *The Chronicle of Lanercost*, trans. H. Maxwell (Edinburgh, 1913), 208; *Chronicon de Lanercost*, ed. J. Stevenson (Edinburgh, 1839), 226–7.

25. *Brut y Tywysogyon or the Chronicle of the Princes. Peniarth MS 20 version*, ed. and trans. T. Jones (Cardiff, 1952), 123; *The Annals of Connacht*, ed. A. M. Freeman (Dublin, 1944), 229–31; *Chartularies of St Mary's Abbey, Dublin and the Annals of Ireland, 1162–1370*, ed. J. T. Gilbert, 2 vols (Rolls series, 1884–6), ii, 344.

26. Duncan, 'War of the Scots', 135; *The Chronicle of Walter of Guisborough*, ed. H. T. Rothwell, Camden Society (London, 1957), 366–7; *The Bruce*, ed. Duncan, 86–93; M. Brown, *The Wars of Scotland, 1214–1371* (Edinburgh, 2004), 197–201; Barrow, *Robert Bruce*, 146–54.

27. For a discussion of Bruce's supporters, see E. Barron, *The Scottish Wars of Independence* (reprinted New York, 1998), 224–35; Barrow, *Robert Bruce*, 154–60, 325–8; Duncan, 'War of the Scots', 137.

28. M. Brown, '*Scoti Anglicati*: Scots in Plantagenet Allegiance during the Fourteenth Century', in A. King and M. Penman (eds), *England and Scotland in the Fourteenth Century* (Woodbridge, 2007).

29. For the ordinance, see E. L. G. Stones, *Anglo-Scottish Relations 1174–1328* (Oxford, 1965), no. 33; F. Watson, 'Settling the stalemate: Edward I's peace in

Scotland, 1303–1305', 127–43, in M. Prestwich, R. Britnell and R. Frame (eds), *Thirteenth-Century England*, vi (Woodbridge, 1997), 127–43; F. Watson, *Under the Hammer: Edward I and Scotland, 1286–1307* (East Linton, 1997).

30. *C.D.S.*, ii, no. 1762; v, no. 492 (v), (vi), (ix), (x); Duncan, 'War of the Scots', 137–8.
31. *C.D.S.*, ii, no. 1782.
32. *C.D.S.*, ii, no. 1779; v, nos 472 (p), 492 (xvi); *The Bruce*, ed. Duncan, 90.
33. *C.D.S.*, v, no. 492 (v), (vi), (ix), (x); Duncan, 'War of the Scots', 137–8.
34. *The Bruce*, ed. Duncan, 90–105; *Chron. Guisborough*, 368.
35. *The Bruce*, ed. Duncan, 102–4.
36. *C.D.S.*, ii, no. 1790.
37. Duncan, 'War of the Scots', 138; *The Bruce*, ed. Duncan, 112–17.
38. *The Bruce*, ed. Duncan, 134–43; Stones, *Anglo-Scottish Relations*, no. 34.
39. *The Bruce*, ed. Duncan, 144–9; *C.D.S.*, ii, nos. 1833–4; v, no. 457.
40. *The Bruce*, ed. Duncan, 153–61; *C.D.S.*, ii, nos 1777, 1780, 1785, 1812, 1829, 1833; v, nos 471(e), 472 (a, c, o); *Scotichronicon*, ed. Watt, vi, 323.
41. Watson, *Under the Hammer*, 185.
42. *C.D.S.*, ii, nos 1757, 1771, 1786, 1857, 1945.
43. *C.D.S.*, ii, no. 1785; v, no. 446.
44. For a list of landowners whose lands were threatened with forfeiture for their support of Bruce, see *Documents Relating to the History of Scotland*, ed. F. Palgrave (London, 1837) i, 301–18. Alan Durward and Alexander Murray, who were taken at Kildrummy, and David Inchmartin, John Somerville, Berrnard Mowat and numerous others captured at Methven were executed. The killers of John Comyn and of an English knight, Roger de Tany, were singled out for execution (*C.D.S.*, ii, no. 1811; *The Bruce*, ed. Duncan, 166).
45. *C.D.S.*, ii, nos 1807, 1829; *The Bruce*, ed. Duncan, 100.
46. Even in 1306 Edward was prepared to allow James Stewart to recover his lands following a submission and fresh oath of allegiance sworn on a relic of the true cross. Stewart does not seem to have joined Bruce in 1306 but his elder son, Andrew, was in Robert's hands and may have been used to raise support among Stewart's affinity (*Foedera*, iv, 62; Stones, *Anglo-Scottish Relations*, no. 35).
47. *C.D.S.*, ii, no. 1786; v, no. 446; Palgrave, *Docs*, 284, 304.
48. *C.D.S.*, ii, nos 1487, 1535.
49. *C.D.S.*, ii, nos 1757, 1771, 1776, 1839, 1857, 1945; *The Bruce*, ed. Duncan, 192n.
50. J. R. Maddicott, *Thomas of Lancaster* (Oxford, 1970), 80–1; K. B. McFarlane, *The Nobility of Later Medieval England* (Oxford, 1973), 261; J. R. S. Phillips, *Aymer de Valence earl of Pembroke* (Oxford, 1972), 22–9; M. Altschul, *A Baronial Family in England: The Clares* (Baltimore, 1965), 157–9.
51. Barrow, *Robert Bruce*, 123–4.
52. R. R. Davies, *Lordship and Society in the March of Wales, 1282–1400* (Oxford, 1978), 15–85.
53. Davies, *Lordship and Society*, 35–40; R. R. Davies, *Age of Conquest: Wales 1063–1415* (Oxford, 1987), 363, 370–1.
54. R. R. Davies, *The First English Empire*, 26–8, 172–3; R. Frame, *The Political Development of the British Isles*, 142–3; *Thomas Wright's Political Songs of England*, ed. P. Coss (Cambridge, 1996), 380.
55. Frame, *Political Development*, 144–68.
56. Davies, *Lordship and Society*, 80–3; Watson, *Under the Hammer*, 66–7.
57. J. Lydon, *The Lordship of Ireland in the Middle Ages* (Dublin, 1972), 89–120; J. Otway-Ruthven, *A History of Medieval Ireland* (New York, 1992), 191–223.
58. J. Lydon, 'An Irish Army in Scotland, 1296', in *Irish Sword*, v (1961–2), 184–9; J. F. Lydon, 'Edward I, Ireland and the War in Scotland, 1303–1304', in J. Lydon (ed.),

England and Ireland in the Later Middle Ages (Dublin, 1981), 43–59; J. Lydon, 'Irish Levies in the Scottish Wars, 1296–1302', in *Irish Sword*, v (1963), 207–17.

59. *C.D.S.*, ii, nos 1841, 1888.
60. *C.D.S.*, ii, no. 1888.
61. *C.D.S.*, ii, nos 1888–9; *Chron. Guisborough*, 368; *Chron. Lanercost*, 178.
62. A. McDonald, *The Kingdom of the Isles: Scotland's Western Seaboard, 1100–1336* (East Linton, 1997); M. Brown, *Wars of Scotland*, 68–88.
63. Brown, *Wars of Scotland*, 255–60. For galloglass, see K. Simms 'Gallowglass', in S. J. Connolly (ed.), *Oxford Companion to Irish History* (Oxford, 1998), 217.
64. *The Bruce*, ed. Duncan, 142–5, 148; *Chron. Fordun*, ii, 335–6; *Scotichronicon*, ed. Watt, vi, 327; McDonald, *Kingdom of the Isles*, 173–5; Brown, *Wars of Scotland*, 261–2.
65. For Gaelic Ireland in the later Middle Ages, see K. Simms, *From Kings to Warlords: the changing political structure of Gaelic Ireland in the later Middle Ages* (Woodbridge, 1987); K. Nicholls, *Gaelic and Gaelicised Ireland* (Dublin, 1972).
66. K. Simms, 'Relations with the Irish', in J. Lydon (ed.), *Law and Disorder in Thirteenth-Century Ireland* (Dublin, 1997), 66–86, 72.
67. For the text of the letter, see R. Nicholson, 'A sequel to Edward Bruce's Invasion of Ireland', in *S.H.R.*, 42 (1963), 30–40, appendix 1. For its attribution to 1306–7, see S. Duffy, 'The Bruce Brothers and the Irish Sea World, 1306–29', in *Cambridge Medieval Celtic Studies*, no. 21 (1991), 55–86.
68. Simms, 'Relations with the Irish', 70–2.
69. *Chron. Lanercost*, 179–80; *Annals of Connacht*, 184–5; Duffy 'Bruce Brothers', 68–76.
70. McDonald, *Kingdom of the Isles*, 81–3.
71. *C.D.S.*, v, no. 472 (u, w).
72. See for example, *C.D.S.*, ii, nos 1895, 1896.

CHAPTER 2

The Bannockburn War (1307–13)

Bruce's war of survival (January–September 1307)

Early in 1307, Robert Bruce began the attempt to win his kingdom which would lead eventually to the plainlands by the Bannock Burn. According to the near-contemporary account of the Englishman, Walter of Guisborough, Robert left the Isles and mustered his forces on Kintyre. With him was a band of fellow exiles which included his brothers, Edward, Thomas and Alexander, the former sheriff of Ayr, Reginald Crawford, and Sir Gilbert Hay.[1] He was also joined by contingents of Irish and Islesmen, among them Malcolm MacQuillan, a local lord in Kintyre. Bruce's allies also provided him with a fleet of galleys.[2] With these Robert may have probed his enemies' positions and gathered revenues to pay his allies by landing small forces in Carrick, Arran and Galloway.[3] What he found encouraged him to proceed with caution. An English garrison of forty men was installed in Ayr Castle, while nearby were Aymer Valence, Henry Percy, acting as earl of Carrick, and John St John, an English knight with local lands, with their retinues.[4]

The dangers of Bruce's strategy were quickly demonstrated. In late January the king's brothers, Thomas and Alexander, accompanied by MacQuillan and Reginald Crawford, landed at Loch Ryan in Galloway. Whether their venture was a further raid or marked the opening of a land campaign, it ended in disaster. They were met and defeated by a local force led by Dugald MacDouall, 'a chief among the Gallovidians'. While MacQuillan and an Irish king were beheaded at once, the Bruces and Crawford were sent to Carlisle where they were put to death in early February.[5] As well as these losses in family, friends and men, the defeat in Galloway demonstrated to Bruce that, as well as the English, he would be fighting many Scots. Alerted by his movements, King Edward and his agents were raising their own forces. Two of his leading magnates, Ralph Monthermer and Humphrey earl of Hereford, were at Ayr by 11 February, while fifteen ships were summoned from Ireland to join John Menteith, who was himself paid for his service with galleys manned by 1,000 men, in the Firth of Clyde. This fleet was to join in 'putting down Robert Bruce'.[6]

Its leaders were also ordered to prevent Robert 'returning to his boats'.[7] For despite his brothers' fate and the forces gathering against him, in late January

Skelbo •

ROSS

Tarradale •   • 1   2 •   4 •
                              BUCHAN
Urquhart • • Inverness   3 •   ⚔
            MORAY   B
                              ⚔
                              C
THE   Aberdeen •
• GARMORAN   MOUNT

• Inverlochy

            Forfar •
• Dunstaffnage   Dundee •
⚔ D   Perth •   • St Andrews
LORN   Cupar •

        Stirling •

        • Dumbarton

ISLAY Sween •   1310 5 Edinburgh •
                6 7   Berwick •
ARRAN   1310
    ⚔ A   Douglas   Roxburgh
Ayr • 1307 THE
Dunaverty • Turnberry • FOREST   TYNEDALE
CARRICK   Dumfries
GALLOWAY
                          Newcastle •
ULSTER   Carlisle   Durham •

Symbol	Legend	Battles		Castles	
•	Castles	A	Loudoun Hill	1	Nairn
⚔	Battles	B	Slioch	2	Elgin
-------	Edward II's campaigns of 1307 and 1310	C	Old Meldrum	3	Balvenie
		D	Brander	4	Banff
				5	Linlithgow
				6	Rutherglen
				7	Bothwell

MAP 2.1 *The Scottish War (1307–13)*

Robert made his landing. His descent on Carrick was a desperate gamble. King Edward at Lanercost Priory clearly expected a rapid result. Twice, on 6 and then 11 February, he dispatched letters to his local commanders expressing 'great wonder' that he had not heard of their success in 'crushing the Scottish rebels'. The king accused Valence, Percy and others of excessive caution and of concealing their failures.[8] They had bad news to hide. Despite their advantage in numbers, Bruce had won first blood. Finding a company of Percy's men camped in a village near Turnberry, Robert launched a sudden attack on them, killing some, dispersing the rest and capturing horses and booty. Percy took refuge in Turnberry Castle and the force of about sixty cavalry from the royal household launched by Edward against Robert in mid-February was probably designed to rescue him and restore contact between Turnberry and Ayr.[9]

The failure of King Edward's commanders to crush the rebels during February meant that the war entered a new phase. There were no further references to Robert and his men returning to their boats. Instead, by mid-March the English reported that Bruce was 'lurking in the moors and marshes of Scotland'.[10] From Carrick eastwards through Galloway to the dales of the Clyde and Annan ran a broad expanse of upland moss and heather. Like other Scottish leaders during the wars, Bruce exploited the rough and broken terrain of the south-west as a refuge and roadway. Realising that remaining static would be fatal, Robert kept on the move. Leaving Carrick, Bruce led his small band of adherents and mercenaries through the hills to upper Nithsdale in March and the following month was back in Glen Trool in the hills of western Galloway.[11] King Edward responded by raising contingents of several thousand foot from the hills of Cumberland and Westmorland who might be expected to adapt well to warfare in the Scottish uplands. More directly, the English king assembled small bands of paid troops to pursue Bruce. Seventy mounted knights and men-at-arms and 180 archers were sent against Robert in Nithsdale, while forty cavalry and 300 archers raided Glen Trool in April.[12]

Against the resources at Edward's disposal, Bruce could not win a straight military contest. The size of the companies dispatched to Nithsdale and Glen Trool suggests that Robert's own force numbered a few hundred men. Though he had avoided defeat, the capture of one of his followers, John Wallace, brother of William, in late March suggests the inevitable effect of attrition on Bruce's party.[13] To survive, let alone advance his cause, Robert needed to win the recognition of Scots, recruiting new men to his banner and collecting revenues and supplies to maintain his small army. There is little evidence to suggest a significant flow of support to Bruce in March and April 1307. Even those who sympathised with his actions may have been waiting the outcome of events before risking an open display of allegiance to their king. At best Robert may have had to compel service and extract supplies from the poor people. However, despite their advantages in manpower, strongholds and authority, the officials of the English king faced their own problems. The survival of Bruce as a military presence within Scotland challenged Edward's claims to rule. Experience had taught Edward the potential fragility of his administration in Scotland. He was clearly sensitive to the loyalty and allegiance of his Scottish subjects. In March he ordered repairs to be made to a number of castles in the north-east, far from the fighting, and instructed his officials not to be 'too harsh and rigorous' in the treatment of Scots, especially those 'compelled' by Bruce to join or supply him. He also showed a readiness to restore lands to Scottish magnates he had forfeited in 1306. James Stewart performed homage to the English king, swearing fealty on a relic taken by Edward from the Welsh prince, and recovered his estates.[14] The continuing war also created problems of logistics. Garrisons at Ayr, Dumfries, Lanark, Bothwell and one newly installed at Cumnock and retinues and companies in the field all needed wages and supplies. These had to be carried through areas haunted by rebels and presented Bruce with an opportunity to augment his own resources.

In early May 1307 the treasurer of England and close royal councillor, Walter Langton, was in south-west Scotland overseeing the supply of his king's forces. On 10 May, in the company of Aymer Valence and a force of cavalry, he was travelling from Ayr to Clydesdale when his escort was confronted by Bruce and an army of about 600 footmen at Loudoun Hill in the moors above Kilmarnock.[15] Drawn by the prospect of Langton's silver, Robert had chosen to face the English king's warden in the field. Bruce had drawn up his spearmen in a close body on a dry field surrounded by mosses. He strengthened this further by digging ditches, which prevented his force being outflanked. Valence could not resist the chance of crushing the rising at a stroke and took the challenge. Charging Bruce's spears head on, the men-at-arms were bloodily repulsed.[16] Valence withdrew towards Ayr. In military terms the battle of Loudoun Hill achieved little. Valence and the treasurer crossed the hills by another route and were at Bothwell by 13 May. If Bruce moved towards Ayr, as several chroniclers believed, it was to emphasise his victory, not to make a serious attempt to take the town. By early June Ayr had been reinforced by 300 footmen led by Patrick earl of Dunbar, while Valence was also in the town with a retinue which included several other Scottish nobles. Valence led this company south into Carrick and Galloway while a second force moved west from Kirkpatrick in Galloway. These bands clashed with Bruce in Glen Trool once again and, though they suffered losses, it was Bruce who retreated, pursued by the enemy.[17]

If Robert's military position remained deeply insecure, Loudoun Hill did mark a political turning point. An English report written from Carlisle on 15 May recounted the effects of Valence's retreat from 'King Hobbe without doing any exploit'. King Edward was 'enraged' by this and the letter writer revealed a sense of confusion and anxiety in his administration. Though David Strathbogie, son of the earl of Atholl who had been executed in 1306, had made his peace, another young noble, James Douglas, who had 'begged that he might be received . . . when he saw that our troops retreated, he chose no longer to keep his word'. There was also talk of 'a wicked alliance amongst some of our people who are siding with the king's enemies'.[18] Further afield there were similar growing fears that Bruce's first visible success would have an impact on allegiances. Another letter, perhaps written by Edward I's Scottish adherent Alexander Abernethy, from Forfar, painted a picture of rising sympathy for Bruce in the north and north-east. Rumours being spread 'by false preachers from Robert's army' of their king's success and of Edward's imminent death fuelled such sentiments and the writer feared for the future.[19] The actions of James Douglas revealed wider cracks in the structures of loyalty which underpinned Edward's rule in Scotland and the opportunities they presented to King Robert. Douglas had been disinherited by Edward, his family lands granted to Robert Clifford. Bruce's success offered Douglas a chance of recovery. After Valence's repulse at Loudoun, only a few miles from Douglas, James made his own move. He entered Douglasdale, raised a force of freeholders and took Douglas Castle from Clifford's garrison. James did not remain and the castle was being repaired by late May, but his actions revealed how widening allegiance to Bruce also spread the focus of warfare.[20]

Edward I reacted to the reports of his men by summoning an army to undertake a full-scale campaign in the south-west. The muster was scheduled for 8 July but on the previous day the old king died. 'Fearless and warlike', 'strenuous and illustrious', the death of the sixty-seven-year-old ruler was an event with massive implications for the peoples of the British Isles.[21] It was not, however, unexpected and preparations for his planned expedition continued. The new king, Edward of Caernarfon, arrived at Carlisle from the south to take up his duties as king of England. In early August Edward II led north an impressive army which contained seven English earls, among them his cousin, Thomas of Lancaster, Aymer Valence and Humphrey earl of Hereford, and Scottish lords like the earls of Buchan and Dunbar. The host reached Dumfries on 3 August, staying ten days before moving up Nithsdale. Edward arrived at Cumnock on 19 August.[22] With a sizeable force, which included numerous Scottish magnates, based at Ayr, the new king was asserting his military ascendancy in the field. However, as he was to learn in the coming years, the ability to put large forces in the field for short periods did not guarantee the defeat of the enemy. As he had been doing repeatedly since February, Robert and his men simply stayed out of the reach of these larger hosts, waiting for them to disperse. Without doing more than waiting at Cumnock for a week, Edward II turned for home.[23]

Throughout the campaign Edward's attention was on his new role. For his adherents, there were worrying signs. He sacked and imprisoned Walter Langton, his father's minister, who had clashed with Edward and his friends in 1305. The chief of these friends, the Gascon knight Piers Gaveston, had been exiled by the old king. With his father's death, Edward was free to recall his favourite. Gaveston swiftly followed Edward north and joined him at Dumfries on 4 August.[24] At this meeting the simple knight was transformed into the earl of Cornwall, a title previously borne by royal kinsmen. Gaveston became the lord of extensive lands in Cornwall, Devon and elsewhere. Though the act was accepted by the other earls, it must have sowed doubts about Edward's abilities, priorities and friendships in the minds of magnates who were ready to serve the new king in his war. Edward left Scotland on 31 August, his attention turning to England and his coronation.[25] It would not be until 1314 that he would be able to assemble such a force of his earls for the Scottish war.

In a tactic which would become a regular part of his armoury, Bruce responded to the departure of an English field army with an attack on his enemies in Scotland. By the end of September complaints were reaching the new king from 'the community, leaders and men of Galloway that Robert Bruce and his accomplices is now come and has perpetrated robberies, murders, burnings and other evils' and was 'inciting and compelling' men to rebel.[26] Edward ordered his Scottish adherents to go to Galloway and drive Robert off but made no wider plans. Further north Douglas and two other barons who now rejoined Bruce's party, Robert Boyd and Alexander Lindsay, were engaged in fighting with Valence and Philip Mowbray in Kyle north of Ayr and near Paisley.[27] While the ambitions of Bruce and his adherents grew, the direct concern and involvement of the English crown with Scotland was on the wane.

THE WINNING OF THE NORTH (OCTOBER 1307–FEBRUARY 1309)

Edward departed, intending to lead a fresh campaign to Scotland in summer 1308. Until then his adherents were left to fend for themselves. Valence had initially been named as lieutenant of Scotland but in September he was replaced by John of Brittany earl of Richmond, a much less active and energetic leader. Letters sent out to Scottish and English lords in September and October make it clear that they were to bear the brunt of the war. In particular, on 18 October, Edward ordered a group of English barons with Scottish estates, including Valence, Hereford, Henry Percy, Robert Clifford and Henry Beaumont, to go to Scotland to defend their lands there.[28] This was the purpose behind the grant of Scottish estates to them but, without clear direction from the king, these magnates remained in England. Garrisons were maintained by Edward in perhaps twenty castles from Inverness to Ayr and by his noble adherents in other locations, but during the winter of 1307–8 the level of military opposition to Robert Bruce and his allies slackened considerably.[29]

Robert was quick to grasp the opportunity this presented. During October he left the hills and moors of the south-west and, accompanied by a force which probably numbered only a few hundred, began a long march northwards. It was a gamble, but a calculated one. After eight months of fighting in Carrick, Galloway and Ayrshire, Robert was still fighting a war of raids and ambushes. Edwardian garrisons still held all the major castles and burghs and

could call on help from England and Ireland. Though his support and his reputation had grown, Robert saw the need to secure a power base from which he
could draw men and supplies. Scotland beyond the Mounth, north of the
Grampians, had the potential to be such a base. Between 1297 and 1303 the
region had lain outside the reach of Edward I, providing resources to his
Scottish enemies. Robert set off for the north with the intention of establish-
ing his authority there before an English field army could return the following summer.[30]

Bruce's plan would not have been a complete surprise to his enemies. Since
March there had been signs of anxiety and preparations in the north and
north-east which suggest an awareness of potential support for Robert in the
region. However, though Bruce did have influential allies in the north, his aim
of winning control of the region was not an easy one. As Barbour put it seventy
years later, 'he had fayis mony ane' beyond the Mounth.[31] In a region traditionally dominated by great magnate families, the leading nobles were almost
all opposed to him. From John of Lorn in northern Argyll, to William earl of
Ross, whose province stretched from the Moray Firth to Skye, to the leading
barons of Moray and Aberdeenshire, like David Strathbogie earl of Atholl,
Duncan Frendraught and Gilbert Glencairnie, there was a hostile coalition
facing Bruce. At the heart of this were the Comyns, established leaders in these
lands. Though the son of the murdered Red Comyn was still a child, his
kinsman, John earl of Buchan, was an experienced, if not particularly gifted,
head of the family. To provide leadership to this group, Edward II had
appointed John Mowbray his lieutenant beyond the Mounth.[32] An outsider from Lothian, Mowbray was expected to act as the king's agent and co-
ordinate opposition to Bruce in the north from this group of lords.

In the months of winter warfare which followed, the lack of co-ordination
between his enemies would, in fact, prove to be crucial. Bruce's march probably took him through the Lennox north of Glasgow and mid-Argyll, both
areas where he had friends, before he reached Inverlochy Castle at the foot of
the Great Glen. On 25 November this Comyn stronghold surrendered to
Robert 'through deceit and treason of the men of the castle'.[33] For a king
seeking to win support, it was an encouraging start which opened the way
north and Bruce followed it up by a rapid march up the glen into the province
of Moray. He rapidly took Urquhart, which had been left ungarrisoned, and
forced the earl of Ross to make a truce. This truce isolated the castles at
Inverness and Nairn, which Robert captured and destroyed. Such victories
probably brought in new recruits and former allies.[34] However, Bruce's run of
successes ended when he failed to take Elgin Castle and, soon afterwards, the
king fell ill while besieging the castle at Banff.[35] Perhaps sensing the stalling of
Bruce's campaign, Mowbray, Buchan and Atholl advanced towards Moray at
the head of a small army. Robert could only travel by litter and command of
his forces was taken by his brother, Edward. The Bruces' host 'left the plains',
taking up a position in the hills at Slioch. Mowbray, Buchan and Atholl

FIGURE 2.1 *Inverlochy Castle was built for the Red Comyn lords of Badenoch and Lochaber in about 1270. Constructed to guard the southern entrance to the Great Glen, it fell to Bruce by treachery on his march north in late 1307. (Crown Copyright. Historic Scotland)*

approached and on Christmas Day there was skirmishing between the armies before the magnates withdrew to raise more foot. They returned a week later and this time the Bruce brothers retreated.[36]

Slioch was a success for Mowbray and his allies which the lieutenant sought to exploit. He harried 'all freeholders and other men that he knew to be of evil repute', seeking to prevent Bruce from winning more recruits among this key group. He also sent the keeper of Aberdeen Castle, Gilbert Peche, to Ross to try to get the earl to lead his men against Bruce from the west.[37] At this crucial point, however, Earl William refused to break the truce he had agreed and Mowbray and the earls were themselves called south to meet with the lieutenant, John of Brittany. They agreed a truce with Bruce until March, which presumably extended to Mar, Garioch and Buchan but left Robert a free hand further west. The king, who had now recovered, began by taking Balvenie Castle before turning against the earl of Ross. His men launched attacks on the borders of Ross. The castle of Tarradale on the Black Isle fell to Robert, while Skelbo in Sutherland was captured by his local adherent, William Wiseman, in early April. Ross fell back before this assault. In a letter to King Edward the earl claimed that Bruce had advanced with 'a great power', forcing him to make a truce until June 'at the entreaty of the good men' of his province.[38] Earl William's further complaint that Lachlan MacRuairi was defying him in the Isles may give a glimpse of a wider picture. The earls of Ross had long acted as agents of Scottish kings in the Western Isles and their activities had brought them into conflict with Islesmen. Lachlan had been a problem for William for over a decade and in early 1308 seized on Bruce's campaign to reject the earl's lordship.[39] The ineffectiveness of the earl in opposing Bruce, a major element in Robert's success, was probably increased by the actions of Islesmen like Lachlan.

Ross also claimed that the absence of Mowbray had left him isolated. However, his truce allowed Bruce to turn back east against Buchan and Mowbray. In late April the king laid siege to Elgin a second time but the castle was relieved by John Mowbray.[40] Despite this, Bruce pressed eastwards into Strathbogie and then across the hills into the Garioch. Mowbray followed and joined up with John earl of Buchan and other nobles at Old Meldrum in Garioch, assembling a force numbered by Barbour at around 1,000.[41] Bruce was encamped a few miles away south of the River Don near Inverurie, between his enemies and Aberdeen. On 25 May David lord of Brechin, one of Buchan's comrades, led a company of men-at-arms into Inverurie, surprising and defeating a group of King Robert's soldiers. Bruce reacted by leading his whole army across the river towards Old Meldrum. Buchan and Mowbray formed up their force with cavalry in front and footmen in a mass to the rear. They probably expected Bruce to halt his advance and prepare for the clash but the king came on 'with baneris to the wynd wavand . . . makand gret fayr'. This display of royal symbols and kingly confidence disconcerted Robert's enemies. Perhaps to make room for a charge, Buchan's knights tried to withdraw a little and Robert led his men in attack under the royal banner. The enemy horse fell back and seeing their retreat, the foot soldiers 'turnyt the bak' and fled.[42] Battle became rout and pursuit. Bruce's men chased some of the enemy to the borders of Buchan. The king soon followed with his whole host. He made camp at Fyvie and 'advancing from there consumed Buchan with fire, he punished some people, brought some to his peace. He scattered his enemies and came away from there as the victor.' This 'herschip of Bouchane' was a calculated act of destruction.[43] It displayed the king's new dominance, the price of adhering to his enemies and the end of the Comyns as leading magnates in the north-east.

Leaving Ross cowed and the surviving garrisons at Banff and Elgin isolated, Robert acted to exploit his victory to the full. At the beginning of July he laid siege to the castle at Aberdeen. The previous year this had held a garrison of fifty-five men. Its keeper, Gilbert Peche, was in England, where he received £100 to lead the relief of the castle by sea.[44] However, Bruce had his own ships, provided by a German merchant, and by the end of July he had taken Aberdeen, probably by blockade.[45] The fall of the castle and control of the burgh gave Robert an east coast port from which he could extend his contacts with traders in Germany and the Low Countries. Exports of wool and hides from the north-east and imports of armour and weapons from the continent would sustain Bruce's war effort. With the fall of Aberdeen and the establishment of his primacy beyond the Mounth, Robert could act as a king in part of his realm.

While his province smouldered, the earl of Buchan fled south accompanied by Mowbray. The news they carried of the sudden collapse of King Edward's lordship north of the Mounth must have come as a shock. Only five days before the defeat at Old Meldrum, the king had sent letters to Buchan, Mowbray and sixteen others thanking them for their 'faithful service' in the north.[46] Edward could hardly complain of his adherents. For months he had given no real help to the many Scottish lords who opposed Bruce as a usurper and murderer. The king's neglect was a result of his preoccupations in England. Though these involved his marriage in January 1308 to Isabelle, daughter of King Philip IV of France, and his coronation the following month, Edward's failure to support his Scottish men with English resources was due to the breakdown in his relationships with his greatest lords.[47] The elevation of Piers Gaveston, who was left as keeper of England when Edward went to France for his wedding, antagonised almost all the other earls. They found the monopoly of influence with the king which this upstart possessed unacceptable. Among those opposed to the king were Valence, Hereford and Robert Clifford, figures who might have been expected to defend Edward's Scottish lordship. In March and April, while the campaign in northern Scotland was in the balance, Edward and his magnates stood on the brink of civil war.[48] It was only after a long and difficult meeting of parliament that, on 18 May, the king agreed to send Gaveston away. Even then Edward tempered the sentence by making his favourite lieutenant in Ireland on 16 June. It was an act which further demonstrated the king's lack of concern for anything except Gaveston's wellbeing. Only a day earlier Edward had appointed Richard earl of Ulster as his lieutenant.[49] Though the earl would be compensated for his dismissal and Gaveston was not a disaster in his role, Edward was clearly not concerned with the smooth running of his dominions.

The same lesson applied to Scotland. The reports of events sent south by Mowbray, the earl of Ross and other Scottish lords were filed away and by the time Gaveston left for Ireland it was too late to stop Bruce winning the submission of the lands between the Mounth and Ross. However, it was probably in June that the king announced plans for an army to muster at Carlisle in late August. Edward meant to lead a major force into southern Scotland to put Bruce and his supporters back on the defensive. Once again English politics intervened. Though the mood was now one of reconciliation between king and earls, the political class remained wholly preoccupied with the fallout from earlier tensions. On 11 August it was announced that the planned Scottish campaign would not take place.[50] The king appointed wardens with small paid retinues to defend his adherents. Buchan and Mowbray were now to be lieutenants in Galloway, while no warden was specifically appointed to the region beyond the Mounth. It was an admission of failure, but also a recognition of worse to come. These wardens were empowered to make truces with Bruce to protect the castles and communities in their charge, though Edward refused to seek a general ceasefire with the enemy. For Edward's Scottish adherents such orders confirmed recent defeats. On 31 October William earl of Ross submitted to King Robert at Auldearn in Moray, receiving his lands back in return for an oath of fealty.[51] In contrast, John Comyn earl of Buchan was an exile from his province and in December he died, leaving behind him two nieces as the heirs to his once-great lineage.[52]

The likely despair of Buchan and the submission of Ross were not just driven by the failure of King Edward to protect them. They also stemmed from the reaction of King Robert to his enemies' weakness and division. It is a mark of Bruce's ability that, despite the exertions of the winter and his own recent illness, he seized the advantages presented by English political crises. He could now also count on the service of able lieutenants who could act on their own. In December 1307, while his king was struggling in Moray, James Douglas remained active in the south. News that the men of Selkirk Forest had joined Robert Bruce marked James's presence in an upland region which had long been a problem for Edwardian officials seeking to control southern Scotland.[53] From this refuge Douglas could lead forays into Clydesdale, the lower Tweed valley and even England. An attempt to dislodge him with a small force led by Scottish nobles was defeated in the summer of 1308 and one of its leaders, Thomas Randolph, was captured.[54] Randolph, who had supported his uncle, King Robert, in 1306, would soon renew his support for the Bruce Cause, rapidly taking up a leading role. Douglas was also harnessed to the renewal of major fighting in the south-west. Immediately after the defeat of Buchan and Mowbray, Edward Bruce was sent south by his brother. Drawing Douglas, Alexander Lindsay and Robert Boyd to his banner and raising a force of Islesmen under Domnhaill of Islay, Edward attacked Galloway.[55] As the defeat of Thomas and Alexander Bruce in early 1307 had shown, the men of Galloway were hostile to the Bruces. Residual antipathy to Scotland, the claims of the Balliol family to the province and a long-standing bloodfeud with the Bruce earldom of Carrick combined to make the Gallovidians opponents of King Robert. On 29 June Edward Bruce met and defeated the men of Galloway, perhaps near the River Cree. He spent the summer in the region, securing the submission of western Galloway, and in early September defeated a force under Ingeram Umfraville in the province.[56]

While his brother was winning fame in the south, Robert was not idle. On the fall of Aberdeen he may have made local truces with Edward's wardens and headed west with an army, for the first time numbering thousands. His target was Lorn, the lordship of the mac Dougalls. Alexander of Argyll and his son, John, were enemies of Bruce who had harried him in 1306 and 1307. Robert now had his revenge. He presumably marched through Breadalbane to the shores of Loch Awe, where he may have recruited local landowners into his host. Probably in mid-September Robert forced the Pass of Brander, defeating an attempted ambush.[57] John wrote to Edward II that 'I am not sure of my neighbours in any direction', suggesting that, like the earl of Ross, the

FIGURE 2.2 *The castle of Dunstaffnage was a key stronghold of Alexander of Argyll and his son John of Lorn at the heart of their lordship in Argyll and the Isles. It fell to King Robert in either 1308 or 1309. (Crown Copyright. Historic Scotland)*

resources of the mac Dougalls were dispersed by threats from both Bruce and local enemies like Domnhaill and Angus Og of Islay.[58] After an initial truce, Alexander submitted. John refused, fleeing by sea to Ireland. In October he was seeking aid to hold onto remaining castles but major resistance was over.[59] By the end of September King Robert was heading east, stopping at Inchmahome and Dunkeld before moving towards English-held Perth. His moves may have been designed to link up with adherents who had carried his cause into Fife. Fighting between Scottish knights and the garrison at Cupar Castle had apparently occurred during the spring and summer and both Cupar and the bishop's castle at St Andrews may have fallen to Robert's men by the onset of winter.[60]

During the last months of 1308 reports were carried to Edward II of attacks into Lothian and the western marches of England. There were even fears for the safety of Berwick.[61] It was a mark of the rapid unravelling of Edward's hold on Scotland under the unrelenting pressure of Robert and his adherents. In December the English king responded to events in the north, appointing a new lieutenant. Gilbert Clare earl of Gloucester was a new presence in English politics. He had only assumed his position in 1307, inheriting the lands not just of a great English magnate, but the lordships of Glamorgan in the Welsh marches and Kilkenny in Ireland, which made him the greatest vassal of the king throughout his dominions.[62] Almost alone among the magnates, Gloucester had not fallen out with Edward over Gaveston, apparently not resenting the favourite's marriage to his sister in 1307. As lieutenant of Scotland he had the prestige to lead a recovery and a degree of enthusiasm for the fight. Gloucester went north in October and was joined by a force of household knights and men-at-arms and Welsh archers to relieve the small castle of Rutherglen in Clydesdale.[63] This campaign may have been successful, but even if so it hardly altered the results of a year which was miraculous for Bruce and disastrous for his enemies. The fall of Forfar Castle to local men in December was a further blow which weakened the positions of a number of Edward's leading Scottish adherents, like Alexander Abernethy and David Brechin, whose estates in Angus were now rendered highly vulnerable.[64] Forfar's capture was the last of a string of losses which marked the contrasting fortunes of the rival kings and their parties.

KING EDWARD AND KING ROBERT (FEBRUARY 1309–JULY 1311)

By the end of 1308 both sides in the war were moving towards a period of truce. The initiative for this had come from King Philip of France who had sent his son, Louis, to Edward and a less prestigious embassy to Robert during November.[65] Philip wished to end the war in the interests of launching an expedition to recover the Holy Land. Talks were arranged between the envoys of the English and Scottish kings and a general truce was agreed to run from mid-February until All Saints' Day (1 November).[66] Both Edward and Robert were keen to respond to the French king's intervention. Edward was anxious to avoid tensions with his father-in-law. The previous year Philip had regarded Edward's relations with Gaveston with displeasure, seeing them as an insult to his daughter, Queen Isabelle. The French king had worked actively with Gaveston's enemies among the English nobility and Edward was keen to avoid him intervening further in English politics or the Scottish war.[67] Bruce hoped for the exact reverse. His murder of Comyn, usurpation and excommunication had made him an outcast among Christian kings. Philip, who had given the Scottish guardians his support up to 1303 and remained the protector of the exiled John Balliol, had offered Bruce no help. His letters to Robert in 1308 did not address him as king.[68] However, for Bruce any contact was an advance which had been won by his successes in warfare. He was keen to exploit the opportunity. A month after the truce had begun, Robert held his first parliament. It met at St Andrews and its main business was to display Bruce as the king of Scots before a European audience. A letter was sent to King Philip from the Scottish nobility which responded to his request for participation in the crusade by reminding him of the alliance he had made with the Scots. Robert was identified as 'our lawful and true leader and prince' who was fighting to uphold their liberties.[69] Similar language characterised a second letter sent from the assembly, the so-called Declaration of the Clergy. This was an effort to win the support, or at least placate the hostility, of the papacy towards the excommunicant Bruce by demonstrating the justice of his cause.[70]

Both Edward and Robert also desired a period of truce from motives which were closer to home. For Edward it seemed a chance to end the run of defeats his men had suffered in Scotland since late 1307. Losses of castles, lands and people from his control had been disastrous and the English king clearly

FIGURE 2.3 *The centre of the Scottish church, St Andrews was probably taken by Bruce's supporters in 1308 and only months later served as the location for the king's first parliament. In 1318 the consecration of the cathedral was turned into a thanksgiving for the victory at Bannockburn. (Author's photograph)*

sought to stabilise the military and political situation in the north, ensuring supplies reached his garrisons and Scottish supporters during spring and early summer 1309. Moreover, the truce terms seemed advantageous. According to the contemporary *Lanercost Chronicle*, both sides agreed to return all lands taken since late July 1308.[71] This would mean Bruce giving up his gains since the fall of Aberdeen, returning Forfar and castles in Fife and Galloway. However, Edward's real concerns in 1309 lay with his relations with his barons and, once again, revolved around Piers Gaveston. In his dealings with the earls the king was ready to make gifts and concessions to secure Gaveston's recall from Ireland. His relations with King Philip and his readiness to accept a truce in Scotland sprang from the same motive. From March until June English politics were absorbed by the question of the return of the favourite, which Edward only secured in late June in return for making concessions about his powers as king.[72]

By this point the true nature of the truce was becoming apparent. It was Robert who benefited from the end of major warfare. As mentioned above, he quickly called a parliament. The first formal meeting of the community under a Scottish king since 1295 was a visible display of Robert's royal title and status. If attendance was, naturally, limited to those barons, clergy and freeholders who had paid Bruce homage, it was a potent symbolic event. By holding it at St Andrews, Robert was demonstrating both his physical and ideological position, at the main ecclesiastical centre in his realm, and in control of a large burgh and port in central Scotland. The parliament may well have seen Robert receive the fealty of his subjects, especially those like Thomas Randolph, James the Steward and John Menteith who had only recently left Edward II's allegiance.[73] For a man whose kingship up to the end of 1308 had been exercised solely in the field of war, the occasion marked the attainment of authority and recognition in the more normal aspects of monarchy.

Robert's readiness to accept the truce may also have stemmed from the strains of war. While we have none of the wealth of material which illustrates Edwardian military organisation for their enemy, the simple fact that Bruce had been engaged in warfare without a break for nearly two years from January 1307 suggests that a halt to major hostilities may have been welcome. If so, by the summer Bruce was ready for a renewal of war. He had never implemented the terms of the truce, restoring nothing from his gains in late 1308, and by the end of July 1309 Edward was complaining that 'the truce agreed . . . with our Scots enemies and rebels lasting for a certain time, the Scots do not observe but break'.[74] Instead they were attacking Edward's liegemen and his castles, lands and tenants 'in those parts', suggesting a fresh wave of forays by Bruce's adherents which intensified during the summer.[75] In response, on 30 July Edward II summoned his barons to perform military service in Scotland, while a week later orders were issued for the raising of 9,000 foot from Wales and northern England. These forces were to assemble at Berwick in late September, when Edward would lead them north 'to chastise the rebellion of our enemies and rebels'.[76] Money and supplies were gathered for the expedition but, as in 1308, such bold intentions rapidly dissipated. By September it was clear that the king no longer planned to go to Scotland in person and the forces summoned were first reduced and then cancelled.[77] Renewed hostility to Gaveston from the barons meant that concern for the defence of Scotland was relegated in importance. Instead of an army, in October Edward informed his Scottish adherents that he was sending a force of only 200 mounted men-at-arms and about 1,600 Welsh foot to defend them through the winter against the enemy under the command of the earl of Hereford, Henry Beaumont and Robert Clifford.[78] Though these were experienced captains, they were no compensation for a royal-led army, and the keepers of Edward's exposed garrisons at Perth, Ayr, Dundee and Banff were given powers to seek local truces which probably extended to a general end to fighting over the winter.[79]

News of Edward's planned campaign may have prompted his enemy into fresh action. In the early autumn Bruce launched a new campaign against Alexander of Argyll. Though Alexander had attended the parliament in March, his son, John, was in the English king's allegiance. This dual loyalty made the family suspect and Bruce was not prepared to risk Alexander's defection. In late summer Robert led another expedition into Argyll, forcing Alexander to flee into exile.[80] The king's fears were natural. The western seaboard had been exploited by Edward I as a region of weak loyalties where his enemies were vulnerable and there are signs that his son attempted to do the same from late 1309.[81] Despite the exile of Alexander and John of Argyll, Edward saw the chance of threatening Bruce from the west. Even while he abandoned his planned campaign in October 1309, the king ordered his English lieges in Ireland to raise a force of nearly 3,000 horse and foot to be at Ayr in late June 1310, challenging Bruce's hold on the west.[82]

However, during the winter Edward's chance of challenging his enemy anywhere seemed slim. The personality of Gaveston, which captivated the king and repulsed almost all the other magnates, once again shaped political priorities in England. By early 1310 the leading nobles were united in opposition to their king, motivated by hatred of Gaveston and a desire to limit Edward's mismanagement. Under the leadership of the king's cousin and greatest subject, Thomas earl of Lancaster, the barons drew up the Ordinances, a document which placed restrictions on the king's use of patronage, his raising of revenues and his household.[83] In March Edward was coerced into accepting these rules and the supervision of his rule by his barons which was involved in them. Ironically, the very restrictions placed on the king may have pushed him towards a more direct role in the Scottish war. The desire to escape close supervision, to protect Gaveston and to divide his opponents may have played a part in Edward's decision to lead his long-postponed expedition to Scotland. A second motive was said to have been Edward's reluctance to pay homage to Philip of France for his duchy of Aquitaine.[84] However, the crucial prompt may well have come from Scotland. On 16 June, a group of Edward's Scottish adherents led by Alexander Abernethy, Ingeram Umfraville and Alexander and John of Argyll attended the king's council at Westminster.[85] They told the king of the loss of his castles and lands, regardless of truces, probably referring to recent setbacks such as the fall of Banff Castle and the defeat of a force of his adherents near Roxburgh, as well as a threat to Perth.[86] Asked about a 'speedy remedy' to the situation, the Scots advised their lord that unless 'we [the king] went thither in person . . . we should lose the country and those who remain faithful to us by our default and negligence'.

These blunt words had the desired effect.[87] Edward gave authority to Umfraville, Abernethy and John of Argyll in Galloway, the north-east and the Isles respectively and wrote at once to his vassals ordering them to bring their quotas of cavalry to serve in his Scottish campaign.[88] More summons for cavalry and foot followed through July and early August which specified Berwick as the muster point. However, when the king reached Berwick in mid-September it was clear that the results of his recruiting efforts were disappointing. In particular, most of the earls stayed away. Lancaster, Hereford and Valence, who had major Scottish interests, refused to come in person, sending small contingents instead. Along with Gaveston, only Earl Warenne and the young earl of Gloucester joined Edward.[89] The force that assembled, though much smaller than the largest armies raised by Edward I, was still an effective size. It has been calculated as containing 1,700 cavalry, 2,500 Welsh foot and 500 English foot.[90] These numbers were probably sufficient to take on anything Bruce could raise and their relative smallness meant it would be easier to secure supplies. By 20 September the English king was at last taking the field.

Further west, Edward's plans had already got off to a faltering start. The employment of exiles from the Isles including John of Argyll and John MacSween raised hopes of a challenge to Bruce's allies in the west. MacSween was from a family which had been driven from Knapdale in Argyll by the Stewarts in the 1260s. In July 1310 Edward granted him his family's lost lands and he led a galley fleet to recover them from their current holder, John Menteith.[91] John of Argyll planned a similar exercise further north and Edward sought to back their efforts with ships from Ireland and western England. However, the Irish army summoned the previous year was delayed, perhaps by bad weather, and, without support, MacSween's attack was driven off.[92] Instead, by December Edward had received news from the west that a fleet had been sent from the 'foreign isles' by Bruce to plunder the Isle of Man. Orders were sent out for ships and men to be sent from England and Ireland to aid the steward of Man, Gilbert MacAsky. English concern for the defence of Man suggests that Bruce had successfully neutralised the threat to his own realm through the Irish Sea and was able to strike back.[93]

The advance of the English king's army proved less easy to divert. During late September Edward's host advanced up the Tweed valley, skirting Selkirk Forest, and by 4 October was at Biggar in Clydesdale.[94] The army then marched up Clydesdale, presumably via the garrisons at Bothwell and Rutherglen, reaching Renfrew on 18 October before turning east. On 24 October Edward was at Linlithgow, where a garrison held the earthwork or pele built by his father. After a brief foray to Glasgow in early November, the king and the bulk of his army was back at Berwick by the middle of the month.[95] During this progress,

Robert and his lieutenants avoided contact with the army, sticking to the moors and hills, but they clearly dogged the march at various points. The *Vita Edwardi Secundi* reports that when small groups of Edward's men were sent to forage they came under attack. On one occasion several hundred English and Welsh were killed by a force of Scots which then retired to refuges in caves.[96] As soon as the army was back in Berwick, Robert assembled his own host and led it into Lothian and 'inflicted much damage upon those who were in the king of England's peace'.[97] Edward immediately took a small force in pursuit, but Robert withdrew. The English king now sent his army into winter quarters at Berwick, Norham, Wark and Roxburgh. A parley was held with Bruce who was at Selkirk, but Robert refused to attend a meeting at Melrose fearing treachery.[98]

That a plot to seize Bruce during negotiations was contemplated is not unlikely and would suggest the bankruptcy of Edward's autumn campaign. His march through the south had achieved little and Robert may have expected his opponent to return south. However, Edward was far from finished. Though English writers put his continued presence in Scotland during early 1311 down to a reluctance to face his baronial critics, Edward and his captains did have a fresh plan. In January Gaveston was sent north with 200 cavalry. His aim was to prevent Bruce from returning from the south to recruit more men. Gaveston reached Perth and then visited Dundee, both major English outposts.[99] He may have found the situation promising. Since the previous summer Alexander Abernethy had been in charge of the region beyond the Forth and his efforts may have made inroads in Angus. *Lanercost* reported that Gaveston was able to 'receive to peace all beyond the Scottish sea' and Abernethy, aided by David Brechin, may have headed a body of renewed opposition to Bruce. The recovery led to plans being made to send siege engines by ship to Aberdeen, suggesting a foray beyond the Mounth was being considered.[100]

This probably did not happen, but Bruce was clearly on the back foot. In early April it was reported by the English that Robert meant to meet Gaveston in battle, a major divergence from his previous strategy. His failure to follow this plan through was ascribed to his lack of confidence in the ability of his men to meet the English on open ground.[101] Gaveston's brief foray had at last made a dent in Bruce's position. Edward was keen to exploit this situation and in April and May was laying plans for a renewed campaign during the summer. An army was summoned to meet at Berwick but, more strikingly, fresh efforts were made for an expedition from the west. A fleet was to be sent under John of Argyll from Ulster into the Isles in a campaign which the king's order described as one of 'the greatest movements in the Scottish war'.[102] Edward's readiness to fight and the plans for a fresh campaign in 1311 belie his usual reputation as lazy and incompetent. However, the real impetus may have come from Piers Gaveston who, for all his failings, showed himself an able and active soldier in both Ireland and Scotland. The winter campaigning also showed that Bruce's position still had shallow roots. There remained Scots who were not prepared to accept his rights as king and, when backed effectively by the English king, they could extract fealty from local communities. Robert lacked the manpower and confidence to risk an open fight with an English field army, even one as small as Gaveston's. Had the war continued on this path Bruce's aggressive strategy of the previous two years would have been replaced by a return to warfare based on defence and evasion.

However, the other lesson from the events of 1310–11 was that warfare did not occur in isolation. In 1303–4 Edward I had remained in Scotland for over a year, grinding down his enemies and raising men and supplies from England to maintain his war. To achieve this, Edward I had used the authority and respect he had built up over decades as king.[103] His son had no such political capital. During his time in Scotland Edward II's relations with Thomas of Lancaster had worsened and talk of civil war was again in the air. Despite pressure from his barons, Edward refused to call a parliament, fearing for his own authority and Gaveston's safety.[104] In these circumstances the king persisted with his plans for the Scottish war. He issued a summons for footsoldiers to muster at Berwick in early August. Without consulting his subjects, Edward asked for a man from each vill and financial aid. His demands aroused further opposition and in mid-June the English king finally agreed to call parliament to meet at Westminster in August. In late July, 'unwillingly enough', Edward left Berwick and headed south.[105] His planned campaign into Scotland would not materialise. It would take until June 1314 for a new royal expedition to go north.

THE HARRYING OF LOTHIAN (AUGUST 1311–NOVEMBER 1313)

It would quickly become clear that Edward II's ten months in Scotland had not altered the shape of his war with Bruce. Within weeks of the English king's departure, Robert led a foray into areas in Plantagenet allegiance. On 12 August this force crossed into England by the Solway and, avoiding Carlisle, moved westwards following the line of the Roman wall. Gilsland, Haltwhistle and upper Tynedale were plundered before the Scots turned for home after eight days driving 'a large booty in cattle'. A fortnight later they were back. This time Robert led his men via Redesdale and Coquetdale before marching south through Northumberland as far as Corbridge. After 'laying waste those parts he had previously spared', Bruce returned up Tynedale to Scotland.[106] The armies Robert led south in 1311 were clearly mobile and were probably quite small, but the contemporary account from the border priory of Lanercost reported that 'the wardens whom the king of England had stationed on the marches oppose so great a force of Scots'. The brief campaigns clearly shocked the men of Northumberland, who paid £2000 to Bruce to avoid any fresh attacks until February.[107]

Money and cattle were exactly what Robert had sought from these forays. His main efforts were still directed at extracting the submission of those lords and communities in Scotland who remained in Edward's allegiance. Despite events since 1307, there were many of these. In the sheriffdoms of Edinburgh, Linlithgow and Haddington, Roxburgh and Dumfries and in the earldom of Dunbar and the lordship of Annandale, administration was carried on in the name of Edward or his adherents.[108] Beyond these areas, the English king's men were active in Galloway, Clydesdale and Angus. Magnates like Patrick earl of Dunbar, David earl of Atholl, Alexander Abernethy and David lord of Brechin continued to play leading roles in the defence of their lands and Edward's lordship.[109] Though, even in Lothian and the borders with England, Bruce had won support since 1309, it would require considerable pressure to win widespread recognition of his kingship from these men and lands.[110] For Edward II the key to defending his remaining people in Scotland was the garrisons he maintained there. The sizeable forces stationed in the castles of Dundee and Stirling and within the walls of Perth supported local adherents and restricted Bruce's movement from north to south. Behind them garrisons at Bothwell, Linlithgow, Dumfries and at Edinburgh, Roxburgh and Berwick were intended to provide military and political support to Edward's Scottish adherents.[111]

However, though this approach had shown signs of success in early 1311, without the kind of field forces led by Edward and Gaveston, the ability of these garrisons to defend themselves, let alone challenge Bruce beyond their walls, was limited. Already cracks were opening in Edward's position. In autumn 1311 the men of the earldom of Dunbar paid a heavy blackmail to avoid having their goods plundered by Robert's forces.[112] Their action reveals the inability of the English king's officials to defend his adherents from the enemy. The fears of these officials were already being expressed to their king in October 1311. Edward responded with promises of supplies and orders for northern English barons to assemble with companies of men-at-arms at Carlisle and Newcastle on 1 November.[113] The king's response marked a return to the insufficient and ineffectual efforts to challenge Bruce from a distance adopted between 1307 and 1310 and, as in those years, this lack of real concern was a product of growing political crisis in England.

Edward II's Scottish expedition had only delayed antagonisms with his barons. He returned south to face demands that he accept the Ordinances and exile Gaveston once again. Though he accepted both demands, Edward was merely prevaricating. During the winter he secured the support of the French king, recalled Gaveston and headed north to York to rally support. Though the king was in the north, the needs of Edward's men in Scotland received little priority. Instead it was even rumoured that he had made contact with Bruce, offering to recognise his kingship in return for Robert's protection of Gaveston. This is unlikely but it suggests the extent to which Edward's obsession with his favourite was seen to undermine his duties as king.[114] For four months Edward negotiated with his enemies, then in May Gaveston was cornered in Scarborough Castle. He surrendered to Aymer Valence in return for promises of his safety. However, as Valence took his prisoner south, Gaveston was seized by the hardline Ordainer (supporter of the Ordinances and opponent of King Edward), Guy earl of Warwick. A show trial ensued before the earls of Warwick, Lancaster and Hereford and then, on 19 June, Gaveston was beheaded. His death opened fresh divisions and left the English realm facing the threat of civil war.[115]

Robert may not have been offered Edward's recognition during early 1312 but, even so, he clearly seized on the renewed crisis of his enemies. It may have been in late 1311 that the castle at Ayr was taken by Robert's adherents and a number of other small castles may also have fallen during these months.[116] By February 1312, Robert had turned against a larger target. The castle and town of Dundee had a clear strategic value to both sides. It had been at the centre of Edward's plans in early 1311 and its garrison included numerous Scots including Atholl, Brechin and Abernethy, all lords of influence in the area. Robert was preparing to lay siege to this key stronghold in early February and by 2 March he had probably been blockading the town for several weeks. On that date the commander of the town was ordered, on pain of death, to break an arrangement with the enemy to surrender if not relieved.[117] Three weeks later plans for that relief were underway. Ships from Berwick and Newcastle were to gather at Holy Island and ferry a force of horse and foot under David Brechin to Dundee. The fleet may have relieved the town, but Brechin's arrival only delayed Dundee's fall.[118] On 7 April Robert was based about six miles away at Inchture, accompanied by the earls of Ross and Lennox. He was awaiting the surrender of Dundee and, only five days later, he was in the town.[119] The fall of Dundee gave Robert control of the Tay and easy access to Fife and Lothian. It left Perth upriver exposed to attack and King Edward's remaining Scottish friends north of the Forth isolated before Bruce. After Dundee's capture, several of these friends made their peace with King Robert or left the scene. David Brechin probably surrendered in the summer, Atholl had submitted by October and Abernethy left Scotland for good in early 1313.[120]

While Edward's last adherents beyond the Forth clustered in Perth, Robert was free to turn south. By July he had travelled to Ayr, where he held what was described as a parliament. While this probably included a formal occasion in which Robert displayed his royal authority, it was also a council of war. The king laid plans for fresh campaigning. He would attack the castles of Dumfries, Buittle and Caerlaverock in the south-west, while he sent his lightly armed forces to raise supplies in a harrying expedition within Scotland. The greater part of the king's forces were to go with his brother, Edward, in an attack on the English marches.[121] Edward Bruce's expedition may have resulted in the burning of Norham on the border and a renewed payment of tribute from the English marches. The ongoing divisions in England encouraged Robert to launch a new attack across the border. Advancing into Tynedale in early August, Robert's men burned Hexham and Corbridge. Then, while the king remained at Corbridge 'in peace and safety', a force was sent south to

Durham, which was attacked on market day. While the bishop's castle was left untouched, the town was plundered and burned. This display of strength led 'the community of the bishop of Durham between Tyne and Tees' to send envoys to Hexham and pay 450 marks for a truce until June 1313.[122] Across the north in Northumberland, Westmorland and Cumberland local communities made similar truces. While their lords quarrelled, the people of the north were left without defence. Lothian experienced the same treatment. By November 1312 the men of Lothian and the borders had bought similar truces from Bruce. In return, all Edward could do was to praise the service of his Scottish supporters, appeal for them to aid his garrisons and make promises of future assistance.[123]

During these months, instead of ordering troops to muster for the defence of his Scottish claims or of the north of England, Edward II summoned forces to bear arms against his enemies at home. The death of Gaveston had, ironically, strengthened the king's position. Hatred of the favourite had been the key element in uniting the earls in opposition to the king, while the way Warwick, Lancaster and other hardliners had seized and executed Gaveston had alienated moderate lords like Gloucester and Valence. The civil war that seemed imminent was averted by the caution of both sides, itself influenced by the flow of bad news from the north. In late 1312 the barons offered to submit to Edward in return for a pardon and his observance of the Ordinances. The barons also promised to work to secure a grant of taxation for the Scottish war and to provide men for the king's next expedition. Edward rejected these terms and negotiations dragged on through the spring and summer of 1313.[124] The king's intransigence was bolstered by the new support of the French king. The removal of Gaveston and the birth of a son to Edward and Isabelle in November 1312 were behind this friendship and, in May and June 1313, Edward left his realm and attended the French king's court.[125] His journey alarmed many of his subjects, who feared that Bruce would be able to march on York or even London.[126] However, Edward hoped to use his influence with King Philip to make Robert accept a truce which would allow him time to settle the affairs of England. Despite the continuing war in Scotland, Edward chose to delay a settlement with his barons, wearing them down in talks until the autumn.[127]

The need to challenge Bruce had failed to end the dispute between the English king and his baronial opponents. Instead Robert remained free to strengthen his position and prepare for new attacks on his enemy's lands, castles and people. In October 1312 Robert had travelled north to Inverness where he met envoys from King Hakon of Norway and renewed the treaty between Scotland and Norway. Bruce may also have made contact with Count Robert of Flanders whose subjects had long been selling weapons and armour to the Scots. The count had poor relations with his own lord, Philip of France, and would not have liked the closer ties between the French and English courts.[128] By the beginning of December Bruce was ready to resume warfare.

The truces he had made with local communities in the summer were said to have allowed his armies free access through their lands. King Robert may have exploited this clause to bring a force through Lothian to the walls of Berwick. On the night of 6 December his men sought to take the town by surprise. Rope ladders were placed against the walls but the defenders were alerted by the barking of a dog.[129] Robert, who could not afford a defeat with Lothian behind him, quickly retreated. He was equally quick to choose another target. Perth was a natural choice. It was Edward's last major stronghold north of the Forth. Like Dundee and Berwick, the town was fortified. Its commander was William Oliphant, who had defended Stirling Castle against Edward I in 1304. Many other Scots were in Oliphant's garrison and at least some of the burgesses of Perth were active adherents of King Edward.[130] Bruce laid siege to the town but after several weeks had made little progress. Robert may have asked for payment to withdraw but this time it was refused. On 8 January Bruce's army broke camp and marched away from Perth. However, Robert returned at night with scaling ladders, reportedly leading his men across the town ditch where it was shallowest. The ladders were placed against the walls and the men climbed up. When a ladder broke, Robert rallied his troops and they gained the rampart. With the walls crossed, the gates were opened and the town was taken. Angered by the defence, Bruce reportedly released the English but imprisoned Oliphant and executed several leading burgesses.[131]

Robert did not delay at Perth. Instead he set out for the south-west. Later tradition credited the king's brother, Edward Bruce, with winning Galloway and Nithsdale for his brother. He had received the title of lord of Galloway in early 1312 and may have been campaigning in the wider region during the winter, perhaps capturing Rutherglen and Buittle.[132] However, it was Robert's arrival which brought about a final collapse in Galloway. On 7 February Dumfries Castle was surrendered by Dugald MacDouall, who six years earlier had handed over two of Bruce's brothers for execution.[133] In contrast, MacDouall was allowed to go into exile. By May the king was looking beyond Scotland. Perhaps drawing on allies from the Isles once again, Robert led a force to Man. The island, which had been part of the Scottish kingdom before 1286, was overrun in five days, the only resistance coming from Rushen Castle which was surrendered by Dugald MacDouall, facing a second personal defeat in five months. Control of Man gave Robert an outpost which guarded approaches to the Isles and western Scotland.[134] Sailing on from Man, Bruce's galleys reached the shores of Ulster. Though they were driven off by the men of the earldom, the raid showed Bruce's attention was shifting back to Ireland, no longer as an exile seeking refuge but as a king seeking plunder and even lordship.[135]

On his return to the mainland, the king prepared for the end of those truces which he had agreed with northern English communities in 1312. As soon as they expired, Robert gathered an army to enter England. This time, however, the people of the northern English counties anticipated Bruce's advance and offered him money for a fresh truce. Their actions were due to the lack of 'defence or help from their king' and show the effect of Robert's sustained pressure since 1311 and the abject failure of Edward to provide any leadership or support to his subjects in these years.[136] These same factors had an even stronger impact in southern Scotland. In late 1313 the Scottish people in Edward's allegiance claimed that since their king's departure in 1311 they had suffered £20,000 worth of damage from the enemy. They had bought truces to protect their lands and lives but now increasingly suffered from plundering by the English king's garrisons. These held local men for ransom and robbed indiscriminately, while other bands carried people off into 'distant parts of Scotland'. Even local barons like Adam lord of Gordon were imprisoned.[137] Not surprisingly, such conditions led some to enter Bruce's peace, among them a previous spokesman for Lothian, Henry Sinclair.[138] However, the local communities as a whole remained in Edward's faith and continued to appeal to him for support. While he maintained garrisons in the south-east, the English king kept the allegiance of most local men. In August 1313 the first serious crack appeared in this position. The pele of Linlithgow had been constructed by Edward I in 1302 as a fortified base between Edinburgh and Stirling. At harvest time it was taken, possibly by local men, but more likely after a brief siege by King Robert's men.[139] With its fall, the grip of Edward II's sheriff of Edinburgh, the Gascon, Piers Lubaud, was weakened. The collapse of allegiance to the English king seemed imminent.

If Edward wished to defend his land of Scotland, he had little time to act. He did, though, have the opportunity. After two years of neglect, Edward was at last in a position to reassert his lordship in Scotland. Finally, and through no great effort of his own, Edward had reached agreement with the increasingly divided opposition in October 1313. Though tensions remained between the two factions, the patched-up agreement raised the possibility of a major royal expedition to Scotland.[140] That it would end in a major battle was due to events in the months from the fall of Linlithgow to June 1314.

NOTES

1. *Chron. Guisborough*, 370. Though Guisborough dates Robert's move to Kintyre and then Carrick to autumn 1306, which is unlikely, his account of the king's movements is plausible.
2. Numbered at thirty-three by John Barbour (*The Bruce*, ed. Duncan, 173).
3. Barbour makes an opportunistic foray against Arran, which Edward I had granted to John Hastings, the prelude to Bruce's landing in Carrick (*The Bruce*, ed. Duncan, 166–75).
4. *C.D.S.*, ii, no. 1895; v, no. 492 (xii).
5. *Chron. Lanercost*, 179–80; *C.D.S.*, v, no. 492 (xvi). MacDouall was rewarded for his victory on 3 February 1307.
6. *C.D.S.*, ii, nos 1888–9, 1896; v, no. 492 (xi, xvi).
7. *C.D.S.*, v, 512 (b).

8. *C.D.S.*, ii, nos 1895–6.
9. *The Bruce*, ed. Duncan, 195–201; *Chron. Guisborough*, 370; *C.D.S.*, ii, nos 1897, 1923.
10. *C.D.S.*, ii, no. 1913.
11. For these movements, see *C.D.S.*, ii, no. 1923 and the discussion of Professor Duncan in *The Bruce*, ed. Duncan, 282–3.
12. *C.D.S.*, ii, nos 1913, 1923.
13. *Chron. Lanercost*, 181–2.
14. *C.D.S.*, ii, nos 1857, 1909, 1912. Henry earl of Lincoln renounced his rights to Stewart's lands in return for a promise of compensation.
15. For this scenario, see *The Bruce*, ed. Duncan, 296–7n.
16. *The Bruce*, ed. Duncan, 295–309; *Chron. Guisborough*, 378; K. DeVries, *Infantry Warfare in the Early Fourteenth Century* (Woodbridge, 1996), 49–57.
17. *C.D.S.*, ii, nos 1776, 1928, 1931, 1935, 1938, 1942; iv, 1829; v, 490; *The Bruce*, ed. Duncan, 282–3n, 297n; *Chron. Guisborough*, 378.
18. *C.D.S.*, ii, no. 1979; *Nat. MSS Scot.*, ii, no. 13.
19. *C.D.S.*, ii, no. 1926.
20. *The Bruce*, ed. Duncan, 200–13; M. Brown, *The Black Douglases* (East Linton, 1998), 14–18.
21. Prestwich, *Edward I*, 182.
22. *C.D.S.*, iii, no. 5; v, no. 497; *Foedera*, ii, 2.
23. *C.D.S.*, iii, no. 1961. Among this group of Scots were Alexander Abernethy, John Menteith, David Brechin and John Mowbray.
24. *Foedera*, ii, 2; Maddicott, *Thomas of Lancaster*, 70–1, 75; Hamilton, *Piers Gaveston*, 37–43.
25. *Chron. Lanercost*, 184–5; *C.D.S.*, v, no. 497.
26. *Foedera*, ii, 8; *C.D.S.*, iii, nos 14–15.
27. *C.D.S.*, v, no. 655; *The Bruce*, ed. Duncan, 290–7.
28. *Foedera*, ii, 4, 6, 8, 9.
29. *C.D.S.*, v, no. 492 (xii, xvi).
30. For the role of the north in this conflict, see Watson, *Under the Hammer*, 116, 175, 177–80.
31. *The Bruce*, ed. Duncan, 311.
32. *C.D.S.*, v, 515 (b).
33. The events of this campaign are traced in a letter written by Duncan Frendraught, one of Edward II's officials in Moray (P. Barnes and G. W. S. Barrow, 'The movements of Robert Bruce between September 1307 and May 1308', *S.H.R.*, 69 (1970), 46–59).
34. *C.D.S.*, iv, p. 400, appendix, no. 14.
35. 'The movements of Robert Bruce', 58–9.
36. 'The movements of Robert Bruce', 58–9; *The Bruce*, ed. Duncan, 318–27.
37. 'The movements of Robert Bruce', 58–9.
38. *C.D.S.*, iv, pp. 399–400.
39. *C.D.S.*, ii, nos 903, 1631, 1633.
40. *C.D.S.*, v, no.518; 'The Movements of Robert Bruce', 59.
41. *The Bruce*, ed. Duncan, 328–9; *Chron. Fordun*, ii, 337; Mowbray was at Kirkton of Alva on 1 May (*C.D.S.*, v, no. 518).
42. *The Bruce*, ed. Duncan, 329–33.
43. *The Bruce*, ed. Duncan, 333–5; *Scotichronicon*, ed. Watt, vi, 342.
44. *C.D.S.*, v, nos 492 (xii), 519; *Rot. Scot.*, i, 55.
45. McNamee, *Wars of the Bruces*, 208–9.
46. *C.D.S.*, ii, no. 43.

47. For discussions of the crisis of 1307–8, see Maddicott, *Thomas of Lancaster*, 70–90; J. S. Hamilton, *Piers Gaveston Earl of Cornwall, 1307–12* (Detroit, 1988), 38–53; M. Prestwich, *Plantagenet England 1225–1360* (Oxford, 2005), 178–81.
48. Maddicott, *Thomas of Lancaster*, 77–80.
49. *C.P.R., 1307–13*, 83, 93; Hamilton, *Piers Gaveston*, 55–6.
50. *C.D.S.*, ii, no. 47; v, p. 79.
51. *A.P.S.*, i, 477.
52. *C.D.S.*, iii, no. 59.
53. *C.D.S.*, iii, no. 28; Brown, *Black Douglases*, 16–18.
54. *The Bruce*, ed. Duncan, 355–9.
55. *Chron. Lanercost*, 188; *Scotichronicon*, ed. Watt, vi, 344.
56. *The Bruce*, ed. Duncan, 344–52.
57. *The Bruce*, ed. Duncan, 360–5; Barrow, *Robert Bruce*, 179–81.
58. Barrow, *Robert Bruce*, 179.
59. *Rot. Scot.*, i, 58.
60. *Scalachronica*, ed. King, 69.
61. *Foedera*, ii, 149; *Rot. Scot*, i, 56.
62. For Gloucester's inheritance, see Altschul, *The Clares*, 159–64, 201–95.
63. *Rot. Scot.*, i, 60; *Foedera*, ii, 155, 161.
64. *The Bruce*, ed. Duncan, 334–5. David Brechin may have come into Bruce's allegiance at this point (*Rot. Scot.*, i, 82).
65. *Foedera*, ii, 136, 144, 161; *Rot. Scot.*, i, 60.
66. *Chron. Lanercost*, 189.
67. Maddicott, *Thomas of Lancaster*, 83–6.
68. Barrow, *Robert Bruce*, 119–22, 183–4; *Foedera*, ii, 145.
69. *A.P.S.*, i, 459.
70. A. A. M. Duncan, 'The Declarations of the Clergy', in G. Barrow, *The Declaration of Arbroath: History, Significance, Setting* (Edinburgh, 2003), 32–49.
71. *Chron. Lanercost*, 189.
72. *Vita Edwardi*, 13–15; Maddicott, *Thomas of Lancaster*, 94–103.
73. *A.P.S.*, i, 459.
74. *Rot. Scot.*, i, 67; *Foedera*, ii, 144.
75. Ayr was said to be 'in danger due to incursions of the enemy' as early as June 1309 (*Rot. Scot.*, i, 66).
76. *Rot. Scot.*, i, 67–70; *Foedera*, ii, 148–9.
77. *Rot. Scot.*, i, 70–5; *Parl. Writs*, II, i, 388–90; Maddicott, *Thomas of Lancaster*, 108–9.
78. *Rot. Scot.*, i, 76–7.
79. *Rot. Scot.*, i, 79–80; *Chron. Lanercost*, 191.
80. *A.P.S.*, i, 459; *R.R.S.*, v, no. 10. For a discussion of the timing of this expedition, see *The Bruce*, ed. Duncan, 366n.
81. For Edward I's involvement with the Islesmen, see Brown, *Wars of Scotland*, 259–62. Robert's father-in-law, Richard earl of Ulster, was given powers to treat with Bruce in August and to this end travelled to Scotland to discuss the possibility of peace. Despite ties of kinship, it is hard to see any grounds for negotiation in 1309 and it is more striking that Ulster met with John Menteith and Neil Campbell. These were Bruce's leading men in Argyll and their discussions with the earl may have been concerned with events in the west (*Foedera*, ii, 150; McNamee, *Wars of the Bruces*, 45–6).
82. *Rot. Scot.*, i, 78.
83. Maddicott, *Thomas of Lancaster*, 109–13; Prestwich, *Plantagenet England*, 181.
84. *Vita Edwardi*, 21–3.

85. *C.D.S.*, iii, no. 95; *Nat. MSS Scot.*, ii, no. 20.
86. *Rot. Scot.*, i, 82, 86.
87. On 18 June 1310 Abernethy was rewarded with the manor of Clackmannan for his service to Edward (*Rot. Scot.*, i, 85).
88. *Rot. Scot.*, i, 82, 83, 90.
89. *Vita Edwardi*, 21–3; *Chron. Lanercost*, 190; *Annales Londoniensis*, in *Chronicles of the Reigns of Edward I and Edward II*, ed. W. Stubbs, 2 vols (Rolls series, 1882), i, 174; Maddicott, *Thomas of Lancaster*, 113–14. For a detailed account of the summons and the army it produced, see D. Simpkin, 'The English Army and the Scottish Campaign of 1310–1', in King and Penman (eds), *Anglo-Scottish Relations 1296–1420*, 14–39.
90. Simpkin, 'English army'.
91. *Rot. Scot.*, i, 90; McNamee, *Wars of the Bruces*, 48.
92. *Rot. Scot.*, i, 90, 93, 99, 100; McNamee, *Wars of the Bruces*, 49, 52.
93. *Foedera*, ii, 180; *Rot. Scot.*, i, 96.
94. *Rot. Scot.*, i, 94–5; *C.D.S.*, v, no. 552.
95. *C.D.S.*, v, no. 552; *Rot. Scot.*, i, 96.
96. *C.D.S.*, iii, no. 166; *Vita Edwardi*, 22–3; Hamilton, *Gaveston*, 84.
97. *Chron. Lanercost*, 191.
98. *Chron. Lanercost*, 191; *C.D.S.*, iii, nos 177, 197; Hamilton, *Gaveston*, 84.
99. *Chron. Lanercost*, 191; *C.D.S.*, iii, nos 201, 246.
100. *C.D.S.*, iii, nos 202, 204; v, no. 562 (b); *Chron. Lanercost*, 191. Lanercost also reports a foray into Selkirk Forest by Gloucester and Warenne.
101. *C.D.S.*, iii, no. 202.
102. *C.D.S.*, iii, no. 203; *Rot. Scot.*, i, 99; McNamee, *Wars of the Bruces*, 52.
103. Prestwich, *Edward I*, 498–502, 536–49; Watson, *Under the Hammer*, 173–94.
104. Maddicott, *Thomas of Lancaster*, 114–17.
105. Simpkin, 'The English Army'; *Chron. Lanercost*, 193.
106. *Chron. Lanercost*, 194–5; McNamee, *Wars of the Bruces*, 53–5.
107. *Chron. Lanercost*, 195.
108. *C.D.S.*, iii, pp. 432–3.
109. *Rot. Scot.*, i, 105, 108, 109–11; *C.D.S.*, iii, nos 219, 220, 229, 238, 241, 255.
110. *C.D.S.*, iii, no. 245; G. W. S. Barrow, 'Lothian in the War of Independence', *S.H.R.*, LV (1976), 151–71.
111. *C.D.S.*, iii, nos 218–19; pp. 393–432.
112. *Chron. Lanercost*, 195.
113. *Rot. Scot.*, i, 105.
114. *Vita Edwardi Secundi*, 39–43; Maddicott, *Thomas of Lancaster*, 117–24; Hamilton, *Gaveston*, 92–4.
115. *Vita Edwardi Secundi*, 42–9; Maddicott, *Thomas of Lancaster*, 125–9.
116. Ayr was in Robert's hands by July 1312 (*C.D.S.*, iii, no. 279).
117. *C.D.S.*, iii, pp. 427–32; *Rot. Scot.*, i, 106, 108–9.
118. *Rot. Scot.*, i, 109.
119. *R.R.S.*, v, nos 17–20. Edward Bruce, Thomas Randolph and John Menteith were also in Dundee with the king and the earls on 12 April.
120. *R.R.S.*, v, no. 24; *C.D.S.*, iii, nos 283, 303, 312.
121. *C.D.S.*, iii, no. 279.
122. *Chron. Lanercost*, 198–200; *R.R.S.*, v, no. 21.
123. *Rot. Scot.*, i, 111.
124. *Annales Londoniensis*, 210–11; Maddicott, *Thomas of Lancaster*, 132–6.
125. Maddicott, *Thomas of Lancaster*, 136, 149–50.
126. *Vita Edwardi*, 67.

127. *Foedera*, iii, 38; *Vita Edwardi*, 72–5.
128. *R.R.S.*, v, nos 24, 25; *Foedera*, iii, 29, 35; A. Stevenson, 'The Flemish Dimension of the Auld Alliance', in G. Simpson (ed.), *Scotland and the Low Countries 1124–1994* (Aberdeen, 1996), 28–42.
129. *Chron. Lanercost*, 200–2.
130. *Rot. Scot.*, i, 105; *C.D.S.*, iii, no. 247, pp. 425–7, 433.
131. *The Bruce*, ed. Duncan, 332–43; *Chron. Fordun*, ii, 338; *Scotichronicon*, ed. Watt, vi, 347–8.
132. *R.R.S.*, v, no. 19; *The Bruce*, ed. Duncan, 400–1.
133. *C.D.S.*, iii, no. 304.
134. *Chronicle of the Kings of Mann and the Isles*, ed. G. Broderick and B. Stowell (Edinburgh, 1973), 46; McNamee, *Wars of the Bruces*, 58.
135. *Chart. St Mary's Dublin*, ii, 342.
136. *Chron. Lanercost*, 203.
137. *C.D.S.*, iii, nos 186, 337, 341.
138. Sinclair was being favoured by Edward II in February 1312 but was with Robert by October 1313 (*R.R.S.*, v, nos 35–6).
139. R. A. Brown, H. M. Colvin and A. J. Taylor, *The History of the King's Works*, vol. 1, The Middle Ages (London, 1963), 409–21; *The Bruce*, ed. Duncan, 370–3; *C.D.S.* iii, nos 330, 682, pp. 411–12.
140. *Vita Edwardi*, 74–7; Maddicott, *Thomas of Lancaster*, 151–6; Prestwich, *Plantagenet England*, 189–90.

CHAPTER 3

Scotland: A Kingdom Divided

The warfare which led up to the Bannockburn campaign of 1314 has usually been regarded as a national conflict between England and Scotland, and Bannockburn itself as a national triumph for Scotland. The reality was more complex. To contemporaries, the war was more easily understood as a struggle between Edward of England and Robert Bruce, rival rulers who both claimed authority over the Scottish realm. Involved in the conflict were not simply English and Scots, but all who owed allegiance to one of these kings. As will be discussed, this meant the involvement of all King Edward's dominions in their lord's efforts to make good his rights in Scotland. The disastrous results of these efforts would also spread across many of the Plantagenet dominions, altering individual and collective fortunes and relationships in the years after Bannockburn. However, between 1307 and 1314, the political impact of the war, in its direct form, would fall most heavily on Scotland. From the onset of war in 1296, until it petered out in a long truce during the 1350s, the struggle always centred on the conflict between the claims of the Plantagenet kings to exercise authority over Scotland and those of Scottish kings to rule the land free from subjection to another monarch. It was in the years leading up to Bannockburn that this dispute reached its most charged and, in many ways, its decisive phase. The choices which faced the Scots in terms of their loyalties and allegiance were most difficult and the divisions within the political class of Scotland were at their greatest. Such divisions were a feature of the Scottish wars from 1296 onwards but, from Bruce's seizure of the throne in 1306, they had an intensity and depth which would open long-lasting scars in the Scottish body politic.

In the years which followed Robert Bruce's return to Scotland in 1307, the bulk of the fighting would be between Scots. The principal objective of this fighting was to win or maintain the sworn allegiance of Scots to one side or the other. Following the submissions of 1304 and, again, after the defeat of Robert's rising in 1306, the overwhelming majority of Scottish landowners publicly accepted the right of the English king to act as their ruler. Bruce's return with a small band of supporters initiated a challenge to this position, both militarily and politically. Robert's survival and then success in war allowed him to present himself as the king of Scots and as a rival source of

52

TABLE 3.1 *The Bruce Connection*

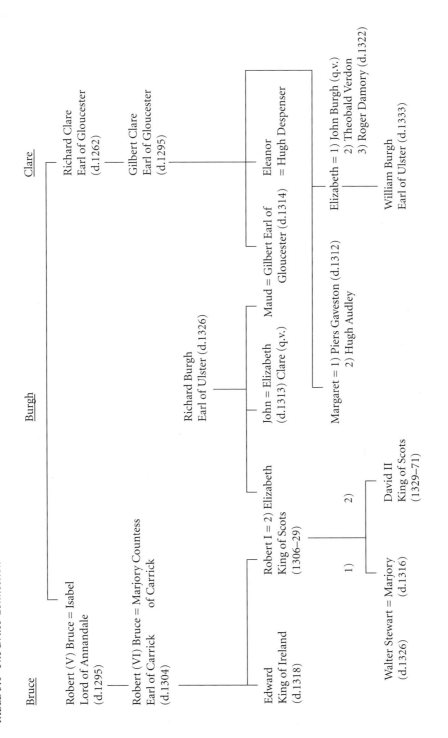

Bruce

Robert (V) Bruce = Isabel
Lord of Annandale
(d.1295)

Robert (VI) Bruce = Marjory Countess
Earl of Carrick   of Carrick
(d.1304)

Edward
King of Ireland
(d.1318)

Robert I = 2) Elizabeth
King of Scots
(1306–29)

1)

2)

David II
King of Scots
(1329–71)

Walter Stewart = Marjory
(d.1326)   (d.1316)

Burgh

Richard Burgh
Earl of Ulster (d.1326)

John = Elizabeth
(d.1313) Clare (q.v.)

Margaret = 1) Piers Gaveston (d.1312)
           2) Hugh Audley

Elizabeth = 1) John Burgh (q.v.)
            2) Theobald Verdon
            3) Roger Damory (d.1322)

William Burgh
Earl of Ulster (d.1333)

Clare

Richard Clare
Earl of Gloucester
(d.1262)

Gilbert Clare
Earl of Gloucester
(d.1295)

Maud = Gilbert Earl of
       Gloucester (d.1314)

Eleanor
= Hugh Despenser

authority to the English crown. The actions of Robert from early 1307 onwards were all directed towards the winning of recognition for his kingship from other Scots. This recognition was expressed not only through the submission of individuals but by claiming the consent of the wider political class. In early fourteenth-century Scotland the term community of the realm or the commune or people of Scotland assumed a significance as the body politic of the kingdom. The assent of those who made up this community could be claimed as a source of legitimate authority by a ruler. This process was evident from 1286, when Scottish government was temporarily assigned to guardians in the absence of an adult ruler. It assumed further significance when two (or more) claimants to royal power were in competition. Not surprisingly, Edward I recognised the vital importance of securing consent from the political class. In 1296 he took care to secure the personal allegiance of over a thousand Scottish nobles, clergy and burgesses and between 1304 and 1305 his settlement of Scotland was carried out with the advice and formal consent of sufficient Scots to claim communal support. Understanding of the term was not completely fixed. In 1306 Edward I's orders for the suppression of Bruce's rising used the phrase 'the poor *commune*' to mean the commons, the peasantry, but in general the community included, and was focused on, the landowning elite.[1]

The rule of Robert Bruce has long been associated with ideas of the community of the realm. Though references to communal consent became more apparent after 1314, the need to stress collective support for his kingship was equally important before Bannockburn. The letters produced at Robert's first parliament, held at St Andrews in March 1309, demonstrate this in different ways. Both the so-called Declaration of the Clergy and the letter written in the name of Scottish nobles and people to Philip of France are statements of communal recognition for Bruce, which proclaim his rights and achievements to an international audience.[2] However, the use of such communal language was not monopolised by King Robert's adherents. In 1313 petitions were received by Edward II from the 'commune of Scotland' and the people of Scotland. Edward's Scottish supporters were clearly capable of identifying themselves as a community and of seeking the good lordship, justice and physical protection from their ruler in return for their allegiance.[3]

Between 1307 and 1314 the Scottish community, the men and women who formed the political class, was divided in two.[4] The letter to Philip IV in 1309 acknowledged this by referring to 'the inhabitants of the whole realm of Scotland recognising the lord Robert, by the grace of God, king of Scotland'. The French king, let alone the Scots themselves, would hardly be fooled by any claims that Bruce enjoyed the recognition of the whole kingdom. Instead the list of lords and communities in Robert's allegiance stresses the extent of division.[5] Only three earls, Ross and Sutherland, who had made peace a few months earlier, and Bruce's long-standing supporter Malcolm of Lennox attended, while, leaving out the recently deceased earl of Buchan, there were

FIGURE 3.1 *The effigy of Sir James Douglas in his family's mausoleum at St Bride's Kirk, Douglas. James joined Bruce in 1307 and would later emerge as one of King Robert's leading lieutenants, his exploits glorified by John Barbour in* The Bruce. *(Crown Copyright. Historic Scotland)*

four in active opposition to Robert, the earls of Dunbar, Angus, Atholl and Strathearn.[6] Two others, Fife and Mar, were growing up in England.[7] Among the barons, the picture was similar. Along with Gilbert Hay, who had returned from the Isles with Bruce, were adherents from the south-west and the north, Alexander Fraser, David Barclay, Robert Boyd, James Douglas and Alexander Lindsay and crucial recent recruits like Robert Keith, Thomas Randolph, James the Steward and John Menteith.[8] However, despite recent defeats,

Edward II could still call on the allegiance of a group of nobles of equal significance. Barons whose principal estates were in Lothian and the south, like John and Philip Mowbray, Henry Sinclair, Alexander Seton, William Soules and Adam Gordon, almost all stood in the English king's camp, while others from further north and west, most notably David Brechin, Alexander Abernethy, Ingeram Umfraville, Dugald MacDouall and the young John Comyn, remained active opponents of Bruce.[9] Such families, the Mowbrays, Umfravilles, Abernethys, Soules and Brechins, were long-established members of the nobility of Scotland, which had played leading roles in the government of the realm for a century.

As we shall see, allegiance to Edward II rested in part on the proven power of the English crown to punish opposition and reward allegiance from Scots. However, it is important to recognise that the division within the community of the realm in 1309 was not simply between those willing and able to renew the war against the English crown and those too cowed or cautious to do so. Instead there was a fundamental political split which led Scottish lords to take alternative views of legitimate authority and allegiances in the eight years before Bannockburn. The nature of these alternative views and the conflict they aroused was evident in the presentation of Robert's position in early 1309. In the Declaration of the Clergy, Robert was portrayed as the rightful king by right of blood and 'in the judgement of the people' who 'has by the sword restored the realm [which had been] . . . deformed and ruined'. Such claims were dependent on the rewriting of recent history in the opening section of the letter. This went back to the dispute over the succession to the throne between Robert's grandfather and John Balliol in 1291–2 and claimed that 'the faithful [Scottish] people always held without doubting' that Bruce was the 'true heir'. Balliol was made king by the 'machinations and plots of [Bruce's] rivals', only to be stripped of his kingdom by Edward I, leaving Scotland 'reduced to slavery'.[10] It was a kingless and enslaved people which Robert stepped in to deliver, reviving his family's claim to the throne. Though written for the consumption of the pope and church council, this account must have contained the basis of Bruce's position from 1306 as both 'true heir' and defender of Scottish liberties against a foreign tyrant.[11]

However, such claims were deeply unpalatable to many Scots in the years after 1306. The declaration claimed that 'if anyone in opposition claims right to the kingdom in virtue of letters . . . containing the consent of the people and community, know that all this took place by force and violence which could not then be resisted'.[12] Though designed, with some justice, to counter Plantagenet claims to rule Scotland based on the submissions of 1296 and 1304–5, there was also an implicit dismissal of the rights of John Balliol to the kingship which, though dormant in 1309, were still important in Scottish politics. There was an alternative view of recent history and legitimate authority in Scotland to that of Bruce. Something of this view may be captured in letters produced by John Balliol's son, Edward, in the early 1330s. This retold history in an attempt to denigrate the Bruce claim. Though, like the Declaration of the Clergy, these letters began with the succession dispute of 1291–2, Edward Balliol naturally regarded the judgement as justifying his family's right to the Scottish throne. The homage paid by John Balliol to the English crown was also stressed, though John's later removal 'for certain excesses' was glossed over. Most importantly, the letters claimed that 'the realm of Scotland . . . was stolen by the heirs of Robert Bruce [King Robert's grandfather] who . . . had no right there'.[13] Though, as will be discussed, attitudes to the rights of Balliol and Plantagenet in Scotland sat uneasily together, rejection of Bruce's claims was more easily justified. To many, Robert was a usurper and a traitor who had broken oaths of fealty to King John and to King Edward and seized a royal office to which he had no legal right.

Members of the Scottish political class had to make a choice between two conflicting claims to their allegiance based on readings of the recent past and current political realities. For many of the core supporters of Bruce up to 1309, the crucial decision may have been made when Bruce took the throne in 1306. Their motives were probably mixed. Some of Robert's key early supporters, like Malcolm earl of Lennox, Neil Campbell and Robert Boyd, had long sympathised with the Bruce claim to the throne and had political associations with Robert prior to his rising.[14] A wider group which probably included Gilbert Hay gave their support to Robert's kingship because he was ready to take on the leadership of the realm in opposition to the English crown.[15] The disaster of Methven and its aftermath meant these men experienced exile, captivity or a release under heavy suspicion, and many who had joined Robert in 1306 proved slow to join him again. James the Steward, who had hedged his bets in 1306, would not recognise Robert as king until late 1308, while a second adherent in 1306, Bruce's nephew and future lieutenant, Thomas Randolph, would only do homage a second time following his capture by Robert's men during 1308.[16] However, the bonds of fealty formed in 1306 did have a significance following the return of Robert in January 1307. Assessments by King Edward's officials that Bruce would 'find the people ready at his will' in certain districts were not simply scaremongering.[17] As Bruce survived the attacks of his enemies in the south-west, his former adherents in the area, Robert Boyd and Alexander Lindsay, rejoined him, as did the young James Douglas. Similarly, when Robert went north he received critical early support from Alexander Fraser, David and Walter Barclay and William Wiseman, minor barons who had backed the 1306 rising.[18] Such men may well have been waiting for Bruce to provide personal leadership before declaring for him. Their actions reveal the importance for Robert of taking the war into new areas of his realm. The very first foray made by Bruce into Lothian, during the autumn of 1308, produced some results. Two local barons, Robert Keith and Thomas Hay, had left the allegiance of Edward II by Christmas 1308.[19] Across Scotland, there were influential local nobles who were drawn to King Robert's cause and his successful war against the English king and his party.

The strength of the Bruce Cause lay in its clear appeal to Scottish liberties and traditions of kingship and, still more, in its run of military successes. The political attitudes of Robert's Scottish enemies were more varied and ambiguous. There was a group of landowners in Scotland who had supported Edward I before 1304 and continued this service to the Plantagenets after 1306. Though the most obvious members of this group were lords like Robert Umfraville earl of Angus, whose main interests lay in England, there were also nobles from Scottish families who adhered to Edward I and II. The best example of this class was Alexander Abernethy, who had been Edward I's keeper of Angus and Perthshire in 1305 and who was given similar powers by his son in the north-east in 1308 and 1311. Though he had initially fought against the English crown, Abernethy built up ties of service to the Plantagenets which led him into exile rather than submission to Bruce when his lands were lost in around 1312.[20] Other barons, like Alexander Balliol of Cavers and the earls of Dunbar, similarly remained consistently in the English kings' allegiance either side of 1306.[21] However, their choices were shaped not solely, or even primarily, by bonds of service as much as the location of their principal Scottish estates in areas of the kingdom close to England.

The largest and most valuable body of Scottish support for the English crown in this period was provided by those lords who found Robert's claims to be rightful king unacceptable. Such men can hardly be dismissed as having little regard for the liberties of the Scottish realm and people. Before the defeat of 1304, Ingeram Umfraville, John Mowbray and John Comyn earl of Buchan had been among the leaders of Scottish resistance to Edward I, while others like David Brechin and Walter Oliphant had also played significant parts in the wars from 1297 to 1304.[22] However, all these lords and many other figures chose to adhere to Edward II rather than pay homage to Robert. Part of their motivation was a result of antagonisms based on family and personal ties. Robert's killing of John Comyn of Badenoch ensured that the wider Comyn family and its extensive network of allies through marriage, which included Mowbray, Umfraville, Brechin and John of Lorn, regarded Bruce as a personal enemy to be hunted down. Yet, as in all medieval societies, such concerns of kinship cannot be wholly divorced from points of principle. The refusal of Malise earl of Strathearn in 1306 to shatter his sworn fealty to Edward I 'like a glass' and join Bruce would have had a wider application.[23] There may have been a reluctance to break sworn oaths of allegiance to the English crown on behalf of a figure like Bruce who had shown such disregard for his own homage to both Edward I and to John Balliol. This was the key for men like Mowbray, Umfraville and Brechin. Their efforts before 1304 had been made in defence of King John's rights in Scotland. Most came from families which had supported the Balliol claim in 1291–2.[24] Though they had submitted to Edward I in 1304, abandoning King John, they felt no obligation or sympathy for Bruce's attempt to usurp John's title. As the later support of many of these families for a Balliol restoration showed, their prime allegiance was to King John, exiled in France.[25]

Between 1306 and John's death in 1314, however, this was not a practical proposition. In this unappealing situation, these Balliol loyalists chose to support the English crown and work for the defeat of Bruce. The efforts of nobles like Philip Mowbray, Ingeram Umfraville, John of Lorn and David Brechin on King Edward's behalf hardly suggests a lukewarm attitude and reveals a deep antipathy to Robert Bruce which both sides would struggle to forget after Bannockburn and the submission of most of these men.

The political choices of individual nobles were not solely based on sympathy or enmity towards one of the royal claimants to Scotland. Allegiance was also shaped by a variety of material considerations. Landholding was central to the status and identity of the aristocracy. Threats to a family's landed inheritance or opportunities to recover or add to these holdings exerted a pull as significant as loyalty to Bruce or Plantagenet. In 1304 the first condition sought by the Scots in their peace negotiations with Edward I was that all their lands, which the English king had forfeited, were to be restored.[26] From 1306 both Bruce and his English rivals used land as a means to secure allegiance and reward support. In this contest as lords and patrons, Edward I and II initially held a clear advantage. The forfeiture of Bruce and many of his leading followers in 1306 gave Edward I a reservoir of land to reward and strengthen those who had given him loyal service in Scotland. However, though Scots like Alexander Balliol, Alexander Abernethy and William Muschet petitioned for new lands, the greatest estates went to English magnates.[27] This demonstrates the other element of Plantagenet lordship. As kings of England, Edward I and his son were the superior lords of the many Scots who held estates in the southern kingdom. As events before 1304 had shown, opposition to the English king inevitably led to the loss of these lands, while, as Bruce himself had recognised in 1302, submission to Edward I meant the recovery of lost lands and possible new holdings. After his rebellion in 1306, the Bruce inheritance in north-east England, Essex and elsewhere was permanently lost, as were the English estates of his followers.[28] In subsequent years, when Robert's successes saw him in a position to deprive his Scottish enemies of their lands, some of these opponents were compensated for their losses with land and pensions in England.

Edward II's need to maintain a body of Scottish support in this way was an indication of the changing balance of lordship in Scotland. The successful campaigns of Robert and his adherents in 1308 gave Bruce the means to reward and threaten in the north and south-west. In both these areas Robert sought to cement his lordship by making enormous grants of lands and powers to close kinsmen. By 1309 Edward Bruce had been made lord of Galloway, receiving the province once held by the Balliols. His principality was extended in 1313 when Robert handed over the neighbouring earldom of Carrick to his brother.[29] A similar process was undertaken in the north, where the earldom of Moray was re-created for Thomas Randolph, Bruce's nephew. This enormous province was formed from the lands of Robert's victim, John

Comyn of Badenoch, in the Highlands, but also gave Randolph the estates and much of the authority of the crown in the coastal districts round Elgin and Nairn.[30] Such patronage showed how Bruce could use his enemies' lands to strengthen his own key lieutenants. Equally important, these great provincial grants were intended to provide trusty leaders of the Bruce party, with their own authority in different parts of Robert's realm. Lesser adherents were similarly rewarded for service with grants or confirmations of land and office, but in the fluid situation from 1308 to 1314 where Robert hoped to win over his Scottish enemies, the king used forfeiture and patronage sparingly. It was only fixed enemies, like the Balliols and Comyns, who were formally deprived of land and only after Bannockburn that Robert took blanket action against those who refused him allegiance. Earlier, enemies like William earl of Ross, who had handed over Robert's wife and daughter to Edward I in 1306, were pardoned and allowed to retain their lands in return for submission and recognition. Bruce even sweetened the deal by turning Ross's custody of some royal lands into heritable possession. Himself born to an aristocratic tradition, Bruce knew the value of land as a political tool and the Ross family were converted into reliable adherents who would serve the king at Bannockburn and beyond.[31]

The experience of William earl of Ross also makes clear that the political choices made by nobles between 1307 and 1314 depended most heavily on military factors. Questions of allegiance were bound inextricably to the course of the war. It had already been shown that Robert's successful recruitment of noble adherents followed the march of his armies. The English king's officials were equally aware of this connection. In 1307 one of these officials, perhaps Alexander Abernethy, reported that 'there are many people living loyally in his [King Edward's] peace so long as the English are in power, otherwise they see that they must be at the enemy's will through default of the king. And it would be a deadly sin to leave them so, without protection among enemies.' It was the English king's duty to protect his loyal people. Should he fail to do so, they would be forced to submit to Bruce. In 1311 Abernethy and others similarly reminded Edward II that, unless he led an army to Scotland, he would lose his 'faithful' Scots. Robert was waging war to secure allegiance. While some lords and lesser men were 'ready' to rush to him when he appeared, it is clear that many were not. The flight of Gallovidians into northern England in 1308, 1311 and 1313, the harrying of Buchan which Bruce unleashed in 1308 and the repeated campaigns into Lothian to plunder and to demand blackmail showed that King Robert knew he had to do more than raise his banner to secure homage. These campaigns were designed to show the price of adherence to Edward II, the failure of that king to protect his liegemen and that these local communities were at King Robert's 'will'. Even so, the winning of Scotland was a hard struggle for Bruce and, even more, for those Scots who opposed him. It took the capture of some nobles, like David Brechin, Earl Malise of Strathearn, William Muschet and even Thomas Randolph, before they would do homage to Bruce. While some Lothian barons, like Henry Sinclair, succumbed to Bruce's pressure and made peace in 1313, numerous southern lords, like the earl of Dunbar, William Soules and Adam Gordon, adhered to Edward II until after Bannockburn. Their decision must have rested, in part, on the judgement that, for all Robert's apparent ability to harry them with impunity, the presence of Edward's garrisons and the resources at his disposal meant that to leave his allegiance would risk the loss of their lands and power. It was only when Bruce appeared as the greater threat to these that many recognised his kingship.

The loyalties of Scotland's nobility were shaped by a variety of issues and interests. Their choices of allegiance were vital to the course of the war. A good example of these statements is provided by the case of John Menteith lord of Arran and Knapdale. Infamous for the capture of William Wallace, Menteith was a leading magnate in the west, who led a retinue of 1,000 men and numerous galleys in 1307.[32] The service of such a lord was valuable to both sides. In 1306 Menteith was the keeper of Dumbarton Castle for Edward I and refused to allow Bruce access to the vital stronghold on the Clyde. As a reward for this, Edward I gave John the earldom of Lennox, forfeited by Bruce's adherent, Earl Malcolm.[33] The Lennox was hostile territory for Edward and Menteith was probably expected to use his own resources and Dumbarton to take possession of his earldom. John probably failed in this task and by late 1308, with King Robert dominant in the neighbouring region of Argyll, he was considering his options. A later story recounted that Menteith entered an agreement with Bruce to surrender Dumbarton Castle in return for being confirmed as earl of Lennox. This tale also stated that a band of English soldiers in the garrison planned to ambush Bruce as he took possession of the castle, but they were revealed by one of the king's men. Robert then imprisoned Menteith until after Bannockburn.[34] However, though the agreement may be real, it is hard to believe that Malcolm of Lennox would have 'freely agreed' to the loss of his hereditary province as the story claims. Instead John's reward was probably custody of his own family's earldom of Menteith, legally held by his great-niece, Mary.[35] Neither was John imprisoned. He quickly took up a leading role in Robert's entourage, serving the king in diplomacy and war. Despite this, the tale contained accurate details and its account of the negotiations reflected the need for Bruce to bargain for support from key Scottish magnates.[36]

Secure within Dumbarton's walls, John Menteith enjoyed a position denied to most Scottish lords. However, he did face a challenge as a result of his change of loyalty. In 1310 John had to beat off an attack on his lordship of Knapdale by a galley fleet led by John MacSween. MacSween's family had been driven from Argyll by Menteith's father in the 1260s, but he returned from Ireland with Edward II's backing 'to punish our enemy and rebel, John of Menteith'.[37] The risks of punishment by one or other royal lord were keenly felt by many noblemen. The Lothian knight Alexander Seton was a good example of this. Seton was clearly drawn to Robert's cause, joining his rising in 1306, but he was captured by John Mowbray in the pursuit after Methven and did homage to Edward II.[38] His action was presumably motivated by the desire to recover his lands and standing, but in September 1308 Seton and his neighbours faced the first of Bruce's campaigns in Lothian. Alexander's reaction to this was to meet with the enemy. A fragment survives of an agreement made between Seton and two of King Robert's long-standing adherents, Gilbert Hay and Neil Campbell. These former allies swore on the Eucharist 'to defend the liberties of the realm and of Robert the recently crowned king against all men, English, Scots or French, for the terms of their lives'.[39] Seton's readiness to promise such support for Bruce probably stemmed from his personal preferences, as well as the physical threat posed by King Robert's army. However, despite the oath, Seton maintained his allegiance to Edward II, even serving on the jury which forfeited those Lothian lords who had defected to Bruce between 1308 and 1312.[40] It would take the first day's fighting at Bannockburn to push Seton into activating the promise sworn six years earlier.

A second noble whose loyalties would change over the two days of Bannockburn was David Strathbogie earl of Atholl. David's father, Earl John, had been an ally of the Bruces since 1290 and joined Robert's rising in 1306. John was captured and became the most important lord to be executed by the vengeful Edward I.[41] David too supported Robert in early 1307 but by May had made his peace with Edward II.[42] As well as doubts about Bruce's chance of success, his defection may have been influenced by family connections. David Strathbogie was married to Joan Comyn, the sister of the Red Comyn killed by Robert Bruce at Dumfries. Joan was also the niece of Aymer Valence and this link may have provided the means by which David returned to King Edward's allegiance. The connection certainly assisted in the recovery of David's inheritance from Ralph Monthermer. Along with John Mowbray and Alexander Abernethy, Valence agreed to help David raise the money to compensate Monthermer for his loss of the earldom of Atholl.[43] During the next six years David remained in EdwardII's camp, fighting Bruce in the north-east. However, the loss of Strathbogie in 1308 and, probably, Atholl some time later, undermined David's loyalties. Though he served in the English king's garrison at Dundee in 1311 and 1312, Bruce's capture of the burgh seems to have led David to switch allegiance. In October 1312 he was at Inverness, witnessing Robert's treaty with Hakon of Norway.[44] Bruce seems to have been keen to secure the earl's loyalty, restoring his lands and making him constable of Scotland, but continued doubts remained. Barbour links them to Edward Bruce's refusal to marry David's sister, Marjory, with whom he had a child.[45] However, David may also have resented Randolph's elevation to the great earldom of Moray, which bordered his own lands and was formed from the lands of his forfeited in-laws, the Comyns. Such grievances, and the tensions of the 1314 campaign, may have led Atholl to make the decision to switch loyalties for a final time. His choice would prove irrevocable.

Men like Menteith, Seton and Strathbogie cannot be dismissed as rogues, cowards or opportunists. They were nobles whose inheritance of land and status and leadership of kin and tenants gave them responsibilities which they sought to fulfil in an era when certainties of obligation and loyalty were hard to chart. Others, such as James Douglas and Gilbert Hay, were fixed in their loyalties by the impossibility of making a settlement after 1307, but most faced choices of allegiance which were informed by a variety of motives. Though the Scottish nobility, with their domination of landholding and war leadership, represented the key level of political society in these years, the factors shaping their loyalties were also experienced by other groups in the community of the realm. In many ways the leaders of the Scottish church shared the outlook of the higher nobility. As lords of extensive estates and of many knightly tenants, Scotland's prelates, the bishops and heads of religious communities, were also magnates. Many came from aristocratic backgrounds and, like their secular counterparts, placed a value on ties of kin and locality. However, they were also ministers of the church and had other duties and loyalties, most obviously to the spiritual wellbeing of their flocks and to their superior in the church, the pope. In the years of major internal conflict between 1307 and 1314, leading churchmen too were forced into hard choices concerning their temporal loyalty.

The Scottish church had long played a role in articulating and defining the existence and liberties which belonged to Scotland as a kingdom and community. In the succession crisis from 1286 to 1292, it was bishops like William Fraser of St Andrews and Robert Wishart of Glasgow who led the defence of Scotland's sovereignty, while after 1296 Wishart, Fraser's successor, William Lamberton, and other prelates took the field in this cause.[46] During the same period, advocates from the Scottish clergy, like Baldred Bisset, presented Scotland's case to the pope and French king with great success. Bruce sought and received the same kind of support. In 1306 Bishop Wishart had propelled Robert into his seizure of the throne, and Wishart, Lamberton and Bishop David Murray of Moray all provided the new king with physical and moral backing.[47] Murray and Wishart were accused by the English king of inciting Scots to rebel by preaching that Robert's rising was as spiritually meritorious as a war against the infidel.[48] In 1309 this support seemed to be expressed in the Declaration of the Clergy, which asserted the support of 'bishops, abbots, priors and other clergy in the kingdom of Scotland' for Robert and his deliverance of the realm. However, this document also illustrates the problems facing these clergy after 1306. Unlike King John before 1303, Bruce did not have papal sympathy. The pope, Clement V, was a Gascon with strong links to the English kings, while Robert was regarded as a usurper who had been excommunicated for his sacreligious killing of Comyn in a kirk. Bruce had been absolved of this crime in 1308, but his title and authority were not recognised by Clement. Scottish churchmen would have to deal with papal displeasure for support of Bruce until the mid-1320s.[49]

There were risks in opposing papal will. These combined with risks closer to home. Though spared the threat of execution, Bruce's supporters among the bishops were not free from danger. Both Lamberton and Wishart were captured in 1306, while Murray had to flee into exile in Orkney. Edward II tried to persuade Pope Clement to have Lamberton and Wishart deprived of their sees, but the pope was unwilling to create a precedent for such an action. Instead Wishart, who had already sworn allegiance to Edward I on eight occasions, according to the English, was kept in custody until released, old and blind, in the aftermath of Bannockburn.[50] Lamberton's subsequent career shows the flexibility required of a political bishop and a certain personal skill in winning royal favour. Unlike Wishart, Lamberton managed to persuade Edward II to release him from custody and even escaped payment of his ransom. Lamberton was clearly trusted by the English king, who allowed him to return to Scotland. However, while formally in Edward's service, Lamberton also sent representatives to King Robert's parliament in March 1309, attended the church council at Dundee in early 1310, and even witnessed acts of Bruce's government in 1312.[51] This ability to keep a foot in both camps was due not just to Lamberton's personality, but also to his role in the running of the Scottish church. Both kings wished to see the performance of the church's spiritual functions run smoothly and the bishop's authority in this sphere was recognised by the hostile parties.

However, this image of the leaders of the clergy standing above the conflict should not be overstated. Many had family and political connections which bound them into the conflict. When Edward II was seeking to depose Lamberton and Wishart from their sees, the candidates he nominated to replace them were Geoffrey Mowbray and William Comyn, kinsmen of two of Bruce's principal Scottish enemies.[52] Similarly, the difficult relationship between King Robert and the bishop of Aberdeen, Henry Cheyne, owed much to the opposition of Henry's family to Bruce, while William Sinclair, who was elected bishop of Dunkeld, made peace with Edward II in 1312 through the intervention of his brother, the influential Lothian baron Henry Sinclair. Henry's defection to Bruce in 1313 may have seen Bishop William adhering firmly to King Robert, who had physical custody of most of the lands belonging to the bishopric.[53] The interests of kin also shaped the actions of Bishop David Murray. He was a member of the influential magnate family which possessed extensive lands in Moray and elsewhere. However, the deaths of David's brothers and nephew between 1297 and 1300 and the absence of his great-nephew in England left the bishop to safeguard these lands as well as his own extensive estates and rights as bishop. His initial support of Bruce may have owed something to the desire to recover the Murray lands, but he made peace with Edward II and, in 1308, he was slow to join King Robert during his northern campaign.[54] For all their identification with the cause of Scottish liberties, the leaders of the church gave patchy support to King Robert in the years of greatest internal warfare.

For kings and their lieutenants seeking to gather armies, the crucial political grouping was probably the section of Scottish society termed '*le menzane de Escoce*', the middle folk. In the late 1290s and early 1300s the support of this group was clearly a matter of political importance for both sides.[55] However, the precise composition of the middle folk is unclear. Probably included were all those knights and lesser nobles below baronial rank, as well as richer peasants, freeholders who held their lands by charter, and the burgesses, the elite who ran Scotland's urban communities. These men possessed arms, armour and even a riding horse and, as will be discussed, formed the core of all Scottish armies. In political terms they enjoyed influence in their locality, which made them a vital group in securing the allegiance of such communities across Scotland. Their importance in the years between 1307 and 1314 was recognised by the appearance of such lesser men in narratives of the war. Barbour's account includes the exploits of Philip, the forester of Platan who gathered his 'freyndis' and captured Forfar Castle in 1308, and of Thomas Dicson, a tenant of Douglasdale, who gave crucial support to the young James Douglas in 1307. Dicson, described as 'ryche off mobleis [goods] and cateill' and 'off freyndis weill mychty', was clearly the kind of local landowner whose influence could deliver wider support.[56] The tale of 'Roland', probably in reality one Oliver Carpenter, who helped Bruce secure Dumbarton Castle, which appeared in the fifteenth-century *Scotichronicon*, suggests that there were many tales of lesser men acting as heroes in the cause of Scotland.[57]

Such stories seem to suggest a level of grass-roots support for King Robert which is backed up by some record sources. The letter from Forfar in 1307 speaks of 'false preachers' whipping up support for Bruce. This may be thinking in terms of the actions of sympathisers like Dicson and Philip the Forester, and suggests anxieties about the appeal of Bruce's leadership to this group. During the northern campaign of 1307–8, John Mowbray, Bruce's opponent, was reported to have taken action against 'all freeholders and other men that he knew to be of evil repute'.[58] These lesser men had probably risen in support of Bruce but had been left exposed when the king fell back after Slioch. By claiming the kingship, and by pressing his claims in war with growing success, Robert was able to activate the strong, traditional allegiance of many Scots to their royal rulers. Lesser nobles and freeholders may have been less concerned about debates over the legitimacy of Bruce or Balliol and more impressed by the success of Robert in warfare. Lacking lands and family contacts in England, many of these middle folk may also have been more ready to regard the English king and his agents as a foreign enemy.

However, it is important not to suggest that the middle folk gave consistent and general backing to Bruce. Earls like Ross and Buchan were able to muster armies numbering several thousand from the men of their provinces to oppose Robert, while barons like Alexander Balliol and Alexander Abernethy led retinues in the service of the English king.[59] Most strikingly, the garrisons maintained by Edward II in Perth and Dundee contained high numbers of

Scots. At Dundee, serving under local lords like Abernethy, David Brechin and David Strathbogie, were considerable numbers of knights and lesser men, especially from Fife and Angus. Some of these individuals were clearly in the following of baronial kin, like Henry Brechin and Christian of Strathbogie, or served as family groups like the five named Ramsays. Others, like John Pitscottie, John Dunmore and Richard Balcaskie, were minor landowners who chose to oppose Bruce.[60] Their motive may well have been the wages paid by Edward II to his soldiers, but they clearly felt no natural affection for the Bruce Cause. Perth presents an equally strong example. Here too, many of the garrison were local Scots, like Philip Lochore and the numerous individuals surnamed Muschet and Cameron.[61] In addition, Scottish accounts of the siege of the burgh all claim that the leading burgesses actively opposed Bruce. Their hostility may have gone back to 1306 when Robert's officials had threatened the bailies of Perth with death until they handed over the burgh rents. In 1312 the burgesses were entrusted with the fortification of Perth. After Robert captured the burgh, he had several of them executed or imprisoned.[62]

The lands between the Grampians and the Tay experienced warfare throughout the period from 1308 to 1313. It was warfare which was not just fought between armies from outside but which pitted local people against each other. Neighbours like Gilbert Hay, John Inchmartin, Alexander Abernethy and David Brechin took up conflicting positions in the fighting. [63] When Bruce besieged Dundee and Perth in 1312 and 1313, he was attacking burghs which were garrisoned by as many Scots as English and which were commanded by local Scottish nobles – William Muschet and David Brechin at Dundee and William Oliphant and Malise of Strathearn at Perth.[64] Nor was this a unique pattern. The sustained warfare in Galloway was equally a conflict between Bruce's adherents, mostly from outside the province, and his local enemies. In Lothian too, the local community was divided between those who risked forfeiture to join Bruce from 1308 and those who chose to continue in King Edward's camp. Despite the military successes won by King Robert up to the autumn of 1313, Scotland remained a divided kingdom. The campaign of the following summer, which would reach its climax at Bannockburn, was waged as the culmination of this internal war for the allegiance of the Scots to Bruce or Plantagenet.

NOTES

1. Palgrave, *Documents*, no. clviii.
2 *A.P.S.*, i, 459; Duncan, 'Declarations of the Clergy', 44–5.
3. *C.D.S.*, iii, nos 186–337.
4. This was not the first time such divisions in the community had been expressed. In 1291 the existence of two parties in Scotland was stated in the 'Appeals of the Seven Earls' (Stones, *Anglo-Scottish Relations*, no. 14).
5. *A.P.S.*, i, 459.
6. For lists of Scots in the English kings' allegiance between 1307 and 1311, see *Foedera*, ii, 8, 119, 124, 149; *Rot. Scot.*, i, 62, 64, 80.

7. *C.D.S.*, iii, nos 8, 302. In 1308 Duncan earl of Fife married Mary Monthermer, daughter of Ralph Monthermer and niece of Edward II.
8. *A.P.S.*, i, 459; *R.R.S.*, v, nos 3, 5, 6.
9. *Foedera*, ii, 8, 119, 132; *C.D.S.*, iii, nos 43, 47, 89, 121, 176, 1147; *Rot. Scot.*, i, 56.
10. Duncan, 'Declarations of the Clergy', 44–5.
11. Duncan, 'Declarations of the Clergy', 32–44.
12. Duncan, 'Declarations of the Clergy', 45.
13. *Foedera*, ii (1), 119.
14. *H.M.C.*, 14th report, Strathmore and Kinghorne, 177; E. L. G. Stones and G. G. Simpson, *Edward I and the throne of Scotland*, 2 vols (Oxford, 1978), i, 82; *C.D.S.*, ii, no. 1471.
15. Hay's position was an interesting one. His family seems to have backed Balliol's claim to the throne and probably backed his rights in the war up to 1304. As a result, Gilbert inherited lands damaged by war and burdened by debt. Edward I allowed him a rebate on his succession duty but Gilbert chose to join Bruce in 1306. His lands were laid waste by the English king's men as a result, committing Hay to the Bruce party (*C.D.S.*, ii, nos 1738, 1782, 1787).
16. Stewart does not appear in any account of Bruce's rising but suffered forfeiture and had to submit to Edward I in late 1306 before recovering his estates (*C.D.S.*, ii, nos 1818, 1826, 1843, 1857). For Randolph, see *The Bruce*, ed. Duncan, 249, 355–9, 373–5.
17. *C.D.S.*, ii, appendix 2, no. 4.
18. *C.D.S.*, iv, p. 400; v, no. 655; *Chron. Lanercost*, 188; 'The Movements of Robert Bruce', 58–9.
19. *C.D.S.*, iii, no. 245.
20. *C.D.S.*, ii, nos 1462, 1694; iii, nos 47, 303.
21. For the Dunbars, see A. J. MacDonald, 'Kings of the wild frontier? The earls of Dunbar and March, c. 1070–1435', in S. Boardman and A. Ross, *The Exercise of Power in Medieval Scotland c.1200–1500* (Dublin, 2003), 139–58.
22. For the roles played by Umfraville, Mowbray and Buchan, see A. Young, *Robert the Bruce's Rivals: The Comyns 1212–1314* (East Linton, 1997), 171–6, 194–5; Watson, *Under the Hammer*, 102, 108, 122; Barrow, *Robert Bruce*, 106, 112–14, 124; Palgrave, *Documents*, 287–90, 293. Oliphant was keeper of Stirling Castle when it was besieged by Edward I in 1304 (*C.D.S.*, ii, no. 1517).
23. Palgrave, *Documents*, no. cxliv.
24. Stones and Simpson, *Edward I and the throne of Scotland*, i, 84.
25. B. Webster, 'Scotland without a King, 1329–41', in A. Grant and K. Stringer, *Medieval Scotland: Crown, Lordship and Community* (Edinburgh, 1993), 222–38.
26. Palgrave, *Documents*, no. cxxiii; Watson, *Under the Hammer*, 185.
27. Palgrave, *Documents*, no. cxlii; *C.D.S.*, ii, nos 1757, 1771, 1776, 1839, 1857, 1945; *The Bruce*, ed. Duncan, 192n.
28. *C.D.S.*, ii, nos 1771, 1776, 1804, 1837, 1841, 1861.
29. No formal grants of these lands survive but Edward held the titles of lord of Galloway and then earl of Carrick in royal records (*R.R.S.*, v, nos 20, 28, 30–2, 34, 36; *A.P.S.*, i, 459).
30. *R.R.S.*, v, no. 389.
31. *A.P.S.*, i, 477; *R.R.S.*, v, nos 77–8; Barrow, *Robert Bruce*, 271.
32. *C.D.S.*, v, no. 492 (xvi); *Chron. Fordun*, ii, 332. Menteith possessed extensive connections in the far west (*The Bruce*, ed. Duncan, 118n; S. Boardman, *The Campbells* (Edinburgh, 2005), 37–9).
33. Stones, *Anglo-Scottish Relations*, no. 34; *C.D.S.*, ii, no. 1786.
34. *Scotichronicon*, vi, 447–8.

35. *R.R.S.*, v, nos 20, 35–7, 39 and p. 358; *C.D.S.*, iii, no. 101.
36. *R.R.S.*, v, nos 6, 9, 20.
37. *Rot. Scot.*, i, 90.
38. Palgrave, *Documents*, pp. 310, 356–7.
39. G. Mackenzie, *The Lives and Characters of the most eminent Writers of the Scottish Nation* (Edinburgh, 1708–22), iii, 210.
40. *C.D.S.*, iii, nos 121, 245.
41. A. Ross, 'Men for all Seasons? The Strathbogie Earls of Atholl and the Wars of Independence, c. 1290–1335, 1', *Northern Scotland*, 20 (2000), 1–30.
42. *C.D.S.*, ii, no. 1926; *Nat. MSS Scot.*, ii, no. 13.
43. *C.D.S.*, iii, no. 5.
44. *C.D.S.*, iii, p. 404; *R.R.S.*, v, nos 24, 28, 29.
45. *The Bruce*, ed. Duncan, 504–5.
46. G. W. S. Barrow, 'The Scottish Clergy in the Wars of Independence', *S.H.R.*, 41 (1962), 1–22; Brown, *Wars of Scotland*, 114–34, 310–12.
47. Stones, *Anglo-Scottish Relations*, no. 35; Palgrave, *Documents*, no. cl; Barrow, *Robert Bruce*, 145–51.
48. Palgrave, *Documents*, pp. 330, 347–8.
49. Duncan, 'Declarations of the Clergy', 32–8, 44; *Scotichronicon*, vi, 318–20.
50. Palgrave, *Documents*, nos cxlviii–cl. For Wishart's career, see D. E. R. Watt, *A Biographical Dictionary of Scottish Graduates to 1410* (Oxford, 1977), 585–9.
51. Watt, *Scottish Graduates*, 323–4; *Rot. Scot.*, i, 80, 108; *R.R.S.*, v, no. 19.
52. *Rot. Scot.*, i, 55; *Foedera*, i, 528.
53. Watt, *Scottish Graduates*, 496–7; *Foedera*, ii, 205.
54. *C.D.S.*, iv, p. 400; Watt, *Scottish Graduates*, 412–13.
55. J. Stevenson (ed.), *Documents illustrative of the History of Scotland*, 2 vols (Edinburgh, 1870), ii, no. ccclii; *C.D.S.*, ii, nos 1204, 1755.
56. *The Bruce*, ed. Duncan, 204–7, 334–5. Other lesser figures who played a significant role in *The Bruce* were Sim of the Ledhouse and William Francis, who aided in the capture of Roxburgh and Edinburgh Castles (ibid., 376–83, 388–93).
57. *Scotichronicon*, vi, 447–8.
58. *C.D.S.*, ii, no. 1926; 'The Movements of Robert Bruce', 58–9.
59. *C.D.S.*, ii, nos 1324, 1356, 1694, 1939; iv, p. 399; *The Bruce*, ed. Duncan, 318–19, 324–5.
60. *C.D.S.*, iii, pp. 427–32; *Rot. Scot.*, 106, 108–9.
61. *C.D.S.*, iii, pp. 425–7.
62. *C.D.S.*, iii, nos 68, 287; *Nat. MSS Scot.*, ii, no. 15; *Chron. Fordun*, ii, 338; *Scotichronicon*, vi, 348–9. Barbour, however, states that Bruce spared the inhabitants (*The Bruce*, ed. Duncan, 342–3).
63. The proximity of these lords to each other in normal circumstances is suggested by the run of charters from the chartulary of Coupar Angus Abbey between c. 1304 and 1320 (*Coupar Angus Charters*, 2 vols, Scottish History Society (Edinburgh, 1947), nos lxv–xcvii).
64. *The Bruce*, ed. Duncan, 336–7; *C.D.S.*, iii, nos 247, 264, 268, 283, p. 425.

CHAPTER 4

The Scottish War and the Plantagenet Dominions (1307–1314)

EDWARD II, SCOTLAND AND THE ENGLISH POLITY

Though the warfare waged in Scotland between 1307 and 1313 was primarily fought by the Scottish supporters of Robert Bruce and those of Edward Plantagenet, the wider picture was of crucial importance to its outcome. The successes won by Bruce and Edward II's gradual loss of the Scottish lordship he had inherited from his father were directly related to attitudes and events in the other parts of his dominions, his kingdom of England, his lordship of Ireland, Wales and the duchy of Gascony.[1] Nowhere are these links demonstrated more clearly than in the connection between English politics and the war against Bruce. The Scottish war was part of the difficult inheritance which Edward II had received from his father. During the last decade of his life Edward I had strained his realm and dominions to wage war against his Scottish enemies. He levied field armies for campaigning in Scotland on eight occasions during the twelve years from 1296 to 1307 and led them in person in six expeditions.[2] The financial and political costs of this commitment were heavy. It has been estimated that waging the war in Scotland cost Edward over £40,000 in 1300, with £13,500 going on garrisons and at least £28,000 being paid for other military wages. The long but apparently decisive campaign from summer 1303 to summer 1304 cost over £75,000.[3] Though such sums were smaller than those expended on the war with Philip IV of France in the 1290s and there were fewer difficulties of persuading English magnates to serve in Scotland rather than overseas, the slow grinding down of Scottish resistance was a heavy drain on the old king's financial and political position. It had taken intense personal involvement and expenditure of resources to impose Edward I's authority on the Scottish realm. Numerous unpopular methods of seeking funds had been employed to pay for the war and the king had run up a huge deficit in his finances in the last years of the reign. To secure money and the service of his barons, Edward had also been forced to make concessions about his rights as king. His apparently successful settlement of Scotland freed Edward to renounce these concessions.[4] Edward's furious reaction to Bruce's rising in 1306 was not just a response to personal betrayal. The renewal of the Scottish war also renewed the problems of finance and political authority in

69

ROSS

BUCHAN

MORAY

● Aberdeen

ATHOLL

THE
WESTERN
ISLES

ARGYLL

Perth ● Dundee
●
Stirling
●

ISLAY

Edinburgh ●

Berwick

LOTHIAN

● Alnwick

CARRICK
GALLOWAY

EARLDOM
OF
ULSTER

O'Neills

● Carlisle

O'Connors

MAN

● Scarborough

York ●

● Roscommon

CONNACHT   MEATH

Pontefract

LOUTH

O'Briens ● Bunratty

LEINSTER

● Dublin

P

Caernarfon
●

Limerick   Kilkenny

WICKLOW

P

KINGDOM OF
ENGLAND

MUNSTER

POWYS

P

PEMBROKE

BRECON
GLAMORGAN

London ●

P   Principality of Wales

Areas outside effective English
lordship in Ireland

MAP 4.1 *The British Isles c.1310*

England which Edward had ridden out. The ailing king's determination to crush Bruce and his adherents may reflect his anxieties about the effect of a long war on the position of the crown in England.

In the event, the death of Edward I at Burgh-by-Sands near Carlisle in July 1307 bequeathed his son a legacy of war and its costs. Though, as has been examined, the new king enjoyed far greater Scottish support in the war against Bruce than his father had received in the conflict before 1304, Edward II's handling of Scotland in the opening years of his reign was disastrous. The most obvious contrast with his father was in the new king's failure to provide leadership in the conflict. In July and August 1307 Edward II took over his father's planned expedition and led an army of several thousand, including the earls of Lancaster, Pembroke, Hereford, Lincoln, Richmond, Warenne and Arundel.[5] However, the campaign which followed lacked direction and lasted little more than a fortnight. Edward II's concern to go south and begin his reign may be understandable but it signalled the end of sustained royal leadership in the campaign against Bruce. The reduced priority accorded to the Scottish war was even more apparent in following years. In June 1308 and July 1309 the king announced plans to muster and lead armies against Bruce, but on both occasions the campaigns were called off.[6] These expeditions, however limited in scale, would have stiffened Scottish opposition to Bruce. Robert's ability to bring about the submission or flight of his enemies in Galloway, Argyll and Angus would have been restricted by the presence of an English field army in the south-west or the Forth valley in 1308 or 1309. Instead, the lack of such support exposed Edward's Scottish adherents to attack.

By the time Edward actually went north to take command in the war in autumn 1310, his position in Scotland had deteriorated significantly. Even then, his personal involvement in the war was limited to a brief march through southern Scotland. However, King Edward's presence in Berwick during the winter of 1310–11 and the active strategy pursued by his lieutenants probably caused Bruce difficulty and strengthened the resolve of men like Alexander Abernethy, David Brechin and David Strathbogie. Had Edward mounted similar expeditions in the months and years which followed, the renewed series of successes and submissions won by Bruce would have been made much harder to achieve. Instead, during the period from August 1311 until the end of 1313 Robert was able to launch attack after attack on the lands, burghs and castles which refused to recognise his royal title. When Dundee was resisting a six-week siege during early 1312, Edward merely dispatched a small relief force by sea to its aid.[7] When his garrison commanders and Scottish adherents asked for his aid, Edward thanked them for their support and advised them to make truces with the enemy. The rapid erosion of support and loss of lordship experienced by the English king in Scotland was an inevitable consequence of this failure of Edward II to take the field or send sufficient forces northwards.

This lack of support for his men engaged in the war did not necessarily indicate a lack of personal commitment to the war by the king himself. Instead it was partly due to the wider financial difficulties faced by Edward II in the opening years of his reign. As we have seen, these problems cannot be separated from the Scottish war but were the legacy of Edward I's pursuit of authority there. Since the end of the 1290s, royal finances had been in a chaotic state. To avoid requesting a grant of taxation from parliament and arousing hostility, Edward I chose to amass a deficit. This debt had reached about £200,000 by the time of the old king's death, leaving many of Edward II's ordinary subjects unpaid for goods and services and resentful about any fresh royal demands.[8] On top of this, the management of the crown's accounts had broken down, leaving the new king to deal with a mass of problems. Even without major royal campaigning, paying the wages and the victualling costs of his garrisons ate up a significant proportion of Edward II's income. Though the new king did receive a grant of taxation in late 1307 specifically to pay for the war in Scotland and a second in 1309 to offset other royal financial demands, the pursuit of a more active military policy was hampered by this underlying quandary.[9]

However, as with much else, Edward II bore a personal responsibility for the difficulty of financing his Scottish war. Most directly, he failed to use the funds accumulated to raise expeditions against Bruce for that purpose. In 1308, having summoned troops to muster at Carlisle in September, Edward had taken foodstuffs and transport from his subjects, using the crown's right of *prise*, the commandeering of goods in a crisis.[10] The routine use of this emergency power by the government, long a source of grievance, was made much worse by the cancellation of the campaign. The following year the process was repeated, inevitably increasing resentment about Edward's policies and demands. In reaction to this, criticism was made in parliament in early 1310 that Edward had misused the taxation granted to him, impoverished his kingdom and people with new financial demands and lost ground in Scotland.[11] Though *prise* was again employed in 1310 and subsidies raised from individual boroughs in 1311, Edward's plans for a campaign later in that year foundered on a lack of money.[12] In the search for funds Edward, like his father, turned to Italian and Gascon bankers who granted the king loans in return for the assignment of royal revenues. By 1312 the payment for his remaining Scottish garrisons had been handed over to such figures in return for further accumulations of debt. The influence of these bankers was widely resented as a drain on English resources, but Edward had left himself little alternative.[13]

If the Scottish war contributed heavily to Edward II's financial hardships, the political problems he faced in England shaped the course of that struggle in the years up to Bannockburn. The repeated and growing series of crises between 1308 and 1313, though they owed something to the disputes aroused by the policies of his father, were largely of Edward's own making. At the heart of these crises was the figure of Piers Gaveston, the Gascon knight who enjoyed a monopoly of the king's favour. From his return from exile to join

Edward at Dumfries in August 1307, Gaveston aroused a general hostility among the English nobility. His presence at Edward's side turned a baronage which had initially been well-disposed towards the king into an opposition party within a few months in late 1307 and early 1308. Over the next five years until his brutal execution by his enemies, Gaveston's influence with the king brought the realm close to civil war on numerous occasions, while the death of Gaveston caused an even deeper crisis. Edward, supported by moderate barons, faced his cousin, Thomas of Lancaster, and more extreme critics. For over a year English political life was in limbo, while the king and his enemies manoeuvred and negotiated to reach a settlement.[14] The disputes over Gaveston had a serious political point. The Gascon's receipt of an earldom, massive pensions and frequent gifts hardly sat well with a king who claimed poverty. His domination of Edward upset the network of personal relationships which lay at the heart of all medieval realms. However, it was the consequences of these antagonisms which were of greatest importance, especially with regard to the war against Bruce. Above all, it was the threat posed to Gaveston in 1308 and 1309 which caused Edward to abandon his planned expeditions to Scotland. To the author of the *Vita Edwardi Secundi* the king's campaign of 1310 was undertaken primarily to avoid leaving Gaveston 'in the midst of his enemies'. The same source also suggested that Edward approached Bruce to give safe haven to Gaveston when these enemies were closing in during early 1312, offering peace in return.[15] Though hardly credible, such a story indicates the atmosphere of suspicion prevailing in England and the belief that the king would do anything to protect his favourite. There is certainly clear evidence that both Edward and his opponents placed the fate of Gaveston above the Scottish war in their priorities. In 1310 almost all the earls refused to take part in the king's planned campaign in Scotland. They claimed to be engaged in drawing up the Ordinances, the rules of good governance. As well as restricting royal use of *prise* and reforming royal financial administration, the Ordinances demanded the exile of Gaveston and other royal servants.[16] The earls also withheld their personal service because they regarded the campaign as an attempt by the king to protect Gaveston and avoid accepting the Ordinances. Gaveston's removal and, more charitably, the reform of the kingdom's government were given priority over events in Scotland by many of the leading magnates.[17]

Edward was equally responsible, not just in 1308 and 1309, but throughout late 1312 and 1313, when he strung out negotiations with his enemies. As early as September 1312 the baronial opposition offered the king their help in securing a financial subsidy from parliament for the Scottish war. In return Edward had to accept the Ordinances. Edward refused these terms, continuing negotiations until the following summer. Though in the final settlement, a year later, in October 1313, the king secured better terms, obtaining the promised subsidy without accepting the Ordinances, the delay had serious implications for events in Scotland.[18] The intervening year had seen the loss of strongholds at Perth, Dumfries, Linlithgow and elsewhere, the submission of Galloway and Man to Bruce and the intense harrying of Lothian and the English marches. Edward's visit to France in June sparked fears in the author of the *Vita* that the Scottish king might overrun the north while Edward engaged in 'constant delays'. The same chronicler stated squarely that 'if he [Edward] had followed the advice of his barons he would have humbled the Scots with ease'.[19]

The course of English politics between 1307 and 1313 raises doubts about the significance accorded to the war in Scotland. While in 1297 news of the defeat of Edward I's forces at Stirling Bridge had served to bring the king's critics and his officials to a swift reconciliation, in the early years of Edward II's reign the king and his opponents repeatedly failed to settle their differences in order to confront Bruce more effectively.[20] Yet the deteriorating situation in Scotland was not unknown or ignored. Though in many southern English chronicles of the period the war received only passing mention up to 1314, the reliable account of the *Vita Edwardi Secundi*, which was probably produced in the west country, reveals real interest and concern about the conflict. In particular, the lengthy description of Edward's campaign of 1310–11 both captures the problems faced by the English king and a degree of admiration for the 'prowess and unremitting perseverance' of Robert Bruce, though the latter is tempered by distaste at his 'evil deeds'.[21] The declining state of affairs in Scotland is mentioned in the next few years, but it is only with the plans for a new royal campaign from late 1313 that the war moves out of the background. Other accounts give much less attention, confirming the sense that events in Scotland, though shocking, were distant from the centre of events, even when King Edward moved his court to York or Berwick.[22] The Ordinances certainly showed concern for Scotland. One of the clauses criticised the king for his failure to maintain his rights in both Scotland and Gascony.[23] Edward was clearly being blamed for the losses of lands and liegemen in Scotland and the flow of bad news must have increased disenchantment with his rule. The *Vita Edwardi* probably conveyed a widely held opinion when it stated that

> the king was really occupied with two projects: one was the defeat of Robert Bruce, in which he acted feebly, because the greater part of the English baronage gave him no help in the affair; the other was keeping Piers Gaveston with him, for whose expulsion and exile almost all the barons of England were working. In these two matters the king . . . could not attain one on account of the other.[24]

The Scottish war was being lost due to the political rivalries within the community. When, as in the summer of 1308, 'councils were held about the defence of Scotland and the defeat of Robert Bruce . . . their outcomes did not . . . result in action'.[25]

Though Edward held the chief responsibility for this, it was not just the king's war. As we have seen, in 1306 Edward I made strenuous efforts to form a body of English magnates with major landed interests in Scotland. Though the rapid submissions of James Stewart and David Strathbogie meant the restoration of their estates and the removal of Henry earl of Lincoln and Ralph Monthermer from their lands, there remained a group of English lords with Scottish estates. The rights of Aymer Valence earl of Pembroke to the lordships of Bothwell and Selkirk, of Robert Clifford to Douglasdale, of John Hastings to Menteith, of Henry Percy to Carrick and of Humphrey Bohun earl of Hereford to Annandale were supposed to commit them to the defence of the English crown's rights in Scotland.[26] To this group can be added Robert Umfraville earl of Angus, heir to an Anglo-Scottish inheritance, and a beneficiary of Edward II's patronage, Henry Beaumont. Beaumont, from a French noble family, enjoyed close links to the king. Since the 1290s, Beaumont had been an active participant in the Scottish wars and he received a personal stake in the conflict when he married Alice Comyn, the niece and heiress of John earl of Buchan, in about 1310. As well as claiming her lost earldom, Beaumont received rights to estates in England and south-west Scotland and pressed his rights to be constable of Scotland. In addition, Henry was given life custody of the sheriffdom of Roxburgh and of the Isle of Man by King Edward.[27] As a landless adventurer, Beaumont saw the Scottish war as the means to achieve the status and resources of a magnate.

Beaumont was frequently engaged by the king in war and diplomacy in Scotland. Similar roles were played by the earl of Angus and by Robert Clifford.[28] Yet even these examples reveal the political problems undermining the English war effort. Beaumont, in particular, was a controversial figure. A political associate of Gaveston, Henry Beaumont and his family were specifically targeted by the Ordainers who demanded their banishment and loss of lands in 1311.[29] The next year Beaumont was active in Edward's moves against his magnate opponents. By contrast, Clifford was from a baronial family with growing interests in Westmorland and Yorkshire. An established and charismatic leader in the old king's Scottish wars, he acted as Edward's warden in Scotland in both 1308 and 1311, having served in the recent campaign.[30] However, though he had enjoyed royal patronage for his efforts, in 1312 Clifford joined the king's opponents in the attack on Gaveston. Under Edward I, Clifford had frequently served in Scotland alongside Henry Percy and their relationship was cemented by a marriage between their children. Percy's own efforts had been rewarded with the grant of the earldom of Carrick, which he had unsuccessfully defended against Bruce in 1307. His defeat by King Robert may have reduced his enthusiasm for the fight but his limited role in Scotland under Edward II was also linked to Percy's growing opposition. By 1311 he was an active supporter of the Ordainers, benefiting from the removal of the Beaumonts.[31] Though he was expected to take charge at Perth in spring 1311, Percy was much less willing to serve in Scotland under Edward II than he had been in the previous reign. The earls of Hereford and Pembroke made similar choices. Both took their rights to major Scottish

FIGURE 4.1 *Robert Lord Clifford commemorated in the stained glass of York Minster. Clifford was a veteran leader in the Scottish wars whose career would end in death at Bannockburn. (By kind permission of the Dean and Chapter of York)*

lordships seriously. Valence had been a leading figure in Edward I's wars and Edward II clearly hoped for the support of these earls in his campaigning. However, when summoned in 1310, neither would join the king's army, sending only their required contingent of cavalry, despite Edward's direct appeal to Hereford. The two earls also joined in the baronial campaign against Gaveston in 1312.[32]

The careers and landed interests of these barons meant that they had strong stakes in the successful prosecution of the Scottish war and this showed through in their political activities. Among the Ordainers, it was the earl of Hereford and Robert Clifford who led efforts to negotiate with King Edward during 1313.[33] During that year they must have been aware of the direct threats posed to their lands in Annandale and Douglasdale by Bruce's advance and may have been behind the proposal to support a grant of taxation to allow the king to lead an expedition to Scotland. When that expedition finally mustered in the summer of 1314, Hereford and Clifford, along with Valence and Beaumont, would take up leading roles in the army. The culmination of the campaign at Bannockburn would prove a decisive turning point for all four.[34]

For Clifford, Percy and many other barons, by 1313 the war with Scotland had become much more immediate. The involvement of Robert Clifford and Henry Percy in Edward I's wars in Scotland had probably encouraged both men to seek new lands in the northern marches. Most recently, in 1310 Henry Percy had acquired the castle and barony of Alnwick in Northumberland, starting his family's rise to their later leading role in the borders.[35] Such interests were immediately challenged by Bruce's first attacks into northern England. As these grew in scale and frequency, and drained incomes and resources from the counties north of the River Tees, the need to oppose Bruce became a priority. Keepers had been appointed to guard the northern march since 1308 but, from late 1311, such measures assumed a much greater urgency and frequency for lords like Clifford. It is not surprising that accounts from the region, like that compiled at the Priory of Lanercost near Carlisle, show a greater awareness of Bruce's rise and the threat he posed to their own districts from 1308.[36] Though Percy would still not serve in 1314, the army that was mustered would contain many knights and far more ordinary foot soldiers mustered from the shires of northern England. The disaster that befell this host would expose the north to warfare of greater intensity and damage than anything experienced since the Norman Conquest.

A clear and growing sense clearly existed in England that the war against Bruce was going poorly and that action was needed to recover the lordship apparently won by Edward I in 1304–5. However, the war and the cost of waging it did not necessarily dictate broader political choices. The dispatch of armies to Scotland was a huge expense. The rewards of the war, for the crown in terms of the revenues it raised from Scotland, or for his magnates in the patronage they received, were always highly uncertain. Unlike Wales, where grants of land had proved secure and profitable, in Scotland major royal gifts had often been reversed by the need to win over their Scottish lords and, if not, their defence was an expensive and uncertain business. For example, in 1311 Edward II took over the defence of Bothwell from Valence to ensure its protection.[37] Some magnates showed a personal commitment to the conflict. Gilbert Clare earl of Gloucester had no personal interests in Scotland. Despite this, from soon after he took possession of his inheritance in 1307 the young earl displayed a desire to become involved in the conflict. In 1308 he took command of a small expedition sent against Bruce and in 1310 Gilbert joined King Edward's campaign, remaining in Scotland until sent south to take office as warden of England. Gloucester's enthusiasm was perhaps motivated by a youthful desire for glory in war but it was well rewarded by the king who assigned him 5,000 marks for his service.[38]

Yet Gloucester was an exception. For most of his peers, the need to reform a corrupt and incompetent government took precedence. Only when Gaveston

FIGURE 4.2 *A stained-glass window in Tewkesbury Abbey depicting the monastery's patrons. Among them (second from left) is an earl of Gloucester, probably Gilbert Clare. The young earl emerged as a leading figure in English politics and the war after 1308. (Crown Copyright. NMR)*

was removed and Edward made to take good counsel could effective action be taken against Bruce. This attitude was exemplified by Thomas earl of Lancaster, the king's cousin and the greatest lord in England. As well as extensive estates in the Midlands, Lancaster held many lands and castles in Yorkshire and Lancashire. The death of his father-in-law, Henry earl of Lincoln, in 1311 brought Lancaster even greater estates, including land in Northumberland, where the earl began work on a new castle at Dunstanburgh.[39] However, despite such northern interests, Lancaster was to refuse to serve under Edward in 1310, 1311 and 1314. He chose to place his opposition to the king and his favourites over the prosecution of the war in Scotland and defence of his own northern lands and tenants. If Edward won a victory against Bruce without accepting the Ordinances then his ability to face down future demands for reform would be greatly increased. Earl Thomas was not prepared to see this happen.

Lancaster's approach was shared by other lords but had its own costs. Just as Edward was criticised for his incompetence and for putting his love for Gaveston over his duties as king, so Lancaster and his hardline allies, Warwick and Arundel, were open to attack for failing in their obligations to defend the realm and people along with their royal lord. Accusations that he was prepared to seek a treasonable alliance with Bruce which followed Lancaster from 1314 probably had their roots in his refusal to serve with Edward in these earlier campaigns.[40] If Scotland was being lost through neglect during these years, it still remained a matter of honour and material importance for the English king and community to turn back the tide of war. The campaign which would be ordered in late 1313 was seen as a key moment in the course of English politics as well as shaping the fate of Scotland.

ALL THE KING'S MEN? WALES AND IRELAND

England was at the core of King Edward's dominions. Apart from his campaigns in Scotland and brief visits to the continent, Edward dwelled solely in England. He drew the vast majority of his revenues from the kingdom and it was the great barons and community of England with whom he had to deal. Yet the kingdom of England did not stand in isolation. The king was also lord of Ireland and ruler of Wales, and in both these lands there were English townsmen and rural dwellers who were as much the king's subjects as their kinsmen inside England. Many of the leading members of the English nobility held estates and possessed personal contacts with the king's Welsh and Irish dominions. Such connections bound these lands closely to the English crown but there were major differences with England. Both contained large native populations whose attitude to the English king was less certain and fixed. Questions of loyalty, fears of rebellion and, in Ireland, ongoing warfare all made for very different political environments from England. These coloured the expectations of the king's officers and limited the contribution they could extract from Wales and Ireland.[41] However, both were expected to play key roles in the war against Bruce and, just as they had done in the fighting up to 1304, the inhabitants of these lands were called upon to give financial and personal support for their king's enterprises. Just as in England, the course of the war would also play an increasingly significant role in the internal politics of Wales and Ireland, shaking the stability of Plantagenet authority.

In June 1310 King Edward issued orders to his subjects to provide him with troops for his campaign to check the 'rebellion and disturbance of Robert Bruce'. As well as the summons sent to his tenants-in-chief to provide cavalry and to the English shires for footmen, the king instructed his subjects in Wales to provide him with troops. Some 5,000 Welsh infantry were ordered to muster at Berwick in September, though only 2,500 seem actually to have served in Edward's campaign through southern Scotland.[42] Neither the summons itself nor the numbers involved would have surprised the king's officials. The previous year over 8,000 foot had been demanded from Wales, and during the last decade of Edward I's reign levies of this kind had been made on an annual basis.[43] In employing Welsh troops in these numbers, the crown was exploiting the traditions of that realm as a land accustomed to regular warfare. Since the arrival of the Normans in the 1060s, and even before, war based on raids and ambushes had been a normal occurrence, producing populations skilled in bearing arms. However, the condition of Wales had altered drastically in recent decades. In 1284 Edward I had inflicted a final defeat on the leading Welsh dynasty, the house of Gwynedd, taking their domains and those of other princes into his hands. Traditions of Welsh princely rule were suppressed and the whole of Wales subjected to the rule of the English king.[44]

Foreign rule brought a kind of peace to Wales but also bound the Welsh into the military and political enterprises of the Plantagenets. Though much changed with the Edwardian conquest, the summons of 1310 also revealed that the divisions which characterised Wales persisted. Unlike England, orders for footmen were not simply dispatched to the king's sheriffs and officials, but were also directed in person to the lords of the march. These lords had inherited or been granted blocs of territory which lay along the eastern border of Wales from Denbigh south to Chepstow and along the southern coast through Glamorgan and Brecon to the cluster of lordships centred on the earldom of Pembroke. Most such lands had originally been carved out in war with the Welsh princes and the status and powers their owners possessed were designed to allow them to act as both a buffer and as a military springboard in continuing conflicts against their neighbours through the twelfth and thirteenth centuries.[45] However, their value to the crown was indicated by Edward I's creation of new lordships in the north-east, like Denbigh and Ruthin, for his English baronial supporters during the 1280s.[46] Above all, marcher lords maintained their powers to raise their vassals and people for military service. They expected their English knightly tenants to follow them on campaign and maintained the right of Welsh lords to demand all freemen to serve in their armies, a right similar to the powers of Scottish army service. The summons of 1310 required lords like Humphrey Bohun earl of Hereford to levy 100 men from his lordship of Brecon and Gilbert Clare earl of Gloucester to provide a contingent of 500 from Glamorgan, suggesting the military potential of such districts. Marcher lords also enjoyed greater judicial and economic powers than their English counterparts.[47] Their ownership of lordships of contiguous territory and with defined, even if disputed, boundaries made them magnates whose powers were closer to the great earldoms, regalities and liberties found in parts of Scotland and Ireland than English earls or barons.

The final defeat of the Welsh princes in the 1280s removed their natural enemies but the marcher lords jealously maintained their rights in the new era which followed. Change was more obvious in the neighbouring regions known as 'pure Wales', which had been ruled by the princes. These areas became known as the Principality of Wales, but rather than native rulers it now belonged to the English crown. Edwardian rule here had been based on long-established local boundaries. New counties had been formed and grouped together under the rule of royal justiciars, English or French servants of the Plantagenets drawn, like Otto Granson and John Havering, from other parts of their dominions.[48] Cemented by the building of castles like Caernarfon, Beaumaris and Conway, as royal centres and the foundation of towns of English settlers alongside them, this new regime began with a colonial character. Its aim was to ensure the Welsh were loyal to the English king and to draw on the resources provided by these new subjects.[49]

The conquest had an ongoing impact on the character of Wales. The wars of preceding centuries were replaced by an apparently more stable environment. Yet, beneath the surface, tensions still existed in the decades after 1284. With typical forcefulness, in these new circumstances Edward I sought to increase the power of the crown. When the two most powerful marchers, the lord of Glamorgan, Gilbert earl of Gloucester, and the lord of Brecon, Humphrey earl of Hereford, engaged in the traditional practice of private warfare in 1290–1, the king stepped into the feud, punishing both magnates.[50] Other marcher lords were subjected to the king's interventions and investigations designed to instil the clear message that royal authority was dominant in both principality and march.[51] The concern shown by Edward I in the march was not simply a matter of increased royal intrusion. The magnates he was dealing with may have been conscious of their special status as marchers but they were not a distinct group. Among them were most of the leading English nobles, the earls of Gloucester, Hereford, Lincoln, Arundel, Pembroke and, after Lincoln's death, Lancaster. These magnates were also the leaders of the English nobility. Neither Edward I nor Edward II could ignore their Welsh interests in his relations with them. Even lords whose principal interests lay in the march, like Roger Mortimer of Chirk and his kinsman and namesake, Roger Mortimer of Wigmore, were bound up by political and family ties with events in England. They also had a stake in royal government in Wales. Initially a minor figure in the marches, Roger Mortimer of Chirk had risen to prominence through the patronage of Edward I and his son. In 1308 he was appointed to be justiciar of both north and south Wales, a post he held until 1315 and again between 1317 and his fall from grace in early 1322.[52] These offices gave Mortimer increased power to act in both royal and marcher Wales, which he exploited in his own interest.

Mortimer of Chirk's career reveals the potential leverage available in Wales for a marcher baron who could employ the crown's authority. It was a sign of things to come on a much larger scale with the dominance of, first, Hugh Despenser and, then, Roger Mortimer of Wigmore between 1317 and 1330.[53] Wales was a land susceptible to the rule of great nobles, where direct coercive tactics were more readily used and more acceptable than in England. Impoverished or friendless barons were at the mercy of powerful lords with royal favour.[54] The environment is illustrated by the dispute over the lordship of Powys which broke out in 1309. Two rival claimants, the English knight, John Charlton, and the Welsh noble, Gruffydd Pole, waged local warfare over

Powys. The king ordered Mortimer of Chirk as justiciar to intervene against Gruffydd and end the feud.[55] The dispute over Powys was not just a display of private warfare in the marches, however. It revealed how Welsh politics were bound up with wider tensions in the Plantagenet dominions. The claimant to Powys, John Charlton, was Edward II's chamberlain and he clearly enjoyed royal support in his case. Charlton was also one of the group of royal councillors attacked by the Ordainers in 1311. As a result, Gruffydd Pole could count on the backing of the king's critics and in early 1313 Thomas earl of Lancaster stepped in to champion Gruffydd. The dispute over Powys now became one of the issues dividing the English king and his greatest subject, hampering efforts for a general reconciliation while Bruce harried Lothian. Though a temporary compromise was eventually agreed, the dispute would rumble on into the 1330s.[56]

A further key element in the political character of Wales was provided by the emergence of a group of Welsh leaders. These nobles of lesser princely stock or of the class of rich freemen later termed gentry did not emerge as enemies of English king and lords but in their service. They provided a vital link between the crown and marchers and their Welsh vassals and subjects who made up the vast bulk of the population. The existence of such men was not entirely new, but after Edward I's conquest they assumed a growing importance and value in the royal principality.[57] The summons for troops in 1309 and 1310 made clear the dependence of the crown on these leaders. As well as English officials like Mortimer of Chirk and Walter Pederton, Edward issued his orders to a group of Welshmen, among them Morgan ap Maredudd, Gruffydd Llwyd and the brothers Philip and Rhys ap Hywel.[58] For the effective recruitment and leadership of Welsh soldiers it was obviously crucial to employ reliable leaders of Welsh birth and speech. Gruffydd Llwyd, for example, had led forces drawn from north Wales in Flanders and Scotland under Edward I and would receive a summons to muster men for the campaign of 1314.[59] Men like Gruffydd Llwyd were also playing an increasingly significant role in the running of Wales. Gruffydd himself had been sheriff of Caernarfon, Anglesey and Meirionydd, while the clerk, Rhys ap Hywel, was appointed deputy-justiciar of south Wales in 1312.[60] Such opportunities were not confined to royal service. Rhys and his brother had begun their careers in the following of the earls of Hereford and great marchers, like Hereford and Gloucester, had their own ties of affinity with local Welsh leaders. The attractions of service were the access to patronage and political support it provided. Rhys ap Hywel received lands from Edward II, while offices came with salaries.[61] In 1306 Gruffydd Llwyd and a second Welshman, Morgan ap Maredudd, even petitioned Edward I for lands in Scotland forfeited by Bruce's adherents.[62]

However, though clearly willing servants of English crown and lords, these Welsh knights and squires also remained part of a recently conquered people, whose relations with their masters retained elements of tension. During the last great rising against Edward I in 1294–5, Morgan ap Maredudd had joined the rebels, while Gruffydd Llwyd, though he remained in English allegiance, was imprisoned for six months in later 1295.[63] For the English in Wales, fears lingered about the loyalties of the Welsh, even those they trusted with authority. However, by the early fourteenth century, for these leading Welshmen the issue was less about an effort to drive out their conquerors than to secure access to their rulers' good lordship. Rewards, protection and fair treatment informed the political choices of these men. Rather than taking up arms, they and the wider Welsh communities sought and received guarantees of their rights.[64] Edward II was equally ready to give such guarantees to the Welsh of the principality, as well as placing trust in key individuals. However, faced by the death of a trusted lord, a minority under royal supervision or marcher lords or royal officials who ignored their interests and petitions, tensions could easily develop. Roger Mortimer of Chirk, a grasping and forceful figure, aroused considerable hostility by his methods, leading to the disaffection of men like Gruffydd Llwyd and, eventually, the king's intervention.[65] As the Scottish war spread after Bannockburn, such tensions would become more worrying for the crown, but up to 1314 Wales operated as a reliable source of manpower for the king's wars.

The lordship of Ireland presented far greater problems to King Edward than did Wales. However, it also had a more direct significance for the king in his war against Bruce. As the warfare from 1306 to 1313 demonstrated, Ireland, and particularly the north-east from Dublin to Donegal, had a strategic importance for both sides. While Bruce had sought refuge and then recruits from the Irish of north-west Ulster, the whole region provided ports and coastlands from which expeditions could be launched towards Galloway, the Firth of Clyde and even the Western Isles, all areas which were shaky in their allegiances for much of these years. Edward I had already recognised this importance, sending fleets from Ireland into Scottish waters, outflanking the king's enemies and harrying their lands.[66] In his struggle with Robert Bruce, Edward II also pinned great hopes on the efforts of his Irish subjects. This was especially the case after the Hebridean magnate John of Lorn was driven into exile in 1308. In 1309 and 1310 John was given authority to pardon King Edward's enemies, especially in Argyll and the Isles. Fleets and men were supplied to John and other Islesmen who were clearly expected to assist the king in his campaign in Scotland, and in 1311 Edward's orders for a fresh fleet and 1,000 men to be mustered at Carrickfergus and placed under John's command indicate that great value was being attached to his efforts.[67] Once again, as the plans for the summer campaign of 1314 were drawn up, the English king would turn to Ireland to provide a base for a renewed campaign by sea led by John of Lorn.

These expeditions did not simply use the king's Irish lordship as a base. Edward II also called on his subjects in Ireland to provide him with ships, men, supplies and money for these ventures. In doing this he was simply following the practices of his father. Edward I had drawn heavily on Ireland to support his campaigns in Wales in 1277 and 1282, and after 1296 made repeated demands for resources to prosecute the Scottish war. Armies raised in Ireland which numbered between 2,500 and 3,500 men campaigned in Scotland on three occasions, their costs met by the Irish exchequer.[68] As with Wales, Edward II expected his officials in Ireland to provide him with the means to wage war in pursuit of his claims to lordship in Scotland. He asked for an army of over 3,000 soldiers in 1310 and for one of 4,000 in March 1314, and sent summons for personal service to lists of named noblemen. The recipients of these letters were twenty-eight English lords in Ireland, including Richard Burgh earl of Ulster, the head of the royal government, Edmund Butler, Richard Clare lord of Thomond and the heads of the powerful FitzGerald kindred, John fitzThomas of Offaly and Maurice fitzThomas of Desmond. A second set of letters was sent to twenty-four leading Irish magnates. Among this group were Aed O'Connor of Connacht and the chief Irish leaders in Ulster and Munster, Donal O'Neill of Tir Eoghain and Donough O'Brien of Thomond.[69] As well as military service, in 1309, 1310 and 1311 Edward II also asked for his officials of Ireland to provide foodstuffs and cash to northern England to supply planned advances into Scotland.[70]

However, despite these efforts to raise contingents of English and Irish soldiers from the lordship, there is little evidence that the bodies of men ever actually left on campaign. Certainly, the king's hopes for significant advances in the Isles and coasts around western Scotland were not fulfilled and his officials had to issue orders forbidding his Irish subjects to supply the Scots. In reality, by making demands on his Irish lordship Edward II was revealing his limited concern for Ireland. Just as Ireland served as a bolt hole for Piers Gaveston in 1308, so its resources were primarily used for royal enterprises in other parts of the Plantagenet dominions. This was not new. No English king had visited his Irish lordship since 1210.[71] The royal administration which operated in his name was headed by a justiciar who sought to run Ireland in the king's absence and who could be a landowner in Ireland, like Edmund Butler, or an outsider, like John Wogan. Though he showed some sense of the needs of his lordship, Edward I had been largely content to draw on the revenues and manpower of Ireland in support of wider interests. His son followed the same approach. Between 1308 and 1314 nearly half of the total revenue raised by the crown from Ireland, some £9,995, was spent on the Scottish war, continuing the pattern of previous years.[72]

This was recognised as a source of difficulty for the king's officials in Ireland, denying them resources which were needed to ensure 'the safety of our land of Ireland'. 'Default of money' was seen as allowing breaches of the peace to the damage of the king and his lieges in the lordship.[73] These problems with keeping the peace were an ongoing and central fact of life in later medieval Ireland. From the intervention of the English crown in 1171, Ireland had never been brought fully under the rule of the Plantagenet king. Instead, in many regions there were Irish dynasties whose allegiance to this foreign lord was, at best, notional and who refused to accept the writ of his officials. In such areas there was frequent, endemic warfare involving both Irish and English communities on the island. The largest such areas lay in the north, in much of Ulster and western Leinster, and further south in Connacht and western Munster. However, there were other points of conflict, even in the Wicklow Mountains within sight of Dublin. The result was that local warfare was endemic in much of the king's Irish dominion.[74] The justiciar was regularly required to mobilise and lead the king's liegemen in warfare against Irish raiders. In the opening six years of the century, at least six expeditions were launched to curb the raiding of the Irish of the mountains. In 1308 and 1309 the justiciars, first John Wogan and then Piers Gaveston, led armies against the Irish of Wicklow and in 1312 Wogan's deputy, Edmund Butler, repeated their efforts, securing the submission of the O'Byrnes.[75]

In such circumstances the ability of these justiciars to spare resources for war in Scotland was severely limited by political geography. Moreover, these direct clashes between the king's officials and Irish enemies were only one part of the problem of local warfare. The core regions of the English lordship lay in eastern Leinster around the cities of Dublin, Dundalk and Drogheda, and further south in eastern Munster, Kilkenny and Wexford. The long and winding fringes of these districts were marchland where English nobles sought to establish and maintain their estates and lordship through warfare. Some like the great earldom of Ulster and the much smaller and more recent lordship of Thomond, north of Limerick, were liberties outside the king's direct administration, but even elsewhere Anglo-Irish nobles were required to act independently to defend their interests in a frontier environment.[76] Though generally reliable adherents of the crown, the management of this nobility was itself not easy. As in the Welsh march, disputes between Anglo-Irish lords could end in private warfare. During the 1290s simmering feuds between three of the greatest English magnates, Richard Burgh earl of Ulster, John fitzThomas and William Vesci, had disrupted the lordship, and in the early years of Edward II's reign there were several direct acts of defiance to the royal government involving English nobles. In 1312 Robert Verdon led a rebellion in Louth winning considerable local support, even defeating a small force raised by Edmund Butler, who had replaced Wogan in charge of the government. The rebels eventually submitted to the crown, making their final peace in 1313.[77]

This kind of violent unrest could not be separated from ongoing warfare involving Irish leaders and kindreds. In Wexford and Kildare in 1309 and 1310, local feuds between English lords drew in the neighbouring Irish.[78] Further west and north, English lords sought to project their influence into areas still ruled by Irish dynasties by intervening in the inevitable conflicts within these families. Earl Richard Burgh had pursued this path with mixed success in Ulster. The head of the O'Neill family in 1314, Donal, had generally opposed the earl's authority, but had secured his position by accepting some degree of control. In his lordship of Connacht, Earl Richard sought to base his position on similar interference and superiority over Irish nobles. His principal adherent was his cousin, William Burgh, who gave crucial backing for Felim O'Connor in his bid for the leadership of his kindred in 1309. William employed mercenaries from Ulster to kill Felim's rival and, though the ongoing feud was hardly resolved, he achieved a brief ascendancy in the province through his Irish ally.[79] William Burgh's forceful methods led him into a larger conflict with an English lord of similar ambitions. Richard Clare had inherited the lordship of Thomond, north of Limerick. The lordship had been the gift of Edward I to Richard's father, and in 1310 Clare arrived to extend his rule, largely at the expense of the O'Briens. To achieve this, Richard backed a claimant for the headship of the O'Brien family, Dermot, against his kinsman, Donough. Donough, in turn, secured the aid of William Burgh, who arrived in Munster with an army of English and Irish from Connacht and Meath. During 1311 there were two pitched battles near Bunratty between these rival leaders, neither of which proved decisive. Both the justiciar and the earl of Ulster stepped in to negotiate a settlement, but the rivalries within both the O'Briens and the English nobility persisted.[80]

The lordship of Ireland was very different to England, or even Wales, in the early fourteenth century. The leading English lords there were required to be more active and robust in the defence or extension of their lands and interests, both against Irish leaders and other English magnates. However, despite this different environment, the leading vassals of King Edward in Ireland remained his loyal vassals, firm in English identity and allegiance. Most of these lords had interests and connections elsewhere in the Plantagenet dominions. Richard Burgh and Edmund Butler both held minor estates in England, while Theobald Verdon, who was justiciar in 1314, was also a lord in the Welsh marches. The inheritance of Trim by Roger Mortimer of Wigmore formed a long-lasting connection between another marcher family, with English holdings, and the lordship of Ireland. Richard Clare of Thomond and his cousin Gilbert earl of Gloucester and lord of Kilkenny were also lords of unimpeachably English backgrounds with major stakes in Ireland.[81] Nor were great English nobles like the Clares necessarily disinterested in their Irish estates. In the early 1290s Gilbert's father had visited Ireland and in 1308 the young earl had married Matilda, daughter of Richard earl of Ulster, while his sister, Elizabeth, wed Ulster's son and heir, John. The double marriage suggests the importance of Irish concerns to the Clares. It may also have been sponsored by the king to preserve good relations with the earl of Ulster. The earl had been appointed as justiciar of Ireland in 1308 but was quickly supplanted in this post by Piers Gaveston. Edward may have worried that Ulster would cause problems for the king's favourite, who was himself married to another Clare sister. The family tie, backed by a payment of £1,000, prevented friction and Gaveston met with Earl Richard at Drogheda in August 1308.[82] The following year the earl was employed to negotiate with his son-in-law, Robert Bruce, and this service may have been linked to the grant of life custody of the royal castles of Athlone, Randown and Roscommon to Earl Richard. These strongholds would significantly augment the earl's position in Connacht.[83]

The anxiety to avoid such tensions reflected the power and status of the earl and the dependence of the king's officials on the support of such great English magnates. However, the image of a royal administration of limited reach and resources should not be overplayed. Though restricted in its range by the existence of Irish lords and English liberties, the justiciar and other royal officers still possessed the power and authority to hold courts through most of Leinster and Munster and mobilise and lead the king's lieges in local warfare, not simply around Dublin, but across Leinster and Munster and less frequently in Ulster and Connacht. The need for the support of great lords in these areas like the Butlers, Geraldines and Burghs may have been more obvious than in England, but such delegation was a normal feature of most medieval realms, like Scotland. The frequency of local warfare and the limited resources at the disposal of the justiciar hardly indicate a political society in danger of internal collapse.[84]

As contemporaries in English Ireland sensed, stresses were being created from the outside by the war in Scotland. The priority accorded to events in Scotland was a normal feature of Edward II's dealings with Ireland. The need to placate Ulster in 1308 was certainly influenced by the earl's importance in the war. Events in 1306 had demonstrated that his lordship in the north was vital both as a route into western Scotland and as a means of preventing alliances between the Bruces and the leaders of the Ulster Irish. The earl was also the father of Robert's captive queen, Elizabeth, and there may already have been anxieties that this family connection could be exploited to tamper with Ulster's loyalties. More immediately, however, King Edward hoped to exploit Earl Richard's link to Bruce by using him as an envoy to the Scots in 1308. This had no results and the earl would be regarded as an enemy by Robert in coming years.[85] Fears for the effect of the Scottish war on the Irish lordship were demonstrated by King Edward in 1311. Perhaps influenced by the criticisms of the Ordainers, Edward tried to ensure greater resources were available to his officials by seeking to recover debts owed to the crown and by ordering the use of the income derived from the customs for 'the safety of Ireland'.[86]

However, such schemes proved short-lived. In 1312 the revenues of Ireland were, once again, assigned to buy foodstuffs for the king's garrisons in Scotland, while during the preparations for his expedition of 1314, Edward sent orders to his Irish treasurer to deliver up all the money received by the exchequer for the raising of troops for the campaign.[87] The summons which was issued to nobles to serve in the king's expedition under the leadership of Richard earl of Ulster revealed the most serious problem facing the lordship of Ireland. While English nobles like John fitzThomas, Edmund Butler,

Richard Clare and William Burgh must have seen the king's call for military service as an unwelcome distraction from their pressing concerns in Ireland, the order to twenty-four Irish leaders was optimistic in the extreme.[88] Donal O'Neill, Felim O'Connor and Donough O'Brien may all have recognised the sovereignty of King Edward and depended on the support of English barons, but their allegiance to the crown was hardly willing or fixed. The endemic rivalries within major Irish kindreds made the search for allies by aspiring leaders a natural process. While this had meant seeking English backers like the Clares, Butlers or Burghs, should another possible source of external aid materialise, it would also be exploited. By late 1313 Bruce may have already been identified as a potential ally. His capture of Man and descent on Ulster opened up the prospect of direct intervention in Ireland. Bruce's long-standing supporters in the Isles, especially Clan Donald, had established contacts with the Irish of Ulster which Robert had already exploited to raise troops in 1306. For Donal O'Neill, and for other Irish magnates, the support of Bruce would be welcomed as a means of escaping the lordship of English king and magnates, but also as a way to secure control of their kindred against Irish rivals.[89] The Scottish war, which had influenced events in Ireland for nearly twenty years, was about to impinge directly on the lordship, exploiting and intensifying the existing problems facing the English administration and community and escalating ongoing conflicts between the two nations and within Irish kindreds.

The road to Bannockburn was not simply about events in Scotland. The mistrust and lack of co-operation between King Edward and the English barons, the demands placed on recently conquered Wales and the complex and unstable environment of Ireland were all related to the course of the king's war against Bruce. Even Edward's distant duchy of Gascony was not wholly separate from the Scottish war. As well as the Gascon knight, Piers Gaveston, Edward employed numerous men from the duchy in his service and in late 1313 they were entrusted with key roles in the Scottish war. Piers Lubaud was constable of Edinburgh Castle, William Fiennes held Roxburgh and Raymond Caillau was a captain in the Berwick garrison. Such men were probably recruited from the friends and associates of Gaveston and his brother Arnaud Marsin. Edward's favour to Piers extended to Gascony, where it also aroused hostility, especially from the king's leading vassal in the duchy, Amanieu lord of Albret. In 1310 Albret complained to King Philip of France that Gaveston and his brother had seized some of his lands and were placing unsuitable men into key offices in Gascony. Albret probably joined King Philip in celebrating Gaveston's death, but the respite was brief. The abrasive approach of the new seneschal, the English baron John Ferrers of Chartley, led Albret to make a fresh appeal to the French king. Private war wracked Gascony, Philip's officers entered the duchy to hear Albret's complaints and, in autumn 1312, Ferrers was assassinated. Faced by hostile barons in England and the relentless attacks of Bruce in Lothian and the borders, Edward could not afford a war with his father-in-law. His attempts to avoid a conflict were aided by Pope Clement, himself a Gascon, who was desperate to prevent a full conflict erupting. In the event, Ferrer's murder removed one abrasive element from the arena and the improved personal relationship between Philip and Edward raised hopes of a settlement. The English king's decision to visit Paris in summer 1313, criticised by the author of the *Vita Edwardi Secundi* as delaying a settlement with his own barons, reflected Edward's prior concern to resolve the dispute with Albret and with King Philip by payment of hefty sums to both.[90]

While the period around Edward's absence witnessed crucial losses in southern Scotland, his priorities in 1313 are understandable. The open rebellion of Albret and the intervention of Philip IV could have precipitated the loss of Gascony, so nearly experienced by Edward I in 1294. An open breach with the French king could also have led Philip to seek an alliance with Bruce, as his son would do in 1326, after a period of war in Gascony. The ongoing need to maintain his rights in Gascony sat alongside the problems recognised in drawing heavily on revenues raised in Ireland and questions of reform and patronage in England to present Edward II with an unenviable set of problems. His failures from 1307 in Scotland were part of this mix and, though the king's poor judgement and relative inactivity were major factors in the disastrous record of his rule up to 1314, the conflicting needs and claims of his various dominions must also be recognised. If the Plantagenets could call on the resources of far greater lands than their Scottish enemies, they were also hampered by the pull of these communities on their resources and attention.

NOTES

1. For discussions of these dominions, see R. Frame, *Political Development of the British Isles, 1100–1400* R. Frame, 'Overlordship and Reaction, c.1250–c.1450', in R. Frame, *Ireland and Britain* (London, 1998), 171–90.
2. Prestwich, *Edward I*, 469–516; M. Prestwich, 'Colonial Scotland: the English in Scotland under Edward I', in R. Mason (ed.), *Scotland and England 1286–1815* (Edinburgh, 1987), 6–17.
3. Prestwich, *War, Politics and Finance*, 175–6.
4. Prestwich, *Edward I*, 523–49.
5. Maddicott, *Thomas of Lancaster*, 70–1, 75; Hamilton, *Piers Gaveston*, 37–43.
6. *C.D.S.*, ii, no. 47; Maddicott, *Thomas of Lancaster*, 108–9.
7. *Rot. Scot.*, i, 109.
8. T. F. Tout, *The Place of the Reign of Edward II in English History* (Manchester, 1936), 73–6; Prestwich, *Edward I*, 534; Prestwich, *War, Politics and Finance*, 221; Maddicott, *Thomas of Lancaster*, 70.
9. Maddicott, *Thomas of Lancaster*, 71, 110–11.
10. *Rot. Scot.*, i, 70–1; *C.P.R.*, 1307–13, 81–2; Maddicott, *Thomas of Lancaster*, 106, 108–9.
11. For opposition to *prise*, see Maddicott, *Thomas of Lancaster*, 106–8, 110–11, 178.
12. *C.P.R.*, 1307–13, 299–300, 303, 321, 325, 339, 341; Maddicott, *Thomas of Lancaster*, 114–17.

13. *C.P.R., 1307–13*, 449, 498, 515, 524; Tout, *Place of Edward II*, 75–6, 85, 87.
14. Maddicott, *Thomas of Lancaster*, 67–159; Hamilton, *Gaveston*, 91–107.
15. *Vita Edwardi*, 22–3, 38–41.
16. M. Prestwich, 'The Ordinances of 1311 and the Politics of the Early Fourteenth Century', in J. Taylor and W. Childs (eds), *Politics and Crisis in Fourteenth Century England* (Gloucester, 1990); J. C. Davies, *The Baronial Opposition to Edward II* (London, 1918); Maddicott, *Thomas of Lancaster*, 106–8.
17. G. L. Harriss, *King, Parliament and Public Finance in Medieval England to 1369* (Oxford, 1975), 168.
18. *Annales Lond.*, 210–11; *Vita Edwardi*, 62–77; Maddicott, *Thomas of Lancaster*, 132–6.
19. *Vita Edwardi*, 68–9, 72–3.
20. Prestwich, *Edward I*, 426–9.
21. *Vita Edwardi*, 22–5.
22. See for example, Trokelowe, *Annales*, 63–84; 'Annales Londoniensis', 151–231; *The Anonimalle Chronicle 1307 to 1334* , ed. W. Childs and J. R. Taylor (Leeds, 1991), 80–89.
23. *English Historical Documents*, iii, ed. H.T. Rothwell (London, 1975), 530.
24. *Vita Edwardi*, 26–7.
25. *Vita Edwardi*, 14–15.
26. *C.D.S.*, ii, nos 1757, 1771, 1776, 1839, 1857, 1945; *The Bruce*, ed. Duncan, 192n; Prestwich, 'Colonial Scotland', 10–11.
27. *C.P.R., 1307–13*, 209, 214–15, 300, 461.
28. *Rot. Scot.*, i, 56, 57, 76, 79–80, 105; *C.D.S.*, iii, no. 114.
29. *Vita Edwardi*, 52–5; Maddicott, *Thomas of Lancaster*, 133.
30. *C.P.R., 1307–13*, 220, 273, 408; *Rot. Scot.*, i, 56, 97; H. Summerson, 'Clifford, Robert, first Lord Clifford (1274–1314)', in *New D.N.B.*
31. J. M. W. Bean, 'Percy, Henry, first Lord Percy (1273–1314)', *New D.N.B.*
32. *C.C.R., 1307–13*, 331–2; *C.D.S.*, ii, no. 1899; iii, no. 226; Maddicott, *Thomas of Lancaster*, 72, 112–13, 123–30; Prestwich, *War, Politics and Finance*, 49, 65–6.
33. Maddicott, *Thomas of Lancaster*, 134–44, 152–3.
34. *Vita Edwardi*, 86–7.
35. J. M. W. Bean, 'The Percies' Acquisition of Alnwick', *Archaeologia Aeliana*, 4th series, 32 (1954), 309–19; J. M. W. Bean, 'The Percies and their estates in Scotland', *Archaeologia Aeliana*, 4th series, 35 (1957), 91–9; J. A. Tuck, 'The Emergence of a Northern Nobility, 1250–1400', *Northern History*, 22 (1986), 1–17.
36. *Chron. Lanercost*, 194–200; *Rot. Scot.*, i, 105. For Lanercost, see A. Gransden, *Historical Writing in England*, ii, 12–17; A. G. Little, 'The Authorship of the Lanercost Chronicle', *E.H.R.*, 31 (1916), 269–79.
37. *C.D.S.*, iii, no. 229.
38. *Rot. Scot.*, i, 58–60; *C.P.R., 1307–13*, 376, 381; Altschul, *The Clares*, 161.
39. A. King, 'Lordship, Castles and Locality: Thomas of Lancaster, Dunstanburgh Castle and the Lancastrian Affinity in Northumberland, 1296–1322', *Archaeologia Aeliana*, 29 (2001), 223–34; Maddicott, *Thomas of Lancaster*, 8–39.
40. *Vita Edwardi*, 166–71.
41. J. Lydon, *The Lordship of Ireland in the Middle Ages*, 89–120; R. R. Davies, *The Age of Conquest, 1063–1415* (Oxford, 1987), 355–88.
42. *Rot. Scot.*, i, 84–5; Simpkin, 'English Army', forthcoming.
43. *Foedera*, i, part 2, 148; Prestwich, *War, Politics and Finance*, 92–9.
44. For a masterly survey of the history of thirteenth- and fourteenth-century Wales, see Davies, *Age of Conquest*, 333–430.
45. R. R. Davies, *Lordship and Society*, 15–62.

46. Davies, *Age of Conquest*, 363, 371–2.

47. Davies, *Lordship and Society*, 67–85.

48. Davies, *Age of Conquest*, 363–70; R. A. Griffiths, *The Principality of Wales in the Later Middle Ages: The Structure and Personnel of Government: South Wales, 1277–1536* (Cardiff, 1972).

49. *Rot. Scot.*, i, 84–5; L. B. Smith, 'The Governance of Edwardian Wales', in T. Herbert and G. E. Jones, *Edward I and Wales* (Cardiff, 1988), 73–95.

50. J. E. Morris, *The Welsh Wars of Edward I* (Oxford, 1901), 220–39; Davies, *Lordship and Society*, 259–60.

51. Davies, *Lordship and Society*, 260–9.

52. Griffiths, *The Principality of Wales*, 97–8; Davies, *Lordship and Society*, 45–7, 274–5.

53. Davies, *Lordship and Society*, 279–84.

54. Davies, *Lordship and Society*, 45–7.

55. Maddicott, *Thomas of Lancaster*, 138–45; Davies, *Lordship and Society*, 286–7.

56. Maddicott, *Thomas of Lancaster*, 143–5.

57. Davies, *Age of Conquest*, 386–7, 408–10; A. D. Carr, 'An aristocracy in decline: The native Welsh lords after the Edwardian Conquest', *W.H.R.*, v (1970), 103–29.

58. *Rot. Scot.*, i, 84–5; *Foedera*, i, part 2, 148.

59. J. G. Edwards, 'Sir Gruffydd Llwyd', *E.H.R.*, 30 (1915), 589–601.

60. Edwards, 'Gruffydd Llwyd', 591; Griffiths, *The Principality of Wales*, 97–8.

61. *C.P.R., 1307–13*, 115, 140; Davies, *Lordship and Society*, 45, 291–2.

62. Palgrave, *Documents*, 311.

63. J. B. Smith, 'Edward II and the allegiance of Wales', in *W.H.R.*, 8 (1976–7), 139–71, 142; Edwards, 'Gruffydd Llwyd', 598–9.

64. Guarantees of their rights were received in 1297 by the men of Glamorgan and Brecon (Smith, 'Edward II and the allegiance of Wales', 144–5).

65. Smith, 'Edward II and the allegiance of Wales', 144.

66. Lydon, 'An Irish Army in Scotland, 1296', 184–9; Lydon, 'Edward I, Ireland and the War in Scotland, 1303–1304', 43–59; Lydon, 'Irish Levies in the Scottish Wars, 1296–1302', 207–17.

67. *Rot. Scot.*, i, 76, 90, 93, 99, 107; *C.D.S.*, iii, no. 203; McNamee, *Wars of the Bruces*, 62.

68. J. Lydon, *Lordship of Ireland*, 102–4.

69. *Rot. Scot.*, i, 78–9, 86, 93, 100; McNamee, *Wars of the Bruces*, 48, 61.

70. *Rot. Scot.*, i, 86, 92, 100.

71. J. Lydon, 'Ireland and the English Crown', *I.H.S.*, 29 (1995), 281–94.

72. Lydon, *Lordship of Ireland*, 96–105; J. Lydon, 'Edward II and the revenues of Ireland in 1311–12', *I.H.S.*, 14 (1964), 39–57, 42.

73. Lydon, 'Revenues of Ireland', 44–5.

74. R. Frame, 'Power and Society in the Lordship of Ireland, 1272–1377', *Past and Present*, 76 (1977), 3–33.

75. *Chart. St Mary's, Dublin*, ii, 330, 335, 336, 338; A. J. Otway-Ruthven, *A History of Medieval Ireland* (London, 1968), 218–19.

76. Frame, 'Power and Society', 195–205; R. Frame, *English Lordship in Ireland* (Oxford, 1982), 13–17.

77. Otway-Ruthven, *Medieval Ireland*, 212–15, 219–20; Lydon, *Lordship of Ireland*, 91–4; B. Smith, *Colonisation and Conquest in Medieval Ireland: The English in Louth* (Cambridge, 1999), 97–104.

78. Otway-Ruthven, *Medieval Ireland*, 219–20.

79. *Annals of Connacht*, 221–3; Simms, 'Relations with the Irish', 99–100; Otway-Ruthven, *Medieval Ireland*, 217.

80. *Chart. St Mary's Dublin*, ii, 339; Otway-Ruthven, *Medieval Ireland*, 221–2.
81. *Chart. St Mary's Dublin*, ii, 329–30; Frame, *English Lordship*, 47–51, 52–4; Altschul, *The Clares*, 190–6, 281–95.
82. *Chart. St Mary's Dublin*, ii, 322, 337–8; F. A. Underhill, *For her good estate: The Life of Elizabeth de Burgh* (London, 1999), 8–10; Hamilton, *Gaveston*, 82–5.
83. *C.P.R., 1307–1313*, 182.
84. Frame, *English Lordship*, 75–123; R. Frame, 'The Defence of the English Lordship, 1250–1450', in T. Bartlett and K. Jeffery (eds), *A Military History of Ireland* (Cambridge, 1996), 76–98.
85. *Chart. St Mary's Dublin*, ii, 338; *Foedera*, i, part 2, 150.
86. Lydon, 'Revenues of Ireland', 42–7.
87. Lydon, 'Revenues of Ireland', 48–9.
88. *Rot. Scot.*, i, 118.
89. *Chart. St Mary's Dublin*, ii, 342–3; Duffy, 'The Bruce Brothers', 73–4.
90. For the Gascon dispute, see M. Vale, *The Origins of the Hundred Years War: The Angevin Legacy 1250–1340* (Oxford, 1990), 164–74.

CHAPTER 5

The Campaign (October 1313–Midsummer 1314)

CAMPAIGN AND BATTLE

The battle of Bannockburn was an exceptional event in the course of the Scottish wars and in medieval warfare in general. Two rulers had mustered armies of a size unmatched in recent years. The target of the campaign which followed was apparently understood clearly by both commanders. After a brief and direct advance by one army, battle was joined on ground chosen by the other. Opposing kings led their hosts in person on the field and the two-day fight was accepted willingly by both leaders. Finally the outcome of the battle was decisive in many ways. While these facts suggest that in its setting Bannockburn conformed to an idealised version of medieval warfare, a fact played up very heavily in the highly dramatised account of the preliminaries of battle described by John Barbour in *The Bruce*, they make the battle almost unique in warfare in Scotland between the 1290s and 1350s, and fairly exceptional in contemporary Europe.[1]

The Scottish wars had seen no clash on the scale of Bannockburn since the battle of Falkirk sixteen years earlier. In 1298 the guardian of Scotland, William Wallace, had held his army at a distance from Edward I's massive host until there were clear signs that the English king's force was experiencing major problems. Lack of food had contributed to an open clash between English soldiers and the massive Welsh contingent who took little part in the coming fight. Wallace may have gambled on these difficulties forcing Edward to retreat or weakening his army's ability to fight. He risked a pitched battle and lost.[2] Falkirk showed that battles, however bloody, were not necessarily decisive events in medieval warfare. The Scots did not capitulate after Falkirk. They chose new leaders and fought on for nearly six years before submitting in 1304. However, in these years Edward's Scottish enemies refused to face him in the open field. They harried his armies and garrisons, defended and besieged castles and kept soldiers in the field but never came close to risking anything like a pitched battle.[3] Traditionally Robert Bruce has been seen as following a similar strategy after 1306. The military precepts remembered as 'Good King Robert's Testament' stressed the use of woods, hills and mosses as refuges, the stripping of supplies from the 'planeland' and the harrying of the

enemy by night and ambush.[4] Both before and after 1314, Robert would not
risk a battle like Bannockburn, and when the leaders of the Bruce regime
abandoned this approach in 1332 at Dupplin Moor and in 1333 at Halidon
Hill they paid a heavy price in defeat. The return to the policy of avoiding
major battles against English armies from 1334 confirmed this as a mainstay
of Scottish warfare in the fourteenth century.[5]

However, a reluctance to risk battle hardly made Robert Bruce and other
Scottish leaders exceptional in their approach to warfare. Though military historians have traditionally liked to stress and dissect battles as the centrepiece
of war, over recent decades studies of medieval warfare have emphasised that
full-scale clashes between armies were relatively rare occasions, rather than
being the natural conclusion and expected outcome of a period of campaigning by rival armies.[6] The careers of militarily active kings of England like
William I, Richard I and even Edward I have been analysed to reveal that these
kings fought a pitched battle on, at most, one occasion in their bellicose
reigns.[7] Despite one Flemish, three Welsh and six Scottish campaigns, as well
as a crusade, Falkirk was Edward's only battle as king. It is clear that forcing
the enemy to accept battle was not the only, or even ultimate, goal of a major
expedition.[8]

Contemporaries who wrote about warfare in the Middle Ages generally
recognised the true nature of campaigning. Stress was placed on the benefits
of damaging the enemy's lands and those of his adherents, on the capture or
fortification of castles in his lands and on the submission of local communities in the face of destruction and the failure of their own lord to defend
them.[9] Such precepts could be applied to Bruce's campaigning from 1307 and
equally apply to Edward's expeditions after 1298. The central military events
of these expeditions were sieges, yet their real objective was the passage of
enemy territory, displaying Edward's strength and his opponents' ineffectiveness. The results were gradual rather than dramatic but it is striking that
the capitulation of the Scottish leaders in 1304 followed not a clash of forces
or even a siege, but Edward's march from Lothian through Fife, Angus and
the north-east in late 1303, before wintering at Dunfermline.[10] It was the
English king's ability to breach the natural barriers of Forth, Tay and Mounth
and his officials' success in feeding his army through the winter which convinced Scottish lords to submit in spring 1304. All that was unusual about the
1303–4 campaign was Edward's success. The great European wars of the late
thirteenth century – the conflict over the kingdom of Sicily waged in Aragon,
southern France and Italy between 1282 and 1295, and the war between
Edward I and Philip IV which consumed huge sums of both kings' money
between 1294 and 1298 – did not produce a single pitched battle.[11] However,
some types of conflict were more likely to result in battle. Wars waged within
a unitary realm like England tended to see rival leaders seeking a rapid resolution on the field of battle. The conflict between Henry III of England and
the barons led by Simon de Montfort in 1264–5 saw two full and bloody

battles after campaigns of a couple of months.[12] This pattern was repeated in English internal conflicts of the fourteenth and fifteenth centuries because in a civil war both parties were keen for a decisive judgement of their rights and hoped a victory in battle would allow them to establish or strengthen their authority.[13] Such motives could exist elsewhere. The rebellion of Flemish townsmen against the French king in 1302 led rapidly to the battle of Courtrai. The readiness of the Flemings to fight stemmed from their position as rebels lacking the means to sustain a long defensive war without a demonstration of their rights.[14]

As these examples and the battles in the later Anglo-French wars show, battles were highly individual events produced by a range of factors, political, economic and military. While many leaders, like Edward I, waged aggressive campaigns which displayed their readiness to accept battle as part of their strategy of wearing down the enemy, it was much less normal for an enemy, like the Scots, to respond to the challenge. The guardians after 1298 had refused battle, presumably on the grounds that they would be defeated by an English army in the open field as they had been at Dunbar and Falkirk. To understand the factors which led Robert I and Edward II to the battle of Bannockburn it is necessary to make an attempt to examine the ways in which the two kings and their adherents operated in the war and to examine the events of the nine months leading up to the battle which have aroused recent controversy.

Armies and warfare

While the course of the conflict has been examined in detail in the preceding chapters, it is important to develop a clearer sense of the resources and aims of the two sides in the years up to late 1313. For Robert Bruce, this task is hard. Not surprisingly, given the nature of his position in the years up to 1309, and even up to 1314, the records of his rule are extremely limited. The great majority of the evidence of his actions and those of his followers comes from his enemies or was produced after 1314. This makes it hard to trace Bruce's movements, let alone his motives, but it seems clear that Robert's military activity in the years after he took the throne was primarily shaped by factors of necessity and opportunity.

Up to 1314 Bruce's access to the traditional means by which the Scottish crown raised an army was probably limited. The ability to call on Scots to serve in war is recorded in a royal order or brieve from 1286. This summoned all those who owed army service in the realm to assemble at a day's notice with their own weapons, armour and victuals ready to serve for forty days. The obligation to bear arms in defence of the kingdom could be related to ownership of land or on the older public duty on freemen to form the so-called 'common army'.[15] Men were mustered by sheriffs or other royal officers, or by their lords. The earldoms were special cases. As heads of provinces, the earls retained rights to call out their own army. Robert Bruce, while earl of Carrick, had raised 'my army of Carrick' and led it in warfare between 1298 and 1302. The sustained warfare of these years must have altered military practices in Scotland. The idea of a Scottish army clearly had a political significance. Wallace and Andrew Murray used the title 'commanders of the army of Scotland' as the basis of their leadership of the realm in late 1297. Wallace raised the army in 1298 and later guardians probably did the same in the period up to 1304.[16] However, other means of raising troops were also adopted. In particular, as was normal across Europe, men also went to war in the retinues of noblemen. Apart from the earls, barons and knights also had their own followings who would attend them in peace and war. In 1299 an army led by the guardians comprised leading lords and their men. When it dispersed, it broke down into the companies of great lords, each noble leaving behind 'part of his people' to defend Selkirk Forest. The English administration clearly expected its supporters in Scotland like Alexander Abernethy and Patrick earl of Dunbar to be able to raise retinues for warfare.[17] Such retinues were probably formed through ties of land, kinship and reward, and the needs of regular warfare, unfamiliar to most Scots, must have given them a military character. With the brief end of warfare in 1304, there were probably bands of men used to bearing arms and living off war roaming Scotland. These may well have provided a pool of manpower on which Bruce could draw after 1306.

Robert certainly needed to find a means to create armies. Though he took the royal title in 1306, his ability to raise men in support of his kingship hardly rested on normal considerations. Instead it depended on his success in winning or coercing recognition of his status from Scots. As Robert continued to face the opposition of many leading Scots through the next seven years, his ability to raise an army using the rights of the crown probably remained limited. In 1306 he enjoyed some success in mustering support, putting an army of several thousand into the field in July composed of his followers and friends.[18] The defeat at Methven and subsequent pursuit scattered this force and Bruce's military position in early 1307 was much weaker. Though later Scottish accounts stress the roles of Robert's friends like Gilbert Hay and the earl of Lennox, it is doubtful if these lords could have led many men into exile and back with the king. Instead, the key to Bruce's return and survival in early 1307 was probably the support he had raised from the Isles, Kintyre and Ulster. Soldiers from the Isles, in particular, had a reputation for tough effectiveness. As galloglass in Ireland they had shown an ability to withstand heavy horsemen, and contemporary depictions and records indicate that they were equipped with mail or quilted armour, axes and spears. A band of these may have provided the core to Bruce's makeshift army and been augmented by the raiding skills of any Irish soldiers who accompanied the king rather than his ill-fated brothers.[19] Robert may have returned to his kingdom at the head of a fearsome band of allies, rather as several lords had attempted in the previous century. Bruce would continue to employ Islesmen through the next decade. In 1308 men from Clan Donald were in the army led by Edward Bruce against Galloway and galley forces from the Isles were raised in 1310 and 1313.

Despite the value of such allies, Bruce's successful capture of the kingship would depend on his ability to raise Scottish forces. This may not always have been a pretty process. In 1307 reference is made, in English accounts, of Bruce compelling local men to join his army during his marches through the south-west. While such recruiting methods were a natural part of medieval warfare, the key to Robert's military advance was the willing recruitment of adherents. The support of local barons like Robert Boyd, Alexander Lindsay and James Douglas, capable, as Barbour's later stories about Douglas show, of raising their own bands from tenants and ex-tenants, gave both a military and polit-ical boost.[20] In the north, the support of local knights like William Wiseman and, more importantly, of the bishop of Moray, David Murray, who had exten-sive lands and tenants through his office, was probably vital.[21] Even as his authority as king developed, the core of Robert's forces probably still rested on the willingness of nobles like John Menteith, Douglas and Randolph to bring out their retinues to support the king's cause.[22] They and their men may have been prepared to serve Bruce on exceptional terms to win the war. It was prob-ably only with the winning of Scotland north of the Mounth that Bruce could think of employing the rights of the crown to call for military service. Reference in 1309 to communities of the earldoms may also suggest that the king was looking to raise the armies of these provinces, even when, like Fife and Mar, their earls were in England.[23] The intensity and frequency of warfare in the years from mid-1309 also raise questions about how Bruce maintained his forces.

The passages of warfare waged by Robert were remarkably long. The des-perate struggle in the south-west in 1307 was followed by a nine-month cam-paign in the north and then continued attacks until the end of 1308. In 1310–11 Robert remained in the field against Edward II and Gaveston and fol-lowed their retreat by raiding Lothian and the English borders before return-ing to besiege Dundee. From summer 1312 until mid-1313 Bruce waged a relentless series of campaigns. Such efforts were impossible for a single force. The reality must be that Robert had the means to call out a series of small armies over long periods. The sequence of truces agreed by Robert in north-ern Scotland may have been to allow fresh musters to be made. In 1310–11 Bruce may have raised a force to harry Edward II during his six-week march across the south and then dispersed it after raiding Lothian. His inability to respond to Gaveston's campaign further north in February 1311 perhaps indi-cates his lack of manpower at that point. The shift from raids on England to campaigns against Dundee, Perth or Galloway also suggests forces being raised from different regions and then dispersed.[24]

These efforts suggest the growing scale and durability of Robert's military resources. They also indicate the critical importance of obtaining supplies as an element in Bruce's plans. From 1307 the need to feed and perhaps reward his troops was an issue for Robert. He was said to descend suddenly on communities and compel them to 'resett' or supply him. The clash at Loudoun Hill was, in part, an effort to seize cash from the English treasurer.[25] As his forces and ambitions developed, the question of supply and recruitment became even more significant. In 1312, at a parliament held during the siege of Dundee, the king agreed to make requests for military service, money and supplies to the burghs only through his chamberlain.[26] The arrangement suggests that royal demands for such things had become frequent and burdensome. Near the end of his reign, Robert would promise to abandon the practice of *prise*, the confiscation of goods to support warfare, which was a common but deeply unpopular practice of the English crown.[27] By 1312 the war may have been putting strains on those communities in Bruce allegiance. Against this background, the growing regularity of campaigns designed to extract money and goods from enemy areas has an obvious purpose. Aside from their political impact, the cash and livestock derived from these ventures supported the ongoing war, feeding and even paying soldiers and buying weapons and grain from Flemish and German merchants.[28] The ability of Robert to win castles and communities in Scotland was directly linked to successful harrying. The sustained siege of Dundee in spring 1312 was supported by the raids of late 1311. The forays at harvest time 1312 probably supplied the siege of Perth. An account of mid-1312 describes Robert's division of his army. Most were sent to harry northern England, his light troops plundered districts within Scotland, while the king led a force to besiege castles in the south-west. This suggests that the collection of resources to support the war was assigned greater forces than the capture of remaining garrisons.[29]

Up to 1314 King Robert waged a war which was suited to his resources as well as his objectives. His aggression stemmed both from the need to obtain supplies and from political factors. Bruce was aware of the need to demonstrate his own ascendancy to his enemies and to exploit continuing English divisions. His approach to war for most of this period was far removed from the cautious model of the 'testament'. In the north and Argyll he had launched a series of attacks against hostile magnates, while his march on Berwick in December 1312 showed a readiness to take risks. The sieges of Dundee and Perth involved blockades of several weeks and indicate that Robert could do more than ambush and raid. At Slioch and Old Meldrum, Bruce also demonstrated a readiness to offer battle, and on the latter occasion Barbour's account of the battle has the king rout his enemies by a rapid advance.[30] However, such aggression was clearest in encounters with Scottish enemies where Robert needed to display his authority as king through warfare. Against major English forces, Bruce had been more cautious. In 1310 he had 'lurked continually in hiding' when Edward II advanced, and in early 1311 was said to have meant to fight Gaveston but 'did not believe he was able to meet the king's forces in a plain field'.[31]

Robert's fears were not surprising. At Loudoun Hill in 1307 he had driven off a cavalry force on a field he had chosen and prepared. He was aware of the difficulties of re-creating the same conditions. His reluctance to risk battle was hardly abnormal among medieval commanders, but it also suggests he recognised the limitations of the forces at his disposal. Evidence from Robert's statute of 1318 specifying the arms and armour to be provided by men of different incomes suggests that Scottish soldiers remained lightly equipped. Men with goods worth £10 were expected to have a 'haqueton', a quilted suit of armour, or a coat of 'good iron', an open helmet, mail gloves and a spear and sword.[32] Such men were surely the 'middle folk', the yeomen, freeholders and burgesses who formed a key group in the politics and warfare of the period. English efforts to win or coerce their support suggests that both sides knew that these men were the core of Scottish armies.[33] However, they formed only the part of Bruce's hosts. The statute also mentioned a much wider group, those rich enough to own a cow, to carry a spear or bow and twenty-four arrows. Though there were special reasons for this statute in 1318, its terms and English chroniclers suggest that many in the armies raised by Bruce wore only light armour.[34] Pictures show the Scots as unarmoured, though wearing helms, and Barbour and others make clear that the fighting men were accompanied by bands of 'small folk', 'poverale' or 'rangaill', peasants equipped with staves who stood with the army's horses and baggage during battle.[35] Such men would likely have been uprooted by warfare and followed Robert's hosts for food and plunder, perhaps assisting in the driving off of cattle on forays.

Though lightly equipped, the warfare of 1307 to 1313 showed the strengths of these troops. Mounted on small riding horses, they could be mobile, fearsome and effective raiders. The repeated calls on their service since 1296 must have given them a greater degree of skill and endurance in warfare and the successes they had won surely bred confidence in their methods and leaders. Despite this, the relative scarcity of archers and the lack of armoured horsemen were major handicaps in open battle. Lacking such resources, the traditional formation of the Scots in battle was the schiltrom, a dense but static mass of spearmen, impenetrable at best but not without weaknesses. If Loudoun Hill revealed the ability of spearmen to resist horsemen, Methven had shown the speed with which footmen could be put to flight by a cavalry charge which caught them unprepared and Falkirk their vulnerability to archery. In 1311 Bruce was reluctant to risk his men and his interests in a battle in which he may have felt he had little to gain. In 1314 he would come to a different conclusion.

In terms of the Scottish war since 1307, the events of late 1310 and early 1311 were exceptional. The expedition was Edward II's only major campaign in Scotland between 1307 and 1314. For the most part he had left the war to much smaller forces who fought a largely defensive war against Bruce and his adherents. The front line in this conflict tended to be provided not by English armies, but by Scottish lords and their retinues. These were presumably raised and equipped in similar fashion to those of King Robert. Such forces could be large. The letter of William earl of Ross in 1308 states that he had 'caused our men to be called out and we were stationed with three thousand men, at our own expense, on the borders of our earldom and . . . Sutherland and Caithness'.[36] The armies raised by Buchan, Atholl and Mowbray in the north do not seem to have been smaller than Bruce's. However, against the ability of Robert to appeal to local landowners as king, these leaders may have found their troops reducing in numbers while their enemy continued to recruit. John of Lorn reported that he had only 800 to oppose Bruce's army numbered at over 10,000, which, even if an exaggeration, speaks of the king's growing access to manpower.[37] The defeat of the northern lords in 1308 and the exile of Alexander of Argyll the next year removed those Scottish magnates able to take the field against Bruce without English support.

Though substantial numbers of Scots continued to serve against Robert, they did so in conjunction with companies retained by the English crown. The majority of these paid forces were in the garrisons which Edward II installed in the key castles of Scotland. Over thirty royal or baronial castles were defended by keepers employed by the English king between 1307 and 1311. Some of these were small holds probably only garrisoned for short periods, but at least half were defended by Edward's administration as the basis of their presence in Scotland. Despite this, most garrisons were small, numbering only a few score soldiers.[38] However, fortified towns like Ayr and Berwick, Dundee and Perth required and could support larger garrisons. Over 100 men-at-arms had their horses valued at Perth and Dundee in 1311, suggesting considerable forces were stationed in these two key burghs.[39] Similarly, as Edwardian castles were lost north of the Forth and west of the Clyde, the size of the garrisons at the remaining key strongpoints was increased. The company at Linlithgow pele rose from thirty to seventy, while Edinburgh and Roxburgh contained garrisons of between seventy and ninety men in 1312.[40] These garrisons included many Scots, and custody of several major castles and towns was committed by Edward II to his Scottish adherents, often men with local connections. David Brechin and Alexander Abernethy at Dundee and William Oliphant and Malise of Strathearn at Perth were expected to use their influence to safeguard their charge and were trusted to remain loyal.[41] At both Dundee and Perth, this trust was well-placed and Bruce's sieges were vigorously, if unsuccessfully, opposed by the Scots in the towns.

The men in the garrisons were probably well-equipped by comparison with their attackers. English payments show the presence of contingents of mounted men-at-arms and hobelars, lightly armoured men on small riding horses, as well as archers and crossbowmen. The numbers of cavalry, who made up half or more of the garrison, indicate the purpose of these small forces. Their role was not simply to sit within the walls ready to defend the castle. Officials like Piers Lubaud combined the role of keeper of Edinburgh with those of sheriff.[42] The increasingly difficult tasks of levying rents and administering justice in Lothian were combined with the military defence of the area from the castle. These relatively small companies were expected to lead and protect the local landowners in war against Bruce's adherents. Despite occasional successes, like those ascribed to Thomas Gray as keeper of Cupar in 1308, the steady fall of castles instead highlights the problems of this reliance on garrisons.[43] Though mostly less than a hundred strong, the efforts of sustaining garrisons year after year was a major drain on Edward II's already strangled finances. It had cost over £1200 to support Lubaud's men in Edinburgh Castle in the year from August 1311 and, facing a backlash over his expenditure at home, the English king clearly found it difficult to pay his troops.[44] In early 1312, just as Dundee was facing siege, Edward was assigning money to pay just a part of the wages owed to David Brechin and his men in the garrison.[45] This was hardly good for morale and there were clearly similar problems in arranging for food and drink to reach more exposed garrisons. This question of supply was linked directly to relations between the soldiers and the local community. In early 1313 Edward II appealed to the men of Lothian, asking them to supply the garrisons at Linlithgow and Edinburgh.[46] Their readiness to do this must have been reduced by the losses they had suffered at the hands of the enemy, from which the garrison had failed to protect them. However, without willing support and supply from the surrounding sheriffdom, constables and garrisons would be tempted to seek such resources directly. The appeal from 'the commune of Scotland' which Edward II received in 1313 complained of the failure of the king's sheriffs to pay for goods.[47] Later in the year a further complaint suggested a breakdown in relations with the garrisons at Berwick and Roxburgh. 'Instead of protecting his lieges' these forces held men for ransom and stole livestock. When the local knight, Adam Gordon, carried this complaint to the sheriff of Roxburgh, Guillaume Fiennes, he was himself thrown in prison.[48]

These problems may have been partly due to Edward's failure to pay and supply his men, but also demonstrated the stresses placed on both garrisons and local communities by Bruce's repeated attacks. Above all, the attacks revealed the isolation of the English king's remaining garrisons. Dundee, Perth and the castles of the south-west had fallen in 1312 and 1313 without any major relief effort. This was the key failing in Edward II's handling of the war. In contemporary warfare it was well understood that the key to effective defence of land and lordship was not simply about placing garrisons in strategic castles. Instead it was necessary to support these castle troops with companies of horse and foot large enough to withstand the enemy in the field and allow the garrisons to operate beyond the walls. To stop Robert's men raiding with impunity and choosing which garrisons to pick off, Edward needed to raise armies of sufficient size and strength to make Bruce concerned about relief efforts and counterstrikes. The deployment of such forces in the field was the obvious way to check Robert's rapid advance. As has been discussed, the events of 1310–11 revealed that Bruce was unwilling to meet such forces in the open. His anxieties were caused by the size of such forces but also by the combination of enemy troops he would face. Above all, it was the cavalry contingent in English armies which encouraged such caution. At Methven in 1306, Bruce's army had been easily routed by the charge of only 300 cavalry.[49] The English kings had the means to put far greater numbers of armoured horsemen into the field. In 1298 Edward I may have raised over 3,000 cavalry for service in Scotland and, despite his problems, it has been calculated that Edward II's army in late 1310 still contained 1,700 cavalry.[50] Only about a quarter of these contingents was raised by calling on tenants of the crown to perform feudal service, providing cavalry in return for fiefs of land or money. Instead the crown increasingly paid for their mounted troops, retaining nobles and their retinues in the royal household or under their own banners. The size of the royal household could be considerable. In 1298 it contained nearly 800 horsemen, though in 1310 it numbered just under 300.[51]

These cavalry contingents were divided into knights and men-at-arms or sergeants. The knights would have been more heavily armoured with a full suit of mail, strenghtened by plate armour on the limbs and a closed helm, and mounted on expensive and protected warhorses. The majority of the cavalry was probably equipped and mounted more lightly and cheaply, but still would have been protected by full mail and metal helmet and armed with lance, shield and sword. The value of forces of knights and men-at-arms in an open battle was accepted across Europe. Their presence, let alone their charge, was designed to intimidate opposing infantry and commanders, even when they were in relatively small numbers.[52] It was with a force of either 200 or 500 men-at-arms that Gaveston campaigned in Angus in early 1311 and which Bruce feared to face in the open. However, a few months later the companies of local men-at-arms numbering 140 and 100, which Edward II stationed in the east and west marches, neither deterred nor defeated Scottish forays into northern England.[53]

The English crown's recent wars in Wales and Scotland also demonstrated the need to support the mounted elite with large bodies of infantry. The immense army which Edward I led to Scotland in 1298 contained nearly 15,000 English foot soldiers and 10,000 Welsh. This was exceptional. In 1300 9,000 English foot served at the siege of Caerlaverock, 7,500 mustered in 1301 and in August 1306 just under 3,000 infantry were raised to pursue Bruce.[54] In 1310 Edward II had a similar number of infantry in the army he led through southern Scotland.[55] These infantry were far from being the skilled and almost professional force which won Crécy and Poitiers. They were levied by commissions of array, bodies of officials who instructed local communities to provide contingents for the royal army. For the Scottish wars such demands were normally centred on the counties of the north and midlands. The system produced bodies of foot which were often poorly equipped and unwilling. Especially in the huge armies of the later 1290s, desertion was a major problem and equipment could be poor. The vast majority of foot raised served as archers, but they were equipped by their own communities and frequently exhausted their supply of arrows on campaign.[56] In quality and training it is hard to imagine that they were any more skilled than their Scottish opponents and, indeed, by 1314 they were almost certainly inferior to many Scots footmen who had become accustomed to serving in Bruce's almost incessant campaigns. As we have seen, for a source of infantry from a more militarised environment, the English crown turned to Wales. Almost all royal armies of this period contained a large proportion of Welsh spearmen and archers. Though prone to desertion and occasionally mutinous, the Welsh contingents were valued for their bravery and skill in warfare in difficult terrain and harsh conditions.[57]

The value of such large infantry forces is not always clear. The favoured account of the battle of Falkirk in 1298 suggests that, following the failure of cavalry charges against the Scottish schiltroms, it was the archery (and even stone-throwing) of the English footmen which caused heavy losses among the closely packed enemy. This broke up the schiltroms and allowed the cavalry to break into and ride down the Scottish foot, causing heavy casualties. The English foot themselves suffered losses of about 2,000, suggesting that they also fought hand-to-hand with the Scots in this extremely bloody and large battle.[58] The use of archers in this way was hardly new or revolutionary, but Falkirk at least shows that the infantry had a clear function in battle. However, encounters like Falkirk were exceptional. Infantry were raised with an eye to the mundane needs of warfare. In the sieges which marked Edward I's Scottish campaigns, infantry were clearly essential for enforcing blockades, for their archery and for storming castles. In rough ground they were equally vital, as in 1300 when they crossed a river in Galloway to attack a Scottish force.[59] Whether such tasks required over 10,000 foot is doubtful. The smaller numbers of foot raised in 1303, 1306 and 1310 may indicate that huge armies were unnecessary and added to problems of supply, which the near starvation of the army before Falkirk had shown.

In 1303–4 Edward I had forced his Scottish enemies to submit by remaining in the field with a small army for over a year. In 1310–11, though he achieved nothing like this success, Edward II demonstrated that he recognised that the maintenance of such an army was the only means to challenge Bruce. The presence of the English king and the active campaigning of Gaveston and others made it more difficult for Robert to raise his own forces, to cross Scotland with impunity and to threaten Edward's adherents and garrisons. Edward II's failure to raise other field forces demonstrated the other factors required to muster armies of cavalry and foot. Armies were expensive to raise and keep in the field.[60] Demands for payment and for personal military service meant that such campaigns depended on the support and consent of the king's subjects. While his father had created, but largely bypassed, major opposition on this score, Edward II lacked the authority to copy him.[61] To launch an army to reverse the defeats since 1311 would require not just the command of King Edward, but the active support of his subjects.

STIRLING CASTLE AND THE FALL OF LOTHIAN
(OCTOBER 1313–22 JUNE 1314)

The long road to Bannockburn began with Robert Bruce's return to Scotland in 1307, but it was a sequence of events during October and November 1313 which set in train the campaign and battle of Bannockburn the following June.[62] As throughout the previous seven years of warfare, at stake was the allegiance of Scotland to Bruce or Plantagenet ruler. Despite their long string of losses, there were still many Scots who opposed Bruce and looked to King Edward for protection. Though some of these had lost their lands already, in Lothian, Clydesdale and the dales of Tweed and Teviot nobles and communities still adhered to the English king. Earl Patrick of Dunbar, William Soules of Liddesdale, Ingeram Umfraville, Roger Mowbray, Adam Gordon and Alexander Seton were leading southern lords in Edward's allegiance in late 1313.[63] However, the position of these men was increasingly desperate. The fall of Linlithgow in August had removed one source of protection, but even before that they had been exposed to the depredations of both Bruce and their own lord's garrisons. As mentioned above, these 'people of Scotland' dispatched a petition to Edward stating their grievances and seeking redress.[64]

Even after five years of Robert's pressure, the local communities of the south-east still looked to the English king for protection, but the letters may have been taken south by Earl Patrick and Adam Gordon with a warning about rival claims on their allegiance. In late October King Robert was at Dundee, where he held a council attended by his leading magnates, including Edward Bruce, Thomas Randolph, John Menteith and David earl of Atholl.[65] At this Bruce may have issued a proclamation demanding the submission of all Scots to him within a year on pain of forfeiture of their lands. This was probably not the first such demand. A year later, those disinherited were said to have been 'often called' to submit to Robert.[66] However, for nobles in Lothian it may have seemed like the tipping point. Earl Patrick and Gordon may have learned of the fresh proclamation and carried their fears to London in November. Like the northern lords, John of Lorn and Alexander Abernethy, who had warned Edward of their losses and asked for immediate military support in July 1310, the leaders of the south-east may have appealed for their king's help.

The king's response to his Scottish subjects developed during November. On 8 November he wrote to the keepers of Berwick and Roxburgh ordering them to protect his lieges and observe the truces they made with the enemy. He also sent letters to a group of southern Scottish lords thanking them for their service. While the king was concerned to answer the complaints contained in their petition, his answer suggested nothing more. By 28 November, however, something had changed. Edward wrote again to 'our liegemen in Scotland . . . replying to those things brought to us by Patrick earl of Dunbar and Adam Gordon'. The king now issued orders to his Scottish adherents to be at Berwick before 24 June 1314 'and we require you to advance with our

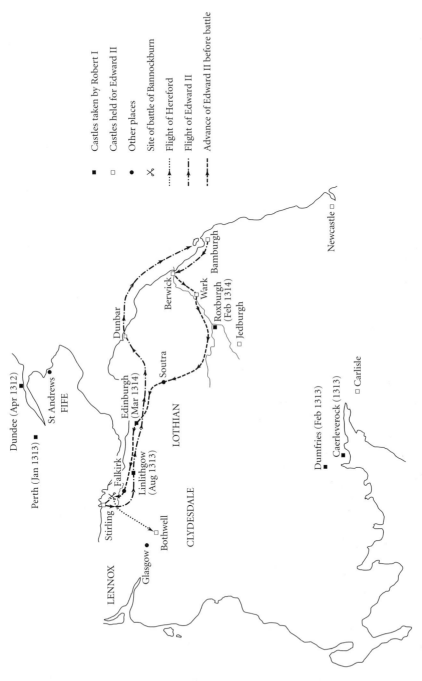

MAP 5.1 *The 1314 Campaign*

Castles taken by Robert I ■

Castles held for Edward II □

Other places ●

Site of battle of Bannockburn ✕

Flight of Hereford ·······▶

Flight of Edward II —·—·▶

Advance of Edward II before battle —··—▶

Dundee (Apr 1312) ■

Perth (Jan 1313) ■

St Andrews ●

FIFE

Dunbar □

Edinburgh (Mar 1314) ■

Soutra ●

LOTHIAN

Falkirk ●

Stirling ●

Linlithgow (Aug 1313) ●

Bothwell □

CLYDESDALE

Glasgow ●

LENNOX

Berwick □

Bamburgh □

Wark □

Roxburgh (Feb 1314) ■

Jedburgh □

Newcastle □

Dumfries (Feb 1313) ■

Caerleverock (1313) ■

Carlisle □

army into those parts [Scotland]'. He further asked for their loyalty up to that point.[67] The planned campaign and appeal for loyalty suggest that Edward had been made aware of the wavering allegiance of his liegemen in the face of Robert's demands for their submission. The English king recognised that his presence at the head of an army was vital to maintain his lordship in Scotland.

In late 1313 Edward II was better placed to lead such an expedition than he had been at any point since 1307. His relations with Philip IV of France were good and in October the threat of open conflict with his baronial opponents had finally been lifted.[68] Though he was still at odds with his leading critics, Thomas of Lancaster and the earls of Warwick and Arundel, and his financial position was weak, Edward could lay plans for a campaign which would have the support of most of his major nobles.[69] For magnates like the earl of Hereford, Aymer Valence and Henry Beaumont who still held interests in southern Scotland, the campaign would serve to safeguard their lands. For northern English lords the expedition offered a means to counter the attacks of recent years. For many of Edward's subjects, after years of neglect the king was at last seeking to defend the rights he had inherited in Scotland. There was also the prospect of ready cash. As part of the settlement with his opponents at the October parliament, a grant of taxation had been made to Edward and, about the same time, the king had arranged to assign the revenues of Gascony to the Pope in return for a payment of £25,000.[70] Such political and financial advances may have persuaded Edward that there was no need to summon parliament to seek formal consent for his campaign. This was against the Ordinances of 1311, but according to the *Vita Edwardi Secundi* the king was persuaded by his 'counsellers and household officials' that, such was the support for the campaign, it was not necessary to go to parliament.[71] Encouraged by his close advisers, men like Edmund Mauley, Hugh Despenser and Henry Beaumont, Edward may have been hoping to use the campaign as a display of his ability to override the Ordinances, as well as his success in war. In late December writs were issued to over eighty earls, barons and tenants in chief ordering them to bring their quotas of men-at-arms with horses and arms to Berwick before 10 June 1314.[72] The preparations for the campaign had begun.

While the machinery of Edwardian military administration ground into action, the Bruce regime prepared its own response. Edward II's promise of support for his Scottish adherents must have been known to Robert. In early 1314 he took action to reinforce his own demands for allegiance. In January 1314 Bruce's favourite, Thomas Randolph, earl of Moray, laid siege to Edinburgh Castle. With 'symple aparaling', light equipment and a company of 'gud men', Randolph may have hoped to take Edinburgh by treachery. The castle's commander, the Gascon Piers Lubaud, was later accused of betraying his charge. He was certainly accepted into Robert's allegiance after Edinburgh's fall and Barbour's account records that Lubaud had spoken with Bruce. However, he also states that, as a result, Lubaud was imprisoned by his men who chose an Englishman as constable.[73] This setback may have forced Randolph to sit outside the walls, blockading the castle.

Typically, as Randolph was bogged down at Edinburgh, Bruce's adherents struck at a second Edwardian stronghold, the 'beautiful castle' of Roxburgh in the borders. This attack was less clearly a result of Robert's strategy. It was undertaken by James Douglas who, despite Barbour's later promotion, was not a leading lieutenant of the king up to 1314. Instead Douglas probably spent his time 'in the Forest', his base in the moors west of Selkirk, harassing the enemy in the surrounding lands. Perhaps aware of Randolph's siege of Edinburgh, Douglas prepared an attack on Roxburgh on its natural site between the rivers Tweed and Teviot.[74] Choosing Shrove Tuesday (17 February), when the garrison were likely to be feasting, Douglas led a band numbered at sixty men to Roxburgh. Disguised in black cloaks, they were able to scale the walls using rope ladders. Once inside, Douglas and his men surprised the garrison while they feasted in the hall, killing or capturing most of them. The keeper, Guillemin Fiennes, another Gascon, escaped to the great tower with a small band. After a night under attack and mortally wounded by an arrow to the face, Fiennes surrendered in return for his garrison's lives and safe conduct.[75]

According to Barbour, this exploit spurred Randolph into action. He found a man, William Francis, who was prepared to guide him up the castle rock. Randolph himself led a band of thirty men up the crag. The walls at this point were only twelve feet high and, as Randolph and his men scrambled over, the main part of the besieging force launched an attack on the gate. After fierce fighting, Thomas was able to open the gate and, after the death of the constable, the surviving members of the garrison surrendered.[76] The fall of both Edinburgh and Roxburgh was a major success for Bruce at a crucial point. It must have raised the confidence of his side, while removing the main means by which Edward II hoped to maintain his hold on loyalties. After Roxburgh's fall, the local men entered Bruce's allegiance. Moreover, Edward had lost two places of strength which would assist his planned campaign in the summer. In conventional warfare, Bruce would be expected to garrison the castles and thus tie down the enemy in long sieges. However, instead King Robert had both castles destroyed. It was a practice which he had followed elsewhere and which was born out of the strains of supplying garrisons and a reluctance to create a situation in which he was forced to choose between the abandonment of a stronghold or the risks of a relief where battle might be forced on ground and in circumstances chosen by the enemy. Robert's policy may have been unpopular. He sent his brother, Edward, to ensure that Roxburgh was demolished and to receive local submissions.[77]

Edward was given another task. He was sent to besiege Stirling Castle. This proved a harder nut than either Roxburgh or Edinburgh. The constable was a Scot, the 'douchty' Philip Mowbray, who had fought long and hard against Bruce since 1306. Though the two sides 'bykyrrit', bickered or skirmished, fiercely, Edward Bruce failed to make any inroads. It was probably in late March that he agreed the famous truce with Mowbray. If Stirling had not been relieved in three months, by 24 June, the castle would surrender.[78] Aware of the existing plans of the English king for an army to muster in early June, this allowed Mowbray hopes of rescue. For Edward Bruce and his brother, however, it was more of a mixed blessing. The capture of Stirling Castle was now a clear test of Robert's military ascendancy. Success in this task was inevitably linked to his demands for the allegiance of his last Scottish opponents. In 1310 Bruce had been able to deny his enemy any clear targets, reducing him to a fruitless march. He would not be able to achieve this in 1314. Instead he needed to prepare for a different kind of campaign.

His enemy's plans were also developing. In late March, perhaps linked to news from Stirling but more likely after word of the loss of Edinburgh and Roxburgh, Edward II's officials sent out a series of orders. Aymer Valence was sent north as keeper of Scotland and the king even announced an intention to be at Newcastle in person after Easter.[79] Though he would not reach the north so quickly, Edward was clearly keen to be on campaign. As in 1311, he again sought to organise a challenge to Bruce from the west. Orders were sent out summoning English lords and Irish kings from Ireland to serve in Scotland under the justiciar, Theobald Verdon, and for ships to transport them. The justiciar was also charged with raising 4,000 foot by Easter to serve in the fleet led by Bruce's old enemy, John of Lorn. John's target was his family's homeland in the Isles and Argyll and he was given power to receive named Islesmen, including Bruce's ally, Donal of Islay, into Edward's allegiance. John had clearly persuaded Edward that Bruce's hold on the Isles was not secure and a display of the English king's strength could win submissions. However, if the fleet ever sailed, it clearly did not distract Robert or deny him the backing of Islesmen during the campaign in June.[80] Another setback may have been the growing awareness that Edward's campaign did not have the complete support of his subjects. For Thomas earl of Lancaster and other hardline opponents of the king, a royal triumph which strengthened Edward's hand would be unwelcome. Using the king's refusal to call a parliament to obtain consent for the expedition, as the Ordinances required, Lancaster and three other earls refused to serve on the campaign in person, merely sending their small quotas of knights. However, the king could, once again, count on the willing service of the young earl of Gloucester who reportedly brought 500 men in his entourage.[81] Unlike 1311, the experienced Aymer Valence earl of Pembroke and Humphrey earl of Hereford, formerly a leading opponent, were ready to raise large contingents to defend their Scottish lands. Once again, though, there would be a direct link between the Scottish war and English politics.[82]

During the spring, the focus of the expedition on Stirling became clear. In March the king had summoned some 10,000 foot to muster but in late May there were fresh demands. These may have been prompted by the arrival of Philip Mowbray from Stirling Castle. Mowbray may have advised the king about both the ground before Stirling and the preparations of the enemy.[83] Just days before the muster date in early June, Edward wrote to the sheriff of York asking for 4,000 men from his county. This was because 'we learn that our Scottish enemies and rebels endeavour . . . to gather with a great crowd of footmen in places strong and vexatious, where horses will find it difficult to enter, between us and our castle of Stirling'. The king stated that he had to 'rescue the castle by the Nativity of St John the Baptist [24 June], as in the conditions agreed with our enemies by the constable of the castle on pain of losing it, which relief we propose to make'. To drive away the enemy 'it is necessary for us to have armed footmen'.[84] The king's determination was clear. Summons for 16,000 English foot and over 5,000 Welsh foot were sent out to muster on 10 June at Wark, just upriver from Berwick. Merchant ships and carts were ordered to ensure the huge force did not starve as it crossed the ravaged lands of southern Scotland and by early May King Edward was in the north of his kingdom.[85]

It is much harder to trace the preparations of King Robert. His one clear move was to launch his brother across the border. In the week after Easter, Edward Bruce entered England in the west, driving off 'a great number of cattle' and even attacking Carlisle, where many refugees from the countryside had gathered. The local *Lanercost Chronicle* states that 'the Scots did these wrongs because the men of that march had not paid them the tribute they had promised'. Perhaps buoyed by the planned royal campaign, the men of Cumberland refused to pay up.[86] Robert was demonstrating his continued ability to wreak havoc. Equally important for the king, he was gathering supplies. The cattle of the English marches would feed any army he could raise in the summer. The only evidence as to this army comes from the later account of John Barbour. He states that, when Edward's army was gathering, he ordered that 'hys men be somound generaly'.[87] This general summons suggests that Robert had called on all owing army service. In the later Middle Ages this could produce forces of well over 10,000 men, and the army at Falkirk may have been of this magnitude. Recent estimates of Bruce's army in 1314 have tended to suggest a smaller army, from 3,500 to 6,000. These may be underestimates but not by much.[88] A major consideration for Bruce may have been the need to supply his host and keep it mobile. His armies up to 1314 had probably been limited in size. To take the field with a larger army, including more unarmoured and inexperienced footmen, would not work to Robert's advantage. As the events of late June would show, the army was neither untrained nor lacking in confidence. It is reasonable to suggest that Robert assembled a host by calling on men who had served frequently in recent warfare. It was an army of spearmen with few archers and mounted men-at-arms, though it was accompanied by bands of 'small folk' and it would be surprising if the herds of horses which carried Scottish forays into England were not gathered for ease of movement. According to Barbour, the muster point was in the Torwood, an area of forest between the River Carron and the Tor burn north of Falkirk. Straddling the approach along the Forth to Stirling, the Torwood had been used as a camp by Bruce as a guardian in 1299.[89] It was an obvious base for Robert in June 1314, secure from sudden attack and with good access to Lothian, Clydesdale and northwards into the more open ground south of Stirling.

The army which Robert would face gathered around Berwick during the first ten days of June. Though much better documented than its opponents, it is still hard to be certain about the size of King Edward's expedition. Over 21,000 infantry had been summoned but it was rare for all of them to appear. In 1318 and 1322 fewer than half of the numbers called had actually assembled, but about two-thirds of the requested number was more normal. The army at Falkirk had contained over 20,000 foot and, though smaller than this total, the infantry at Bannockburn probably numbered more than any Edwardian army since then.[90] In terms of the cavalry, there has been greater consensus. The *Vita Edwardi Secundi* gives the sober figure of 'more than two thousand' for the number of cavalry which has generally been accepted. Again, this force was as large as in many of Edward I's armies and the largest force of armoured cavalry put in the field against Bruce as king.[91] The absence of Lancaster and his allies had clearly not limited the resources available to Edward II too much. This was not just an English army. While Barbour's purple verse names Gascons, French, Poitevans, Hainaulters and Bretons, these were just individual adventurers and mercenaries like the famous knight Giles d'Argentan, who had been rescued from a Greek prison by Edward in time for him to serve in Scotland.[92] More substantially, some of the Irish contingent called in March may have reached Berwick, perhaps even led by Richard earl of Ulster, Bruce's father-in-law.[93] Certainly there were several thousand Welsh, raised by royal officials and by marcher lords, the greatest of whom, Hereford, Gloucester and Valence, were in the host. Also ready to serve were a number of Edward II's Scottish adherents. Ingeram Umfraville certainly fought at Bannockburn, as did Thomas Torthorwald, once a vassal of the Bruce family in their lordship of Annandale. Also there was John Comyn of Badenoch, the son of Bruce's victim.[94] For such men, the 1314 campaign was another episode in their ongoing war against the usurper.

While at Berwick, King Edward was clearly thinking ahead. In anticipation of success, he granted the lands of Thomas Randolph to his rising favourite, the young Hugh Despenser. More immediately, the plan for the campaign must have seemed obvious. Edward needed to be within three miles of Stirling Castle by 24 June. However, he was preparing for a longer campaign. Supplies were being called for and stocked which would allow the king to campaign until early August.[95] In 1310 he had been in the field against Bruce for such a period and clearly intended that, having relieved Stirling, his army would recover lost ground and renew lost loyalties. Bruce had not stood to fight in 1310, so why would he do so now faced by a much larger and more imposing force? With time to relieve Stirling running short, the infantry and 'multitude of carts and baggage wagons' began to move across and then west along the Tweed before marching up Lauderdale.[96] On 18 June the king was at Soutra, a small religious house at the summit of the Pentland Hills, where the road ran down into Lothian.[97] The king reached Edinburgh on 19 or 20 June. Probably after a pause to allow the army to reassemble, Edward ordered a march west towards Stirling. Informed of the enemy's advance, on Saturday, 22 June King Robert moved his men north from the Torwood to the New Park. This was a royal hunting preserve about two miles south of Stirling and, like the Torwood, it straddled the main approach to the castle. By nightfall on 22 June, the English king and his army had reached Falkirk, just south of the Torwood, and within a day's march of their target and their enemy.[98] After over seven years of warfare the test of battle was approaching.

NOTES

1. *The Bruce*, ed. Duncan, 400–13.
2. *Chron. Guisborough*, 327–8; M. Prestwich, *War, Politics and Finance*, 109; Barrow, *Bruce*, 102; Watson, *Under the Hammer*, 66–7.
3. Watson, *Under the Hammer*, 108–9, 122–3, 151, 175–7.
4. Barrow, *Bruce*, 186; C. Oman, *A History of the Art of War in the Middle Ages*, 2 vols (London, 1928), ii, 99.
5. See Brown, *Wars of Scotland*, 234–43.
6. See for example, R. C. Smail, *Crusading Warfare 1097–1193* (Cambridge, 1965); S. Morillo, 'Battle Seeking: The Contexts and Limits of Vegetian Strategy', in B. Bachrach (ed.), *Journal of Medieval Military History*, 1 (Woodbridge, 2002), 21–42; Prestwich, *Armies and Warfare*, 305. For a different view, see C. J. Rogers, 'The Vegetian Science of Warfare in the Middle Ages', in *Journal of Medieval Military History*, 1, 1–20.
7. J. Gillingham, 'Richard I and the Science of War in the Middle Ages', in J. Gillingham and J. C. Holt (eds), *War and Government in the Middle Ages* (Woodbridge, 1984), 78–91; J. Gillingham, 'William the Bastard at War', in C. Harper-Bill, C. Holdsworth and J. Nelson (eds), *Studies in Medieval History presented to R. Allen Brown* (Woodbridge, 1989), 141–58.
8. For Edward I's military activities, see Prestwich, *War, Politics and Finance*, 1–40.
9. Morillo, 'Battle Seeking'.
10. Watson, *Under the Hammer*, 173–94; M. Haskell, 'Breaking the Stalemate: The Scottish Campaign of Edward I, 1303–4', in M. Prestwich, R. Britnell and R. Frame (eds) *Thirteenth Century England* (Woodbridge, 1999), vii, 223–42.
11. J. R. Strayer, *Medieval Statecraft and the Perspectives of History* (Princeton, 1970), 107–22; Prestwich, *Edward I*, 376–435.
12. D. Carpenter, *The Battles of Lewes and Evesham* (Keele, 1987).
13. Morillo, 'Battle Seeking', 29–30; Carpenter, *Lewes and Evesham*, 12–18, 52–9; A. Goodman, *The Wars of the Roses: Military Activity and English Society, 1452–97* (London, 1981).
14. J. F. Verbruggen, *The Battle of the Golden Spurs*, 20–6.
15. G. Barrow, 'The army of Alexander III's Scotland', in N. Reid, *Scotland in the Reign of Alexander III, 1249–86* (Edinburgh, 1986), 132–47; A. A. M. Duncan, *Scotland: The Making of the Kingdom* (Edinburgh, 1975), 378–83.

16. A. Grant, 'Aspects of national consciousness in medieval Scotland', in C. Bjorn, A. Grant and K. Stringer (eds), *Nations, Nationalism and Patriotism in the European Past* (Copenhagen, 1994), 68–95.
17. *Nat. MSS Scot.*, ii, no. 8; *C.D.S.*, ii, nos 1321, 1694. For a later period, see M. Brown, 'The development of Scottish Border Lordship', *Historical Research*, 70 (1997), 1–22.
18. *The Bruce*, ed. Duncan, 93.
19. A. McKerral, 'West Highland mercenaries in Ireland', *S.H.R.*, 30 (1951), 1–29; J. F. Lydon, 'The Scottish soldier abroad: the Bruce invasion and the Galloglass', in S. Duffy (ed.), *Robert the Bruce's Irish Wars* (Stroud, 2002), 89–106.
20. *Foedera*, ii, 8; *C.D.S.*, ii, no. 1909; *The Bruce*, ed. Duncan, 201–13.
21. *C.D.S.*, ii, no. 1926; 'The movements of Robert Bruce', 59; *A.P.S.*, i, 477.
22. Douglas and Randolph were repeatedly identified in Barbour's *Bruce* as having their own bands of followers, while in 1307 Menteith had been able to raise ships and men for Edward II and presumably did so in defence of Knapdale against MacSween in 1310 (*The Bruce*, ed. Duncan, 205–7, 243, 313, 355, 373–7; *C.D.S.*, v, no. 492 (xvi)).
23. *A.P.S.*, i, 459.
24. Duncan, 'War of the Scots', 147–8.
25. *The Bruce*, ed. Duncan, 296–7n; *C.D.S.*, ii, no. 1912.
26. *R.R.S.*, v, no. 18; Duncan, 'War of the Scots', 147.
27. *A.P.S.*, i, 475–6.
28. Stevenson, 'The Flemish Dimension of the Auld Alliance', 28–42; W. S. Reid, 'Trade, Traders and Scottish Independence', *Speculum*, 29 (1954), 210–22.
29. *C.D.S.*, iii, no. 279.
30. *The Bruce*, ed. Duncan, 331–3.
31. *C.D.S.*, iii, no. 202; *Vita Edwardi*, 23.
32. *A.P.S.*, i, 473; Duncan, 'War of the Scots', 145.
33. *C.D.S.*, ii, nos 1204, 1755.
34. *Vita Edwardi*, 90–1; *A.P.S.*, i, 473.
35. *The Bruce*, ed. Duncan, 301, 305, 417, 427, 497; Duncan, 'The War of the Scots', 145–6.
36. *C.D.S.*, iv, pp. 399–400; *The Bruce*, ed. Duncan, 319–27, 329–35; 'The Movements of Robert Bruce', 58–9.
37. Duncan, 'War of the Scots', 142–3; *C.D.S.*, iii, no. 80.
38. For places garrisoned between 1307 and 1311, see *C.D.S.*, iii, nos 121, 176, 218; v, nos 492 (xii, xvi), 515 (b), 562, 566 (b); *Rot. Scot.*, i, 80.
39. *C.D.S.*, iii, pp. 425–33.
40. *C.D.S.*, iii, no. 259, pp. 405–12.
41. *Rot. Scot.*, i, 105–6, 109; *The Bruce*, ed. Duncan, 337.
42. *C.D.S.*, iii, p. 432.
43. *Scalachronica*, ed. King, 69.
44. *C.D.S.*, iii, pp. 408–10. In 1300 Edward I spent £13,574 on the wages and supply of his Scottish garrisons (Prestwich, *War, Politics and Finance*, 175).
45. *C.D.S.*, iii, no. 238.
46. *Rot. Scot.*, i, 111.
47. *C.D.S.*, iii, no. 186.
48. *C.D.S.*, iii, no. 337.
49. *Chron. Guisborough* 368; *The Bruce*, ed. Duncan, 99–103.
50. Prestwich, *War, Politics and Finance*, 91; Simpkin, 'English Army', 14–39; M. Prestwich, 'Cavalry Service in Early Fourteenth Century England', in Gillingham and Holt, *War and Government*, 147–58.
51. Prestwich, *War, Politics and Finance*, 52–5; Simpkin, 'English Army', 14–39.

52. Prestwich, *Armies and Warfare*, 13–37, 51–2.

53. *C.D.S.*, iii, nos 201–2; *Chron. Lanercost*, 99, 195; *Rot. Scot.*, i, 106.

54. Prestwich, *War, Politics and Finance*, 93–8.

55. Simpkin, 'English Army', 14–39.

56. Prestwich, *War, Politics and Finance*, 96–107; J. E. Morris, *The Welsh Wars of Edward I*, 88–105; M. Powicke, *Military Obligation in Medieval England* (Oxford, 1962), 118–33.

57. Prestwich, *War, Politics and Finance*, 92–100, 108–10; Davies, *Lordship and Society in the March of Wales*, 67–85.

58. *Chron. Guisborough*, 327–8; Prestwich, *War, Politics and Finance*, 109–10; P. Armstrong, *Stirling Bridge and Falkirk* (Oxford, 2001).

59. Prestwich, *War, Politics and Finance*, 110.

60. Prestwich, *War, Politics and Finance*, 176.

61. Prestwich, *Edward I*, 517–55.

62. The traditional view of events leading up to Bannockburn has, like much of Robert I's reign, been shaped by Barbour's *Bruce*. This poem makes the sole reason for Edward II's campaign of 1314 the siege of Stirling Castle. The siege is said to have begun in Lent 1313 and was suspended by a truce between its keeper and Edward Bruce. They agreed that if the castle was not relieved by Midsummer 1314 it would be surrendered. Warned of this, Edward II began his preparations for Stirling's rescue and, though initially annoyed, Robert nobly accepted the challenge. Recent discussion of this by Professor Duncan has, however, clearly articulated the flaws in this account. A truce of over a year to allow for the relief was unique and inexplicable. At most a few months would be considered. The contemporary English accounts of *Vita Edwardi Secundi* and the *Lanercost Chronicle*, moreover, date the siege to spring 1314, after the fall of Edinburgh and Roxburgh castles. It is likely that Barbour extended the truce to make the fight for Stirling a suitably chivalric cause for the battle and to allow him, once again, to portray Edward Bruce as brave but dangerously rash – both themes of his work. Duncan's alternative explanation of the battle forms the basis of the account here (Duncan, 'War of the Scots', 149–50; *The Bruce*, ed. Duncan, 401–9).

63. *Rot. Scot.*, i, 113; *C.D.S.*, iii, nos 245, 338, 721.

64. *C.D.S.*, iii, no. 337.

65. *R.R.S.*, v, nos 35–7.

66. *A.P.S.*, i, 464. Duncan argues that the passage in Barbour which states Bruce gave a year for men to pay homage for their lands after Bannockburn is an understandable error. Instead it was after Bannockburn, in October 1314, that the year ran out, allowing Robert to issue the statute forfeiting all those who had died outside his allegiance or not done homage (*The Bruce*, ed. Duncan, 519; Duncan, 'The War of the Scots', 149).

67. *Rot. Scot.*, i, 112–13.

68. Haines, *King Edward II*, 309–10.

69. Maddicott, *Thomas of Lancaster*, 150–3.

70. Maddicott, *Thomas of Lancaster*, 151, 157. Edward also received support from Philip VI's minister, Enguerrand de Marigny (Haines, *Edward II*, 92–3).

71. *Vita Edwardi*, 87.

72. *Foedera*, ii, 59.

73. *Vita Edwardi*, 85; *The Bruce*, ed. Duncan, 376–9; J. Stevenson (ed.), *Illustrations of Scottish History* (Glasgow, 1834), 6.

74. *The Bruce*, ed. Duncan, 355, 379; Brown, *Black Douglases*, 14–28. Though James Douglas witnessed a charter issued by Robert I in 1309, he does not appear on royal acts in subsequent years up to 1314 (*R.R.S.*, v, no. 7).

75. *The Bruce*, ed. Duncan, 379–87; *Chron. Lanercost*, 204; *Vita Edwardi*, 84–5.
76. *The Bruce*, ed. Duncan, 387–97; *Chron. Lanercost*, 204.
77. *The Bruce*, ed. Duncan, 387.
78. *The Bruce*, ed. Duncan, 401–3; *Vita Edwardi*, 84–5; *Chron. Lanercost*, 205. As Duncan notes, though Barbour suggests a twelve-month truce, both contemporary English works make clear that it was only after the fall of Roxburgh and Edinburgh that Stirling was besieged (*The Bruce*, ed. Duncan, 402–5n). Soon before 25 March, Mowbray sent out a servant to buy provisions for his men, indicating the truce was in force (*Rot. Scot.*, i, 121).
79. *Rot. Scot.*, i, 117–20.
80. *Rot. Scot.*, i, 118–19, 121; McNamee, *Wars of the Bruces*, 61.
81. *Vita Edwardi*, 90–1.
82. *Vita Edwardi*, 86–7; Maddicott, *Thomas of Lancaster*, 157–9.
83. *The Bruce*, ed. Duncan, 405; *Vita Edwardi*, 84–5.
84. *Rot. Scot.*, i, 126.
85. *Rot. Scot.*, i, 126–7.
86. *Chron. Lanercost*, 205–6.
87. *The* Bruce, ed. Duncan, 415.
88. Barrow, *Robert Bruce*, 208–9; *Barbour's Bruce*, ed. McDiarmid and Stevenson, i, 88. For the size of later Scottish armies, see A. McDonald, *Border Bloodshed, Scotland, England and France at War* (East Linton, 2000), 151–5; N. Barr, *Flodden* (Stroud, 2001), 41–68; G. Phillips, *The Anglo-Scottish Wars, 1513–1550* (Woodbridge, 1999), 42–103.
89. *The Bruce*, ed. Duncan, 415, 441; Barrow, *Robert Bruce*, 409; *C.D.S.*, ii, no. 1109; Watson, *Under the Hammer*, 92.
90. *The Bruce*, ed. Duncan, 410n; Morris, *Bannockburn*, 36–41; Prestwich, *War, Politics and Finance*, 94–7.
91. *Vita Edwardi*, 87–9; Prestwich, 'Cavalry Service', 148–52; Prestwich, *War, Politics and Finance*, 91; Morris, *Bannockburn*, 25–35; Barrow, *Robert Bruce*, 207.
92. *The Bruce*, ed. Duncan, 409.
93. *C.P.R.*, 1313–17, 121. This may suggest that Earl Richard was with King Edward in late May 1314.
94. *Chron. Lanercost*, 206; *C.D.S.*, iii, no. 406.
95. *Rot. Scot.*, i, 127;
96. *Vita Edwardi*, 87; *The Bruce*, ed. Duncan, 411.
97. *C.D.S.*, iii, no. 365.
98. *The Bruce*, ed. Duncan, 423, 427. The site of Bruce's camp may have been near the Borestone.

CHAPTER 6

The Battle (23–4 June 1314)

The first day (Sunday, 23 June)

On the morning of Sunday, 23 June it was still far from certain that a battle would take place. The armies were still about eight miles apart, enough distance for Robert to move northwards beyond the Forth or westwards up the river into a district of mosses and hills. This option was probably in Bruce's mind throughout the day and was also likely to have influenced the plans of King Edward and his leading lords. Given his declared objective and the approach march of the previous week, it was certain that 23 June would see

FIGURE 6.1 *The Prize. Stirling Castle seen from the King's Park to the south was the immediate goal of King Edward's advance on 23 June. Its rock would also draw many fugitives after the defeat. (Crown Copyright. Historic Scotland)*

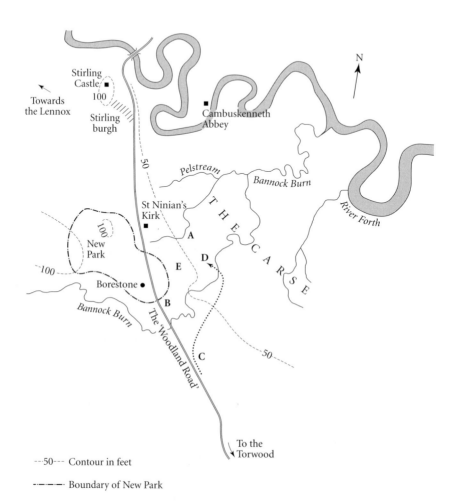

--50--- Contour in feet

-·—·—· Boundary of New Park

A Possible location of clash between Randolph's battle and cavalry of Beaumont and Clifford
B Fight between English vanguard and Robert I's battle
C Move of English army down into the Carse
D Probable camp site of English army
E Possible site for battle on 24 June

MAP 6.1 *The Battle of Bannockburn (23–4 June 1314)*

the English king resume his advance to Stirling. Indeed, the *Vita Edwardi Secundi* complained that in the effort to rescue the castle Edward 'hurried day after day' like a pilgrim rather than the leader of the army and, as a result, 'horses, horsemen and infantry were worn out with toil and hunger'. Nearly seventy miles had been covered in a week, a pace which was determined but hardly amounted to a forced march.[1] Now Edward was within reach of Stirling, he made plans for battle. Whatever the abilities of the king himself, Edward did not lack for experienced advisers. Aymer Valence earl of Pembroke, Henry Beaumont and Robert lord Clifford were veterans of the Scottish war who had fought with the king's father at Falkirk. Though from a younger generation, both Humphrey Bohun earl of Hereford and Gilbert Clare earl of Gloucester had also campaigned in Scotland before, as had many of the bannerets and knights in the army.

However, the plans for the army's advance had two flaws. Firstly, the political tensions of Edward's reign had not been wholly left behind in England. When the king gave out commands, he may have opened old wounds. In particular, Gilbert earl of Gloucester was given command of the vanguard, an appointment which, in one English account, led to a quarrel with Hereford, the hereditary constable of England. As neighbours in the Welsh march, the families of the two earls had waged private war against each other in the 1290s and they had taken different positions in recent disputes.[2] The king's favour to Gloucester may reflect that earl's recent support, but Hereford was also placed in the vanguard. If the two earls had recently quarrelled, this was hardly a move destined to foster unity and leadership. The second problem may have been that plans were laid on the expectation that Bruce would not fight. His reputation with English chroniclers was as a lurker in the hills. Faced by a large army, Edward and his captains probably expected Robert to move off ahead of them, as he had already done by leaving the Torwood for the New Park the day before. It may have been with this in mind that the English king would put Clifford and Beaumont in command of 300 men-at-arms with orders to ride ahead and reach Stirling Castle, apparently bypassing Robert's army.[3] Similar hopes of catching Bruce and forcing him to fight possibly explain other actions by his enemies on 23 June.

Bruce's intentions on 23 June are impossible to know. Barbour states that, by moving to the New Park, Robert intended to block the obvious route of Edward's host or force them to 'beneuth us ga and our the merrais pass'.[4] The New Park lay across the main road from the south into Stirling.[5] Both wooded park and road stood on top of a bank below which lay the 'merrais' or marsh, referred to as the Carse or the Pows running down to the Forth. This was regarded by contemporary writers as either a plain or a swamp, but it was clearly intersected by water courses, above all the Bannock Burn, described as 'a foul, deep, marshy stream'.[6] Barbour also describes King Robert ordering the digging of 'pottis', holes a foot across which were concealed with grass 'in a plane feld be the way', on open ground next to the road where he thought the 'Inglismen' would pass. The digging of these pots, which an English account says were actually in the 'wood', may have been designed to restrict the ability of the enemy to form up against Bruce's forces in the park, like the trenches dug at Loudoun Hill, but they played no further part in Barbour's account.[7] Instead the poem concentrates on the preparations of the army, describing the Scots hearing mass on the Sunday morning and Robert sending the 'smale folk' with the horses and supplies deep into the park.[8]

Accounts of coming events suggest that the main part of Bruce's army was formed up at the edge of the park on the fringe of the woods. The woods themselves would hardly have been suitable ground for an army equipped with long spears, but would give the Scottish foot a route through which to escape rapid pursuit by cavalry. However, understanding the precise nature, equipment, organisation and leadership of the army which stood in the New Park on 23 June 1314 throws up a number of gaps and problems. As was mentioned in the preceding chapter, the size of the host, like all medieval Scottish armies, is a matter of guesswork. Barbour, who reckons it was 30,000 strong (and the English 100,000), gives the only lengthy description of the force.[9] There are problems with what he says. Bruce orders his men 'to gang on fute to this fechting armyt bot in littil armyng'.[10] The decision to fight on foot is also a feature of English accounts, at least two of which say clearly that all were on foot, 'not one of them was on horseback'. One chronicle specifically states that they did this because, at the battle of Falkirk, the Scottish cavalry, 'seeing the vast multitude of the enemy horse, fled, leaving the footmen to die on the field'.[11] Clearly the Scottish army fought on foot, but later on Barbour produces a band of Scottish horsemen who play a vital role in the battle unmentioned by other writers.[12] The geographical origins and composition of Bruce's army is, irritatingly, obscure too. Barbour only identifies the make-up of the king's 'battail', saying that it included the 'men of Carrik . . . Arghile and of Kentyr and off the Ilis quharof wes syr Angus of Ile' and 'a mekill rout' from 'the plane land', the Lowlands.[13] Intriguingly, this suggests that Robert was again relying heavily on men from the Isles and west Highlands for the core of his host, but the lack of further information is frustrating. Assumptions about the other battles and their composition have frequently been made but are just guesswork.[14]

Even the basic organisation of the army is problematic. Barbour states that there were 'four bataillis' led by King Robert, Edward Bruce, Thomas Randolph and Walter Stewart, because of whose youth command really rested with James Douglas.[15] Though this account is accepted by most writers, it has recently been pointed out that it conflicts with almost all other near contemporary descriptions of Bannockburn.[16] In particular, three English chronicles from subsequent decades, all generally reliable in their discussion, the *Vita Edwardi Secundi*, the *Lanercost Chronicle* and *Scalachronica*, all specifically state that Bruce formed his army into three battles. This was the normal division of a medieval host into vanguard, main battle and rearguard.[17] Though there is not complete agreement among these accounts on the leaders

PLATE 1 *Taken from the manuscript of Walter Bower's* Scotichronicon *produced in the 1440s, this is the earliest representation of the battle of Bannockburn. (By permission of the Masters and Fellow of Corpus Christi College, Cambridge)*

PLATE 2 *A drawing of the wheel of fortune from an early fourteenth-century English bible, the Holkham Bible. The extreme shifts of fortune experienced by both Robert Bruce and Edward II of England were inevitably linked to turns of fortune's wheel by near-contemporary writers. (British Library, Add MS 47682)*

PLATE 3 *Built by the Maxwell family near the Solway Firth, Caerlaverock lay close to both Galloway and the main routes from England into south-west Scotland. King Robert captured the castle in 1312 and 1313, demolishing it to prevent its future use by his enemies. (Crown Copyright, Historic Scotland)*

PLATE 4 A copy of the coronation of St Edward as depicted on the walls of Edward I's painted chamber in the Palace of Westminster. The original painting and the palace were destroyed by fire in 1834. The making of a new king in Scotland was the most important ceremony for any medieval realm. (By permission of the Society of Antiquaries of London)

The story of Elijah and Ahaziah.
Vetusta Mon. Vol. VI. pl.xxx.

C.A. Stothard del.

PLATE 5 *Edward I chose to decorate the walls of his palace at Westminster with scenes from the Old Testament. The choice of the prophet Elijah and the downfall of King Ahaziah was an interesting one. Ahaziah's fall was due to his pride, a sin of which Edward was accused. Other scenes showed the Israelite hero Judas Maccabeus, who was later used as a model for Edward's enemy, Robert Bruce. (By permission of the Society of Antiquaries of London)*

PLATE 6 *This communal drinking cup known as the Bute mazer was probably made in the years after Bannockburn. The arms inside it are those of western adherents of King Robert, including his son-in-law Walter Stewart (between the lion's paws), James Douglas (to the left of Stewart's arms), John Menteith (to the right of Stewart) and Walter fitz Gilbert (to the left of Douglas). (000-190-001-147c Copyright National Museums of Scotland. Licensor www.scran.ac.uk)*

PLATE 7 *As the traitor who handed William Wallace to the English king and, eventually, a major backer of Robert Bruce, John Stewart of Menteith has troubled historians but probably acted like many of his peers. This effigy is at Inchmahome Priory. (Crown Copyright. Historic Scotland)*

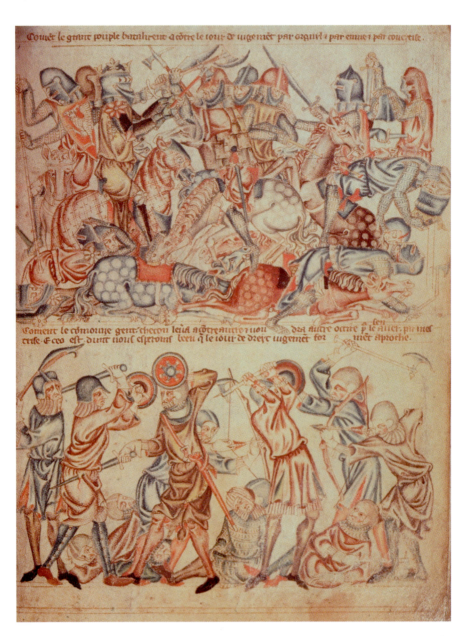

PLATE 8 *Taken from the pages of the Holkham Bible, these illustrations convey a sense of the carnage and confusion in medieval battles. The risks of such conflicts explain the reluctance of commanders to engage in battle in normal circumstances. (British Library, Add MS 47682)*

PLATE 9 *'The tower of the Proud Conqueror': Edward I's castle at Beaumaris was one of the great strongholds built by the English king as centres of his authority and symbols of his conquest in north Wales. (Cadw. Crown Copyright)*

PLATE 10 *The immense fortress of Caerphilly in the Clare lordship of Glamorgan was built as a display of marcher power. After the death of Gilbert Clare at Bannockburn, the castle was caught up in the Welsh rebellion of 1316. (Cadw. Crown Copyright)*

PLATE 11 *Sir Edmund Mauley from his family's window in York Minster. Mauley was steward of King Edward's household and a hardline supporter of the king. Though probably in the king's entourage in the battle, when Edward fled northwards Mauley was caught up in the southward rout and was drowned or crushed in the Bannock Burn. (Reproduced by kind permission of the Dean and Chapter of York)*

of these battles, it is striking that, while Edward Bruce and Thomas Randolph were earls with regional powers under King Robert by 1314, Douglas was a young man of limited importance.[18] With this in mind, it seems likely that the king, his brother and his nephew led the three battles of foot which made up the Scottish king's army in June 1314. Douglas and Stewart, whose role in Barbour's account is largely superfluous, were probably present but did not command major forces.[19] Similarly, if there were Scottish cavalry, perhaps under Douglas and the marischal of Scotland, Robert Keith, they were very few in number and the decision had probably been taken that the vast majority of knights and men-at-arms in the host should stand alongside the king and his earls in the battles of foot spearmen.[20]

Such difficulties with finding answers to even the most basic questions about the Scottish king's army reveal fundamental problems with forming a clear and coherent account of Bannockburn. Battles are the hardest kind of historical event to explain. They are confused and unpredictable, easy neither to describe nor understand for those involved in them, let alone by later writers. Medieval battles are especially so, given the nature of evidence, its scarcity and the usual distance in space and time from the events that are described.[21] Above all, it needs to be understood that medieval accounts of battles were not produced to allow a reconstruction of the events described by their audience. The purposes of such works tended to be more complicated than simple relation and explanation of fighting. The fullest account of Bannockburn was that produced in the 1370s by John Barbour in his epic poem, *The Bruce*. Though a cleric, Barbour was writing for an audience which included the king and his nobles. While claiming that his work was 'suthfast', truthful, Barbour was most concerned with 'plesance in heryng', the pleasure of his audience for his story. Where it seemed to add to the tale, Barbour was clearly happy to adjust or add to the facts to improve his narration of the heroism of Bruce and his captains. Such changes were clearly done with an eye to the 'ofspring' of these men in the 1370s.[22] This feature was especially true of James Douglas, whose son and nephew were both leading magnates and both keen to act as heirs to James's reputation. Perhaps using an existing set of tales about James, Barbour wove Douglas into his poem but, when this source failed to give James a suitable role in the actual fighting at Bannockburn, Barbour developed one for him.[23] Satisfying the audience and creating heroes for late-medieval Scotland took precedence over a narrow relation of events.

Concerns of this kind are not confined to works of chivalric romance like *The Bruce*. The account of the battle provided by *Vita Edwardi Secundi* is similarly dominated by the glorification of a participant. The focus of this text is on the young earl of Gloucester and the shame of his death, abandoned by almost all of his immense entourage. It makes Gloucester's death the key moment in the battle and is linked to the equally heroic and futile end of Giles Argentan, whose end is placed much later in the fight by all other writers.[24] The account of *Scalachronica*, which, uniquely, was written by a knight,

Thomas Gray, is also focused on one individual. Gray's father was in Henry
Beaumont's retinue in 1314 and was captured in the fighting on 23 June. Not
surprisingly, *Scalachronica* gives a much fuller description of the events of the
elder Thomas Gray's capture than to the decisive clash the next day.[25] In
general, chronicle accounts of the battle are concerned with ascribing causes
for victory and defeat rather than producing a forensic analysis of the fight.
The piety of the Scots and the justice of their cause are set against the pride
and boastfulness of the English and their king's lack of respect for his church
and his unwarlike character. Above all, the English defeat was because 'the
hand of the Lord was not with you'.

With this in mind it is optimistic of many of the long sequence of writers
on Bannockburn to expect that these fourteenth-century accounts of the
battle will provide unambiguous answers to the, wholly modern, set of questions they ask about the battle. Issues of formation, morale and equipment
were clearly understood by contemporaries, especially of those who had par-
ticipated in warfare like Sir Thomas Gray. However, trying to reconstruct the
precise organisation and deployment of the various parts of the two armies
when the basic division of these hosts is a matter of uncertainty is probably
not going to yield more than opinion. Accounts of the battle, filtered through
the minds of men unaccustomed to battle who had no direct knowledge of the
landscape, are equally an unreliable basis for the detailed mapping of the
various phases of Bannockburn. The *Lanercost Chronicle's* likely confusion of
Torwood for the New Park is only one example of this. Use of terms like '*beau
chaumpe*' (translated as open field) by Gray, 'plane feld', 'plane', 'merrais',
'Kers' and 'hard feld' by Barbour and reference to woods in all the sources have
led historians for nearly two centuries to locate the battle on various sites in
the lands south of Stirling. Detailed arguments have been constructed about
the terrain on these shaky foundations which largely ignore the implications
of changes in the landscape in the last 700 years. These include the draining of
the Carse during the eighteenth and nineteenth centuries, the removal or
addition of woodlands and extensive construction all over the area from
Stirling to the Bannockburn and beyond in the last hundred years. With this
in mind, conclusions relating current landscape to contemporary topograph-
ical references have to be treated with caution, as do maps which show not
merely Douglas's 'phantom division' but precise dispositions and movements
of the forces. Any credible account of the fighting of 23 and 24 June has to
recognise the limitations of the evidence and rest on the words of near contemporaries.[26]

What all these accounts make clear is that the English king's army advanced
northwards through most of the day. According to *Scalachronica*, Edward was
met on the march by the constable of Stirling, Philip Mowbray, who told him
that by approaching so close the king had relieved the castle. Mowbray pointed
out the strength of the enemy position and advised Edward to halt. Gray adds
that 'the young men would not stop, but held their course'. This charge is

implicitly aimed at the young earl of Gloucester in the vanguard.[27] However, it is unlikely that Edward, having assembled such an army and come so near, would have been content with a technical success in relieving Stirling. Stirling could only be defended in the long term and the king's lordship in Scotland restored with a more resounding victory against Bruce. It was at about this point, probably after dinner on 23 June, when the armies were two miles apart, that Clifford and Beaumont with 300 men-at-arms were sent ahead. *Lanercost's* account says this force was ordered 'to make a circuit of the wood to prevent the Scots escaping by flight', while both Gray and Barbour state that the cavalry was sent towards the castle.[28] Their move probably allowed them to attempt both. If they reached Stirling Castle, Clifford and Beaumont would unequivocally relieve the garrison and place a mounted force behind the Scottish host, making retreat more difficult. The route the cavalry took was across 'open fields', that is not through the woods, and, in Barbour's words, 'newth the New Park . . . and the kyrk', beneath the park and St Ninian's Church on top of the bank. This implies that Clifford and Beaumont were moving across the Carse, below kirk and park.[29]

Seeing this, King Robert turned to Thomas Randolph, who had been told to position his men 'besid the kyrk to kepe the way', telling him 'rudly that a rose of his chaplete was fallyn'. Barbour's tableau of king and earl may be fiction but it may also capture some sense of alarm in the host. Randolph, whose men were presumably on the eastern edge of the New Park, 'came out of the wood with his battle and took the open field'.[30] While his advance could hardly have cut off the cavalry from the rest of Edward's army as *Lanercost* says, Randolph may have deliberately offered a challenge designed to divert Clifford's advance and precipitate a fight. In *Scalachronica* there is a dispute between Beaumont and Thomas Gray over how to respond to the advance. Beaumont accuses Gray of cowardice and the latter then charges the Scots with only one companion, William Deincourt. Deincourt is killed and Gray unhorsed and captured.[31] In the subsequent fight, the English cavalry, unsupported by foot, found it impossible to break up Randolph's men in their schiltrom. Barbour's dramatic account of the fight describes the cavalry surrounding the Scots, impaling their horses on the spears and being reduced to hurling swords and maces at the enemy who respond by throwing spears and even darting out of their ranks to stab the mounts of the enemy.[32] At the end of this savage, but probably brief, encounter the Scottish battle defeated Beaumont and Clifford's cavalry 'utterly. Some of these fled to the castle, others to the king's army.'[33]

At around the same time a second, less intense clash occurred further west on the line of what Gray calls 'the woodland road'.[34] King Edward's main army was now approaching the New Park where the battle of King Robert was forming up. According to Barbour, it was at this point, when he was in sight of the enemy, that Edward halted to discuss whether to camp for the night or to prepare for an immediate attack on Bruce's host.[35] Either unaware of this or disregarding it, the vanguard under the earls of Gloucester and Hereford pressed on to the edge of the New Park. The *Vita Edwardi Secundi*, which was well-informed about Gloucester's actions, states that 'the Scots were seen straggling under the trees as if in flight'.[36] This may have encouraged the earls to advance. In particular, Henry Bohun, a kinsman of Hereford, with a contingent of Welsh troops probably from the earl's lordship of Brecon, set off 'a bow-schote' ahead in pursuit. However, entering the trees he found King Robert forming up his men. While the *Vita* says Bohun then tried to escape, in Barbour's famous account, 'Henry the Boune the worthi' charged the king who was mounted on a 'littil palfray', not a trained warhorse. 'Schyr Hanry myssit the noble king' in his charge and Robert 'raucht him a dint' which cut his head open to the brains. Bohun's squire and, probably, the Welsh were overwhelmed by the sudden advance of the king's battle.[37] It may have been in the sudden retreat which followed that Gloucester was 'thrown from his horse'.[38]

The results of these clashes are not entirely clear. The *Vita Edwardi*, which confuses them, states that 'though our men long pursue the Scots, many are killed on each side'. More plausibly, Barbour describes the enemy vanguard falling back rapidly when confronted by King Robert's battle but losing few men. According to *The Bruce*, the effect of this rebuff was to persuade Edward to avoid a direct confrontation with the enemy until the morning. Plans were therefore made for the army to camp for the night. Barbour places this camp 'doun in the Kers', on the low-lying Carselands to the east of the road. He describes the English crossing the streams, using thatch taken from nearby houses to bridge them. They are assisted in this by the men from Stirling Castle who bring windows and doors, presumably from the burgh, to allow them to cross. By daybreak, Barbour says that the army had 'passyt our' the streams and the horse were on 'the hard feld'. This account is supported in essentials by English chronicles, especially *Scalachronica*. Gray describes how 'the king's army . . . had already left the woodland road and had come to a plain near the river Forth, beyond the Bannockburn, a foul, deep, marshy stream'. On this plain, the English halted.[39]

The purpose of King Edward's decision to move onto the Carse and the route the army took is a matter of conjecture. Rather than a retreat to await battle on the apparently open ground south of the Bannock burn, an evening march onto the Carse and across the burn looks suspiciously like an advance towards Stirling which followed close to the route taken earlier by Beaumont and Clifford. Barbour's account suggests that by taking his army down the slope Edward made full contact with his garrison in Stirling Castle. Is it possible that, though they had been driven off, Clifford and Beaumont's advance had shown the anxiety of the Scottish army and its leaders about the enemy moving to the east, around their flank? If the vanguard's experience at the entrance to the New Park proved the difficulty of forcing Bruce and his host from the woodland, Randolph had shown that they would risk battle to prevent the English crossing the Carse. The English king and his leading lords and advisers may still have been expecting Bruce to retreat, rather than risk a full battle in the open. Such an expectation lies behind most of their moves on 23 June. The dispatch of cavalry round the New Park and the belief of the vanguard that the Scots were in flight both suggest that the main concern of Edward and his captains was to hinder Bruce's escape. If their confidence had dipped by evening, the decision to advance down onto the Carse may have been a conscious challenge to Robert, designed to force him to retreat or, at last, bring him to battle. The risks for the English king's army in this plan would become clear in the morning.

THE SECOND DAY (MONDAY, 24 JUNE)

Given the time of year, there must have been little real darkness. Barbour implies that the advance of the English host across the Carse and over the Bannock burn was completed not long 'befor the day'. The army halted when the horse had reached the 'hard feld', a phrase which suggests they had left the Carse, or perhaps just the marshy banks of the burn. This movement may account for the English 'spending the whole night sleepless', but as *Vita Edwardi Secundi* states there were also fears that the Scots would attack by night, presumably encouraged by the series of nocturnal escalades which Bruce and his captains had launched against Edward's castles.[40] Though one English account speaks of the army's drunken arrogance, most chronicles speak of anxiety, *Scalachronica* describing the force as being 'in a very poor state from the day's fighting'. Gray compares this with the atmosphere among Bruce's men in the New Park. 'The Scots in the wood reckoned they had done well enough in the day's fighting', he states. However, he goes on to add that, as a result of their success, they 'were on the point of decamping to the Lennox, a more defensible country'.[41] Barbour implies the same situation when he has Robert ask his lords whether, after the 'fayr beginning' they have achieved in repulsing the vanguard and 'yone othyr joly rout' (Clifford and Beaumont's company), they should fight or leave.[42] This seems to confirm that, as late as the night between the two days of the battle, Bruce was still considering a withdrawal. The Lennox was friendly ground and a move there would take his army away from the English whose rough handling on the previous day would probably make them cautious in any pursuit. The successes won on the Sunday would allow Robert to claim victory and ride out Edward's subsequent campaign from the Lennox, ready to counterattack as he had done in 1310 and 1311 and would do again in 1319 and 1322.

On the other hand, a clear chance of victory lay before the Scots. Barbour has the lords reply to King Robert with a single voice, telling him to prepare for battle until 'we have maid our countre fre'.[43] *Scalachronica* gives a different account of the decision. Bruce's planned retreat is halted when Alexander Seton, who was in Edward's army, crossed 'secretly' to the New Park during the night. Seton told the king that 'the English have lost heart and are defeated' and expected a 'sudden, open assault'. It was Seton's advice which persuaded Robert and his lords to prepare such an assault in the morning.[44] These tales of events during the night inevitably rest heavily on foreknowledge of the 'calamitous day' to come, but the events of Sunday afternoon and evening had clearly tested the loyalties of some in the two armies.[45] Seton, who had remained in Edward II's allegiance during the ravages of recent warfare, responded to an apparent sense of impending defeat and changed sides. Bruce's party was not immune to such tensions. Though mentioned only at the end of his account of the battle and hardly fitting in with the overall tone of his description, Barbour relates that during the same night a treacherous attack was launched on Robert's camp at Cambuskenneth Abbey by David Strathbogie earl of Atholl. Atholl was a late and reluctant adherent of Bruce, only joining the king in 1312, but he was constable of Scotland in 1314 and his defection was a major embarrassment to Robert. It may have been more than this. Atholl killed one knight and many other men and seized victuals which would have been of value to either side. His desertion may have been due to a personal grievance against Edward Bruce, as Barbour suggests, but it suggested that loyalty to Robert could evaporate under pressure too.[46] Had Bruce lost the next day, Atholl's defection would be better known and be held up as the first sign of the divisions which undermined the king's effort.

Dawn on 24 June, the feast of the Nativity of St John the Baptist, must have come at about four in the morning. All accounts agree that it was at daybreak that the Scots came out of the trees of the New Park and began to form up. The *Vita Edwardi* and Barbour add that they had a brief meal and it was probably at this point that Robert knighted some of his followers, among them Walter Stewart and James Douglas.[47] It may also have been at this time, as the *Vita* says, that Bruce 'briefed his company'. Though the speech put into the king's mouth by Barbour was probably a poetic device, such addresses were not unusual. The promise, which Barbour quotes, that the heirs of all killed fighting for Bruce in the battle would receive their lands without payment of relief, a charge owed by a tenant on the inheritance of estates, or wardship, the rights to all revenues of an estate while the heir was a minor, does ring true. A similar concession would be made to those who fought at the battle of Harlaw in 1411 and before Flodden in 1513, designed to encourage men that their estates would be unencumbered should they be slain.[48] However, Robert's other words may have focused more on the practical orders for the fight, rather than the exhortation to defend liberty quoted by Barbour. After this the Scots formed up, almost certainly in the three battles described by Thomas Gray, the *Vita* and *Lanercost*, and began their advance onto 'the plane'.

At the emergence of Bruce and his men from the park, Edward's army also began to form up. As all the main sources indicate that the English had not rested but remained on the march or at arms through the night, the force was hardly taken by surprise. The *Vita Edwardi* records another divisive English council where the king was advised to refuse battle on that day by his 'experienced' captains, this time including the earl of Gloucester, but 'the younger men' challenged this as 'lethargic and cowardly'. Though such debates between rash youths and cautious veterans are a common theme in chronicle accounts of battle, if such arguments were taking place round the king, involving the leaders of the host, they may explain the apparent problems experienced by the army in forming up, problems which would become fatal. Gray states that the English 'mounted on horseback in great consternation', and though *Lanercost* says that 'archers were thrown forward before the line' by both sides, any such event is unnoticed by other writers and had no discernible effect on the battle.[49] More revealing is Barbour's remark that, while the Scots were in 'gud aray', the English 'war nocht arayit on sic maner for all thar bataillis samyn wer in a schilthrum'. Here the term schiltrom is employed to described a dense mass of men with no clear divisions or organisation. Barbour speculated whether this formation was intended to overawe the Scots or was due to 'the gret straitnes of the place', the confined ground on which the English stood.[50] However, he is clearly presenting the English forming up in a disorganised fashion and on unsuitable ground.

The reason for the apparent problem lay only partly with continued signs of debate and uncertainty among King Edward's councillors. The real cause lay with Bruce's actions. In the account of Thomas Gray, the only fighting man to give an early impression of Bannockburn, the Scots 'came out of the wood in three battles, and steadily held their course towards the English army' and then 'the Scots came quickly lined in schiltroms, and attacked the English battles, which were crushed together'. His clear summary is echoed in other sources. In the *Vita Edwardi* the Scots 'advanced like a thick-set hedge', while *Lanercost* says that 'they had so arranged their army that two columns went abreast in advance of the third'. Interestingly, Barbour describes a surprised English reaction. 'Quhen the king of Ingland swa the Scottis . . . takand the hard feyld sa openly and apon fute he had ferly [he was astonished] and said, "Quhat, will yone Scottis fycht?"' Barbour suggests that Edward still did not believe the Scots would fight in the open.[51] Edward's surprise may have been that, unlike the previous day, Robert would risk bringing his full army out into the 'hard feyld' away from the protection of the woods and where the English cavalry could charge. However, by advancing across this ground, Bruce may have recognised that he was denying his enemy both time and space to form up their large numbers of foot and horse.

It was the steady approach of the Scots, apparently broken only when the whole army knelt in a brief prayer, which led to the English men-at-arms mounting 'in great consternation'.[52] Barbour implies that, the night before, the cavalry had camped ahead of the main army on the 'hard feld'. If this was the ground over which the enemy now advanced, the cavalry were being given little room to make a full charge. Recognition of this may explain the *Vita*'s stories of King Edward rebuking Gilbert earl of Gloucester and recriminations between Gloucester and Hereford. The leaders of the vanguard, who had done poorly on the previous day, were now being caught out again. The *Vita* states that, according to 'some', while Gloucester disputed with Hereford, 'the Scottish forces were approaching rapidly' and 'Earl Gilbert dashed forward in disorder, seeking to carry off the glory of the first clash'. The headstrong charge of the young earl is a good story but, in his own version, the author of the *Vita* presents Gloucester's ranks being 'vigorously attacked' by 'the first division of Scots'. 'The earl withstood [them] manfully, time and again he penetrated their wedge', but 'at a sudden rush of Scots, the earl's horse is killed and the earl falls to the ground. . . . Without a defender and burdened by the weight of its [the horse's] body, the earl cannot easily rise, and . . . he was killed.' The *Vita* places the blame, not on its doomed hero, the young earl, but on his men who failed to save him when his horse fell.[53] Though written with Gloucester's posthumous reputation in mind, the description also suggests that, though the attack of the vanguard may have been poorly organised, Earl Gilbert was reacting to the vigorous advance of the Scottish battle. The fighting in which he was killed may have been intended to halt the advance of Bruce's first two battles.

This clash between the English vanguard and the Scottish battle under Edward Bruce is also described by Barbour, who goes on to chart the entry of Randolph's force into a general attack on the enemy. The account he provides with, first, James Douglas and, then, King Robert entering the fray is dramatic and exciting with blows being struck, blood flowing, rich clothes being trampled and knights tumbling to the ground. However, the sense develops of a literary set piece being unrolled, with the heroes of Barbour's narrative all taking their due place on the stage. It is amid this story that the poet unleashes the Scottish cavalry in their charge. While the battles are engaged with the enemy, Barbour describes the English archers shooting so fast that if they had continued 'it had bene hard to Scottismen'. To stop them King Robert sent 500 armoured horsemen under Robert Keith who rode them down, allowing the Scottish archers to begin to cause losses among the enemy who then grew confused.[54] This episode is described nowhere else and seems to contradict what all the writers, including Barbour, state about the Scots all fighting on foot. It is hard to see how the English archers could have managed to shoot once the armies were engaged or how, if they did, the Scottish cavalry could find room to charge, which Edward's horse were not able to use to make an attack of their own. Instead, the episode probably arises from a minor event, either during the battle or in the campaign, or, as with at least one story in *The Bruce*, from another time altogether. Its purpose was, perhaps, to give a role to Robert Keith, whose family retained their status in the 1370s and may have provided stories to be included in the poem.[55]

The understandably sombre accounts of the battle produced in near-contemporary English chronicles describe the growing difficulties of King Edward's army in more credible terms. The *Lanercost Chronicle* states that 'the English in the rear could not reach the Scots because the leading division was in the way, nor could they do anything to help themselves', while Gray explains that 'the English battles . . . were crushed together so that they could not move against' the Scots. By advancing rapidly and successfully forcing back the English vanguard, King Robert's battles had forced the much larger army of King Edward to fight in a cramped piece of ground, beside or behind which lay the 'Bannockburn ditch'. The Scots seem to have continued to press forward, perhaps, though this is nowhere stated, aided by higher ground and pushed English cavalry and foot into a confused mass. Gray reports that 'the men in the English rear fell back on the Bannockburn ditch, falling over one another' and under this pressure the army 'began to flee'.[56]

Amid the growing chaos, the position of King Edward was now at risk. All the accounts agree that the men assigned to guard the king, holding the reins of his horse, led Edward away. Though the *Vita Edwardi*, inevitably, makes the king's retreat a reaction to the rout of Gloucester's men, the other sources place it later after a sustained fight between all of the Scottish battles and the front of the English host. There is disagreement, however, about the English king's conduct. Gray describes Edward being led off 'against his will' and striking out with his mace at Scottish knights who tried to stop his horse which was wounded, while John Trokelow speaks of Edward fighting 'like a lion'. However, in the *Vita* the king flees with 'two hundred knights and more who had neither drawn their swords or struck a blow', while *Lanercost* describes the flight of Edward and his companions as being 'to their perpetual shame'.[57] While the hostile accounts are perhaps a natural product of anger at the defeat, it would not be surprising if Edward, like many of his men, was caught up in the rout without coming within reach of the enemy. One of those responsible for guarding the king, Giles Argentan, 'a renowned knight', abandoned Edward's care at this point and turned back into the fight, charging at the Scottish vanguard and meeting a heroic death. The king, now probably in the care of Aymer Valence, headed north towards Stirling Castle, perhaps confirming their position to the east of the New Park.[58]

King Edward also decided to flee northwards to escape the fate of the rest of the army further south. As the English wavered, Bruce's battles continued to advance, in Barbour's tale crying 'on thaim, on thaim, on thaim, thai faile'. According to *Lanercost*, the English were pressed by the Scots into the 'great ditch called Bannockburn'. 'Many nobles fell into it with their horses in the crush . . . and many were never able to extricate themselves from the ditch.'[59] Abandoned by their king and with 'thar fayis thaim pressyt fast', the enemy advancing, the English broke, says Barbour, 'and fled sa fast . . . to the water of Forth . . . and Bannokburne betwix the brays', where many drowned. So many, in fact, that the burn could be crossed dry-footed. Caught between the enemy and the 'slyk' and deep ditch, the slaughter may have been terrible, with the advancing Scottish battles now joined by Barbour's 'small folk' leaving the camp to take part in the pursuit and plunder.[60] In the words of the *Vita*, 'amongst all their misfortunes this one thing at least turned to the advantage of our army, that while our people sought safety in flight, a great part of the Scottish army turned to plunder'. The flower of the English nobility and their king did not come to war without comforts and the *Vita* valued the goods, the horses, the arms and armour, the rich cloths and golden plates and vessels taken by the Scots on the field at £200,000.[61] For men from a poor land who had endured years of war, such rewards would hardly be passed over and, Barbour says, 'many man mychty wes maid off the riches that thair thai fand'. For the 'laddis, swanys and rangaill' who followed the host, the ordinary spear-men and even the knights and nobles in the army this plunder was the real fruit of the victory.[62]

ROUT AND PURSUIT (24–5 JUNE 1314)

The immediate pursuit of the English host by the bulk of Bruce's soldiers ended at the baggage train, allowing many of their enemies to leave the field. However, it would prove another matter for these fugitives to get out of Scotland. In one case, Robert's men mounted a dogged chase. King Edward had fled to Stirling Castle, only to be turned away at the gates. Barbour, who writes well of the constable, Philip Mowbray, has him warn his lord that he will face siege and capture if he takes refuge in the castle. Though the *Vita* confirms this, it also suggests that Mowbray was accused of treason by some English.[63] Turning south, the king passed to the west of the New Park and the Torwood, riding for Linlithgow. English accounts record a hot pursuit, which Barbour attributes to James Douglas with sixty mounted men. Despite its hero, Barbour's story is detailed and credible. Douglas, with too few men to attack King Edward's company, hounded them past Linlithgow, killing or cap-turing stragglers and shouting insults at them. Edward halted at Winchburgh, having covered over twenty miles from Stirling, before riding on through Lothian until he reached Dunbar, the nearest castle still in the hands of his adherents.[64] Though Earl Patrick of Dunbar was to submit to Robert within days, he acted honourably to his current lord, allowing Edward access to his castle and, according to *Scalachronica*, 'leaving the place with all his men' so that the king would have 'no doubt or suspicion' of treachery.[65] Taking to 'an open boat', Edward and 'his chosen followers', among them Hugh Despenser, Henry Beaumont and, perhaps, Aymer Valence, sailed south to Bamburgh. The bulk of those who had guarded the king on his flight were left to make their own way. 'Holding bravely together' they came 'safe . . . through ambushes' and rejoined Edward at Berwick.[66]

Most of those fleeing the field were less successful in escaping Scotland. Barbour includes a revealing story which relates that a great many fugitives headed north, like their king, to the refuge of Stirling Castle. 'The craggis . . . about the castell' were packed with men seeking a safe haven and their

FIGURE 6.2 *The great tower at Bothwell was the basis for an Edwardian garrison between 1301 and 1314. Seen as a refuge by a group of lords fleeing Bannockburn, it rapidly became a trap due to the treachery of its keeper, Walter fitz Gilbert. (Crown Copyright. Historic Scotland)*

numbers were so great that King Robert feared they would regroup and renew the fighting. Barbour says that Robert kept a force together nearby against this possibility. In reality there was no fight left in these men, and it was probably early on 25 June that Philip Mowbray rode out and surrendered Stirling Castle, at the same time recognising Robert as his rightful king.[67] The largest party which escaped from the field was numbered by *Lanercost* at 600 men-at-arms and 1,000 foot. Its leaders were the earl of Hereford, Ingeram Umfraville, his kinsman Robert Umfraville earl of Angus, and John Segrave. These were major figures. The last two had been lieutenants of Scotland for Edward II, Ingeram was a mainstay of Scottish opposition to Bruce and Hereford was a great marcher magnate and English baron. They led their large company, not through Lothian, but south-west into Clydesdale, seeking to reach Bothwell Castle which was held by a friendly garrison. However, unlike Earl Patrick, its constable, Walter fitz Gilbert, determined to exploit the situation. Barbour describes how Walter, a Scottish knight, allowed the leaders and a company of fifty men within the walls, but took care to disperse them in different buildings.[68] Word was then sent to Robert that 'the riche erle of Herford' was at Bothwell and the king dispatched his brother with 'a gret menye'. Walter agreed to surrender the castle and hand over his guests to Bruce. The rest of the, now leaderless, band of fugitives sought to escape south but few reached home. 'Many . . . were taken wandering round the castle, and many were killed', while Barbour estimates that three-quarters of them were slain or captured.[69] Across southern Scotland other bands were straggling towards England, harried as they went. A few made it. Both *Lanercost* and Barbour record the escape of a 'gret rout off Walis-men', probably led by Maurice Berkeley, a retainer of Aymer Valence. The Welsh, who were easily recognised because of their near nakedness, travelled swiftly but still lost many men before reaching England.[70] Stories in English chronicles told of women capturing knights and complained that 'the inhabitants of the countryside, who had previously feigned peace, now butchered our men' until ordered by King Robert to hold them prisoner. Such tales speak of the harsh revenge of peasants on soldiers during late June and early July 1314.[71]

While Bruce's army lost only two knights, the Lothian landowner William Vipond and the earl of Ross's son Walter, the numbers of those killed in King Edward's army are impossible to calculate.[72] Among the nobility in the host the battle had taken a heavy toll. Barbour records that 200 pairs of red spurs were taken from dead knights on the battlefield, a fact which recalled the stripping of golden spurs from the French nobles slain by the Flemings at Courtrai in 1302. The estimate of 200 knightly dead may not be an exaggeration. The *Annales Londonensis* gives the names of thirty-seven dead knights and a chronicle from a friary in Dorset records eighty named dead. At the head of all the lists was the name of Gilbert Clare earl of Gloucester.[73] As a great landowner and as the nephew of King Edward, Gloucester was seen as the most notable of the slain. He was also a kinsman and the brother-in-law of King Robert. Robert mourned Gloucester's death and had his body carried to a church and appointed men to stand vigil over the corpse.[74] Many of the knightly dead may have fallen with Gloucester in the clash between the two vanguards. The *Lanercost Chronicle* says that the steward of King Edward's household, Edmund Mauley, and one of the king's baronial critics, Payn Tibetot, were also killed there, as was the young John Comyn. Among the other dead was Robert lord Clifford, whose long participation in the Scottish wars had finally proved fatal.[75] There were plenty of other northern knights among the dead and prisoners and their loss may have increased the problems of the region in the coming years, while the victory of Bruce also claimed the lives of some of the Scots who fought against him. As well as John Comyn, his kinsman Edmund Comyn of Kilbride was slain, as was the Annandale knight James Torthorwald and the son of Dugald MacDouall.[76] While the bodies of Gloucester and Clifford were apparently handed back to their kin without ransom, the bulk of the dead were buried on the field, 'the gret lordis in haly place honorabilly' and the rest flung into 'gret pyttis'.[77]

Of greater value to King Robert were the captives. As well as those like Hereford, Angus and Segrave who were taken at Bothwell were many others captured on the field or in the days that followed. Among this group were many of the king's household. The keeper of the privy seal, Roger Northburgh, was captured with two of his clerks with the seal still in their hands. Another clerical captive was the Carmelite friar Robert Baston, who had come north in the royal entourage to write verses to celebrate Edward's deeds but who was made by the Scots to compose a poem which related the defeat of the English army.[78] The *Vita Edwardi Secundi* says that 'more than 500 were thought to be dead, but were taken captive and later ransomed', among them powerful marcher barons like John Giffard and Roger Mortimer of Chirk, and English lords like William Latimer.[79] The ransoms of these rich nobles added to the plunder to make Bannockburn a hugely profitable victory for the Scots and their king. As will be discussed, in some cases English prisoners were exchanged for Scottish captives and, according to different stories, Robert released some prisoners without ransom. The veteran Yorkshire knight Marmaduke Thweng, and Ralph Monthermer, Gloucester's stepfather, were reputedly both set free without payment. In English accounts as well as Barbour, Robert receives praise for his behaviour in victory.[80] He and his followers would hardly have been treated as generously had they been defeated. This was the point Bruce was making, however. Rather than pure chivalry, Robert was showing that he was no rebel leader, lurking in moors and mosses. He had proved himself to be a king capable of winning on the plain field of battle, putting his skill and his cause to the ultimate test in contemporary eyes. In victory he behaved as a king, honouring the fallen and respecting the rules of war between sovereign realms.

Though respect may have been accorded to Bruce, the overwhelming tone of English accounts of Bannockburn is shock and remorse. The *Vita Edwardi Secundi* captures this mood. 'Oh! Famous race unconquered through the ages, why do you, who used to conquer knights, flee from foot soldiers? At Berwick, Dunbar and Falkirk, you carried off the victory, and now you have turned your backs to Scottish infantry.'[81] Comparison is made, and perhaps consolation sought, by reference to the battle of Courtrai in 1302, 'when the flower of France fell before the Flemings'. The parallels between this battle and the fight at Bannockburn also occurred to Thomas Gray in *Scalachronica*, who says that 'the Scots had taken the example of the Flemings, who had previously defeated the forces of France at Courtrai'.[82] As a fighting man Gray's view must carry weight, but the Scots had traditionally fought on foot and his real concern may be to emphasise that, unlike his own experience during the 1340s and 1350s, the English nobility in 1314 mounted to meet the enemy. The value of the link with Courtrai is clearest in its social and psychological context. The narratives of both battles stress the superior wealth, numbers, arms and social standing of the defeated armies and the piety and simple strengths of the victors. Descriptions of both also describe the doomed host holding councils where cautious advice is rejected in favour of rash attack. Such themes are staples of battle descriptions and much of this may come from literary concerns.[83]

However, Courtrai and Bannockburn, along with other contemporary clashes, seized attention as victories won by footmen over the flower of a great kingdom's chivalry. As such they were events which threatened to upset the perceived natural order. In truth, at both Courtrai and Bannockburn the foot soldiers, burghers and peasants were led by nobles and Bruce's behaviour after the battle stressed his membership of the noble elite and adherence to its rules.[84]

Does the basic similarity between the battles, observed by contemporaries, mark these fights as part of a new era of warfare in which the supremacy of the mounted knight on the battlefield was assumed? In reality, such assumptions were always unrealistic and may have owed more to social values than practical warfare. The two battles do have some points in common. At Courtrai the Flemings restricted the ground available to the enemy cavalry by forming behind ditches and with a river to their own rear. The Flemish fought as dense bodies of foot and their solidity and refusal to break repulsed the attacks launched on them by the French men-at-arms. The final rout of these horsemen led to many being trapped or drowned in the watery ditch in front of the Flemings. Like Bruce's army at Bannockburn, Flemish success rested on the ability of well-formed foot with polearms to withstand the unsupported attack of armoured horsemen, especially on difficult ground.[85] Randolph's repulse of Clifford and Beaumont on the first day at Bannockburn and, still more, Loudoun Hill in 1307, were clashes of this type. However, the two-day battle at Bannockburn was a more complex affair. While Courtrai occurred less than two months after the outbreak of a rebellion in Flanders against French rule, Bannockburn came after seven years of warfare between Bruce and his enemies. The experience of this conflict had an effect on the course and outcome of the battle. Past campaigns had not led Edward II and his advisers to think that they would win an easy success against Robert, as the French may have thought before Courtrai. The setbacks against Bruce since 1307 would hardly have bred overconfidence in the outcome of the campaign in 1314.

However, Robert's conduct of war may well have led English leaders to assume he would be difficult to bring to battle in the open. The decisions of the English king and his captains on 23 June, in seeking to bypass Bruce with a cavalry force, in mistakenly thinking he was falling back and, finally, that in advancing onto the Carse they would either encourage the enemy to retreat or fight, all rested on this belief in Robert's elusiveness. That by coming to rest on ground which was cramped and hemmed in to flank and rear the English leaders were giving Bruce a major advantage, does not seem to have been considered. The next day, there seemed to be an equal assumption that, if he fought, Robert would merely stand on the defensive, like the Flemings at Courtrai. This had been Scottish practice at Loudoun Hill and Falkirk and the ability of Robert's men to advance without losing cohesion may have been a product of their increased skill after long periods in arms.

Several contemporary accounts of the battle state that the Scots made an unbroken advance, forcing the English to fight where their numbers and horsemen proved to be, not decisive advantages, but additional problems. In later battles, like Dupplin Moor, Halidon Hill and Neville's Cross, Scottish armies attempted to advance in the same manner and close with the English. These tactics were modelled on Robert's at Bannockburn but met with disaster. Bruce exercised a much clearer grasp of the situation than his heirs. As during the previous seven years, Robert showed himself a master at recognising his enemies' weaknesses, knowing when and how to fight them and how to employ his own limited forces to best effect. There is no reason to think that Robert was following a master plan during these two days in late June. Instead his achievement was one of flexibility of response, confidence in his lords and his men and, above all, the art of timing in battle.

NOTES

1. *Vita Edwardi*, 89. In 1300 Edward I's army had only managed about seven miles a day, while in 1346 on the Crécy campaign the English army covered from ten to fifteen miles on a single day. Fifteen miles was about as much as a full army with baggage train could possibly manage (Prestwich, *Armies and Warfare*, 130–1).
2. 'The Chronicle of Robert of Reading', in *Flores Historiarum*, ed. H. Luard, 3 vols (Rolls series, 1890), iii, 158; *Vita Edwardi*, 93; Morris, *Welsh Wars*, 224–7.
3. *Scalachronica*, ed. King, 73.
4. *The Bruce*, ed. Duncan, 419.
5. For the location of the New Park, see Barrow, *Robert Bruce*, 212–14; *The Bruce*, ed. Duncan, 441; T. Miller, *The Site of the Battle of Bannockburn* (London, 1931).
6. *Scalachronica*, ed. King, 75; Barrow, *Robert Bruce*, 211–12.
7. *The Bruce*, ed. Duncan, 423; *Scalachronica*, ed. King, 73.
8. *The Bruce*, ed. Duncan, 427.
9. *The Bruce*, ed. Duncan, 410, 419.
10. *The Bruce*, ed. Duncan, 419.
11. *Scalachronica*, ed. King, 75; *Vita Edwardi*, 91; John de Trokelowe, *Annales*, 84.
12. *The Bruce*, ed. Duncan, 481–3.
13. *The Bruce*, ed. Duncan, 421–3.
14. See for example, Barrow, *Robert Bruce*, 210. Barrow acknowledges that his suggestion that Edward Bruce led men from the south-west, Stewart from 'Strathclyde' and Randolph from the north rests on 'commonsense reasoning, not contemporary evidence'. However, more recent works have assigned the battles geographical characters as if a proven fact (A. Nusbacher, *The Battle of Bannockburn, 1314* (Stroud, 2000), 85; P. Armstrong, *Bannockburn 1314* (Oxford, 2002), 28).
15. *The Bruce*, ed. Duncan, 421–3.
16. S. Cameron, 'Keeping the Customer Satisfied: Barbour's *Bruce* and a Phantom Division at Bannockburn', in E. J. Cowan and D. Gifford (eds), *The Polar Twins* (Edinburgh, 1999), 61–74.
17. *Vita Edwardi*, 91; *Scalachronica*, 75; *Chron. Lanercost*, 207.
18. Cameron, 'Phantom Division', 62, 65–6; Brown, *Black Douglases*, 18–20; S. Vathjunker, 'A study of the career of Sir James Douglas: the Historical record versus Barbour's *Bruce*' (unpublished PhD thesis, University of Aberdeen, 1992).

19. Cameron, 'Phantom Division', 66–7.
20. Keith and Douglas act as Robert's scouts before the battle and Douglas leads the pursuit of King Edward after it, leading Duncan to suggest a role for Douglas as the leader of cavalry (*The Bruce*, ed. Duncan, 429, 452, 509).
21. J. Keegan, *The Face of Battle* (London, 1976), 13–116.
22. *The Bruce*, ed. Duncan, 16–32, 47, 773; Cameron, 'Phantom Division', 70–1.
23. Cameron, 'Phantom Division'; Brown, *Black Douglases*, 53–75.
24. *Vita Edwardi*, 91–3.
25. *Scalachronica*, ed. King, 73–5.
26. For such descriptions and depictions, see J. E. Morris, *Bannockburn* (Cambridge, 1914); W. M. Mackenzie, *The Battle of Bannockburn* (Glasgow, 1913); W. Seymour, *Battles in Britain* (London, 1975), 2 vols, 1, 83–104; W. W. C. Scott, *Bannockburn Revealed* (Rothesay, 2000); A. Nusbacher, *The Battle of Bannockburn, 1314*, 101–44; Armstrong, *Bannockburn*, 44–72, 91.
27. *Scalachronica*, ed. King, 73. This debate probably came after Beaumont and Clifford had been sent north.
28. *Lanercost*, 207; *Scalachronica*, ed. King, 73; *The Bruce*, ed. Duncan, 431. Though *Lanercost* talks of the Scots being in the Torwood, Barbour and Gray make it clear that Clifford was to bypass the New Park.
29. *Scalachronica*, ed. King, 73; *The Bruce*, ed. Duncan, 431–3.
30. *The Bruce*, ed. Duncan, 427, 433.
31. *Scalachronica*, ed. King, 75; *Chron. Lanercost*, 207.
32. *The Bruce*, ed. Duncan, 433–5.
33. *Scalachronica*, ed. King, 75.
34. Barbour puts this clash after Randolph's fight with the cavalry but *Scalachronica* reverses this order and *Vita Edwardi* only really mentions the fight between Robert and the vanguard under Gloucester (*The Bruce*, ed. Duncan, 449; *Scalachronica*, 75; *Vita Edwardi*, 89–91).
35. *The Bruce*, ed. Duncan, 449.
36. *Vita Edwardi*, 91.
37. *Vita Edwardi*, 91; *The Bruce*, ed. Duncan, 449–51.
38. *Vita Edwardi*, 92; *The Bruce*, ed. Duncan, 451–3.
39. *Scalachronica*, ed. King, 75. *Lanercost* also makes clear that Edward's army had crossed the Bannock burn (*Chron. Lanercost*, 208).
40. *The Bruce*, ed. Duncan, 467–9; *Vita Edwardi*, 91.
41. *Scalachronica*, ed. King, 75.
42. *The Bruce*, ed. Duncan, 457.
43. *The Bruce*, ed. Duncan, 457–9.
44. *Scalachronica*, ed. King, 75.
45. *Chron. Lanercost*, 207.
46. *The Bruce*, ed. Duncan, 505–7; *R.R.S.*, v, no. 41; A. Ross, 'Men for all seasons? The Strathbogie Earls of Atholl and the Wars of Independence, c.1290–1335, 2', *Northern Scotland*, 21 (2001), 1–15.
47. *The Bruce*, ed. Duncan, 469; *Vita Edwardi*, 91. The knighting of Douglas only in 1314 further supports the idea that he was too junior a figure to be given effective command of one of the army's battles (Cameron, 'Phantom Division', 65–6).
48. *The Bruce*, ed. Duncan, 465; *Vita Edwardi*, 91. For the Act of Twizelhaugh in 1513, see N. Macdougall, *James IV* (Edinburgh, 1989), 272. For a similar promise for those at Harlaw (which was probably granted after the battle), see *Registrum Episcopatus Aberdonensis*, Spalding Club, 2 vols (Aberdeen, 1845), i, 214–15.
49. *Scalachronica*, ed. King, 75; *Chron. Lanercost*, 207.
50. *The Bruce*, ed. Duncan, 469–71.

51. *The Bruce*, ed. Duncan, 417; Trokelowe, *Annales*, 84; DeVries, *Infantry Warfare*, 66–85.
52. *Scalachronica*, ed. King, 75.
53. *Vita Edwardi*, 90–3; *The Bruce*, ed. Duncan, 473–5. The *Vita* names the leader of the Scottish vanguard as James Douglas, contradicting Barbour, but, admittedly, strengthening the idea that James was, after all, in a leading role. A compromise would be to suggest, as Duncan does, that Douglas was fighting under Edward Bruce's leadership, as he had in 1308 (*The Bruce*, ed. Duncan, 481).
54. *The Bruce*, ed. Duncan, 483–5.
55. *The Bruce*, ed. Duncan, 26–8.
56. *Chron. Lanercost*, 208; *Scalachronica*, ed. King, 75–7.
57. *Chron. Lanercost*, 208–9; *Vita Edwardi*, 94–5; *Scalachronica*, 77; *The Bruce*, ed. Duncan, 495–7; Trokelowe, *Annales*, 86.
58. *The Bruce*, ed. Duncan, 495–7; *Scalachronica*, ed. King, 77.
59. *Chron. Lanercost*, 209.
60. *The Bruce*, ed. Duncan, 497.
61. *Vita Edwardi*, 97.
62. *The Bruce*, ed. Duncan, 497. One Scottish noble, John Murray, was said to have captured twenty-three knights, as well as esquires and others, and to have 'taken a very heavy ranson for them' (*Lanercost*, 215).
63. *The Bruce*, ed. Duncan, 499, 503; *Vita Edwardi*, 95.
64. *The Bruce*, ed. Duncan, 499–501.
65. *Scalachronica*, ed. King, 77.
66. *Chron. Lanercost*, 209; *The Bruce*, ed. Duncan, 513.
67. *The Bruce*, ed. Duncan, 503, 507–9.
68. *Chron. Lanercost*, 209–10; *The Bruce*, ed. Duncan, 501.
69. *The Bruce*, ed. Duncan, 501, 515; *Chron. Lanercost*, 210.
70. *Chron. Lanercost*, 209; *Annales Londoniensis*, 231; *The Bruce*, ed. Duncan, 501–3. *Lanercost* states that Valence led the Welsh himself but he was also recorded as being with King Edward and Barbour, whose account of the rout is generally consistent and well-informed was probably right that Valence's retainer was in charge (Phillips, *Aymer de Valence*, 74–5). The *Vita* names Berkeley among those captured (*Vita Edwardi*, 97).
71. *Vita Edwardi*, 95; *Chron. Lanercost*, 210.
72. *The Bruce*, ed. Bruce, 505; *Scotichronicon*, ed. Watt, vi, 365.
73. 'Annales Londoniensis', 231. The west country chronicle is 'The Continuation of Nicholas Trevet's *Annals*' in *Chrons Edw. I and Edw. II*, ii, 25–151.
74. *The Bruce*, ed. Duncan, 507. For the earl, see Althschul, *The Clares*, 163–4.
75. *Chron. Lanercost*, 208; 'Annales Londoniensis', 231.
76. *C.D.S.*, iii, nos 331, 406, 1522.
77. *The Bruce*, ed. Duncan, 515; Trokelowe, *Annales*, 87.
78. Cont. Trevet, 14; *Scotichronicon*, ed. Watt, 366–75; Tout, *The Reign of Edward II*, 92, 317; Barrow, *Robert Bruce*, 231.
79. *Vita Edwardi*, 95–7; *C.D.S.*, iii, no. 419; Cont. Trevet, 15. The Roger Mortimer captured at Bannockburn was probably not the future ruler of England, Roger Mortimer of Wigmore, but his uncle, Mortimer of Chirk. The lord of Wigmore issued a charter from Wigmore on the Welsh borders dated 17 June 1314, making it unlikely he was at Bannockburn (J. B. Smith, 'The Middle March in the Thirteenth Century', in *Bulletin of the Board of Celtic Studies*, 24 (1970–2), 77–93, 91–2, no. 10).
80. *The Bruce*, ed. Duncan, 507–9; Trokelowe, *Annales*, 87.
81. *Vita Edwardi*, 95.

82. *Vita Edwardi*, 97; *Scalachronica,* ed. Gray, 75.
83. For the best analysis of Courtrai in English, see Verbruggen, *The Battle of the Golden Spurs.*
84. For other contemporary clashes, see DeVries, *Infantry Warfare.*
85. Verbruggen, *Battle of the Golden Spurs,* 152–243.

CHAPTER 7

The Aftermath (July 1314–May 1323)

THE WAR WIDENS (SUMMER 1314–SUMMER 1316)

Bannockburn did not end the war between Robert Bruce and Edward of England. It was to be nearly nine years before the long truce which halted the ongoing conflict begun in 1306 and another five before a short-lived peace was agreed. However, as will become clear, Bannockburn did have an impact on the course and character of the war. Symbolically and materially it transformed the conflict. After the battle the scale and reach of the fighting grew greater and wider, impacting on much of the north and west of the British Isles. Questions of immediate warfare and of loyalty and identity, with which the Scots had been wrestling for two decades, now faced individuals and communities in northern England, Ireland and Wales as well.

The quickest and clearest results of Bannockburn came in Scotland. The surrender of Stirling Castle was followed by the capitulation of the remaining Edwardian strongholds at Dunbar, Bothwell and, finally, Jedburgh.[1] By early 1315 only Berwick remained outside Robert's control and the capture of what had been Scotland's largest burgh would form a major objective of the king in the next phase of the war. The castles he had taken in 1314 were demolished to prevent them being recovered by the enemy. More important for Robert was the submission of their lords and keepers to his authority. Bannockburn brought to an end not just the manning of Scottish castles against Bruce, but open opposition to his royal rights and title within Scotland. The battle had claimed the lives of some leading enemies, like John and Edmund Comyn, but still more made the decision to recognise Bruce's kingship in the weeks that followed. Patrick earl of Dunbar rapidly made peace with Robert, as did Philip Mowbray, Walter fitz Gilbert and the Scottish keeper of Jedburgh, William Prenderguest. Captured in Bothwell, Ingeram Umfraville also chose to pay the king homage, and his example was followed by southern nobles like William Soules and Adam Gordon.[2] Time would reveal that the enthusiasm with which some of these influential lords acted was limited, and in late 1314 they recognised the inevitable.

The alternative to paying homage to Robert was exile and disinheritance. In early November 1314 the king held a parliament at Cambuskenneth Abbey,

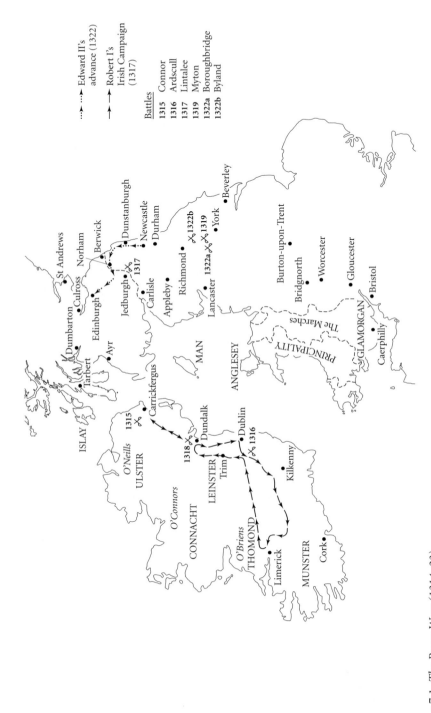

Edward II's advance (1322)

Robert I's Irish Campaign (1317)

Battles
1315 Connor
1316 Ardscull
1317 Lintalee
1319 Myton
1322a Boroughbridge
1322b Byland

St Andrews
Culross
Dumbarton
Norham
Berwick
Dunstanburgh
Newcastle
Durham
Edinburgh
Jedburgh
1317
Carlisle
Appleby
Richmond
1319
1322b
York
Lancaster 1322a
Beverley
Ayr
Tarbert
ISLAY
Carrickfergus
1315
O'Neills
ULSTER
MAN
ANGLESEY
Burton-upon-Trent
Bridgnorth
Worcester
Gloucester
Bristol
The Marches
PRINCIPALITY
GLAMORGAN
Caerphilly
Dundalk
1318
Trim
LEINSTER
Dublin
1316
Kilkenny
O'Connors
CONNACHT
O'Briens
THOMOND
Limerick
MUNSTER
Cork

MAP 7.1 *The Bruce Wars (1314–23)*

TABLE 7.1 *The Comyn Connection*

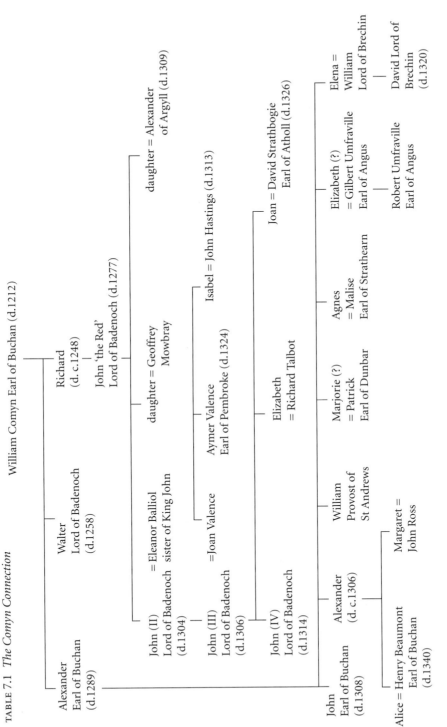

within sight of the battlefield at Bannockburn. In parliament and 'with the consent and assent of the bishops, prelates, earls, barons and other nobles of Scotland and also the whole community of the realm', Robert passed a sentence of 'perpetual disinheritance' on all 'who had died in war outside the faith and peace of the lord king [or] who had not come to his faith and peace by this day'.[3] Victory in battle allowed Robert to enforce his claim to the homage of all Scottish landowners. The price of treachery was quickly demonstrated. At Cambuskenneth, the site of his betrayal, a sentence of forfeiture was passed on David Strathbogie earl of Atholl. The office of constable, given to him by Robert in 1313, was now returned to Gilbert Hay who, unlike Strathbogie, had stuck loyally to Bruce since 1306. Atholl was not there to face the king's judgement. He had fled to England where he joined a band of other nobles who had been denied or stripped of their lands by Robert's victory.[4] This group included Scottish enemies of the king like John of Lorn, but also numbered men such as Henry Beaumont, who claimed the earldom of Buchan by his marriage to Alice Comyn, and Robert Umfraville earl of Angus.[5] These disinherited lords would have a strong interest in reversing the results of Bannockburn in coming years.

In late 1314, however, such lords were in no position to challenge the victorious king. Instead, Robert was able to exploit his victory at Bannockburn by releasing his most prominent captive, Humphrey Bohun earl of Hereford, not for ransom, but in exchange for Scottish captives. Such a plan was being discussed in July. In late September Hereford returned to England in return for the release of the aged Bishop Robert Wishart of Glasgow and of Robert's female relations, his sister, Christina, his wife, Elizabeth Burgh, and his daughter, Marjory. Earl Duncan of Fife was also set free at this point, though Robert's nephew, Donald of Mar, chose to remain at Edward II's court.[6] Another exchange saw John Segrave liberated in return for a number of Scots nobles. Among this group was Andrew Murray, who twenty years later would lead a defence of the Bruce Cause as skilful as King Robert's.[7] The return of these lords and ladies brought benefits to the king. With his queen and his daughter back in Scotland, Robert could make dynastic plans, arranging a marriage between his daughter and Walter steward of Scotland.[8] This match cemented a long-standing affiliation between the Bruces and the Stewarts and would give this great and influential family a fixed place in the Bruce regime. However, a Stewart succession was not an imminent prospect. In April 1315 at a council in Ayr, a statute was issued making Edward Bruce heir to his brother, should Robert die without a son.[9] Marjory consented to her uncle preceding her in the line of succession. Despite the greater security which followed Bannockburn, this was an act which recognised the need for an adult king, proven in war, to replace Robert. Edward must have been recognised as heir during the years before Bannockburn, when he was the only hope for the dynasty should Robert die. The statute reflected Edward's reluctance to step aside and the wider desire for an experienced leader of the Bruce name. It recognised the uncertainty felt by many Scots about the future, uncertainty which would prove to be well-placed.

Scottish anxieties were surpassed by those of King Edward's subjects, especially in the northern shires of England. For these localities, Bannockburn opened a period of unparalleled Scottish invasion, far beyond the raids and blackmail experienced since 1309. This began just over a month after the battle. In early August Edward Bruce, accompanied by James Douglas and the recent recruit William Soules, led an army of horsemen and foot soldiers across the Tweed. Bruce devastated Northumberland, extracted a payment from the men of Durham and then pressed south across the Tees, plundering Richmondshire and Swaledale. Crossing the hills, the Scots returned home through Brough and Appleby.[10] By marching with impunity across a wide region, the Bruces demonstrated the vulnerability of the north in the aftermath of Bannockburn. Robert clearly hoped the campaign would influence opinion in England, rapidly following it with an offer of peace to Edward II who had summoned parliament to York in October. However, though the English agreed to talk, Edward's continued refusal to recognise Bruce as king, which was Robert's key goal, made any settlement impossible.[11] In response, Robert renewed attacks, but with a different purpose. The *Lanercost Chronicle* recorded that in January 1315, 'the Scots occupied both north and south Tynedale . . . and Tynedale did homage to the king of Scots'. Bruce was no longer entering England just for money and goods, he now sought allegiance and granted lands to his men. English border communities, like the men of Lothian in previous years, had no protection against the enemy, and were forced to make peace with the Scottish king.[12] The deaths or capture of many northern knights at Bannockburn deprived the wider region of leaders and there were growing signs of disorder, much of it linked to men hired by Edward II for the defence of Northumberland.[13]

It was against this background of military and political crisis that King Edward faced his critics in the months after Bannockburn. The Scottish war had come home to roost. Defeat had cost Edward much of his remaining authority and gave his opponents, led by Thomas of Lancaster, an opportunity to direct affairs. In response to the crisis in the north, parliament met at York in September.[14] Edward was forced to accept the Ordinances once more and agree to a purge of his household. While these moves were made and talks arranged to discuss a truce or even a peace with the Scots, some effort was made to restore the military situation. Powers were given to new officials in the north and, more importantly, Lancaster sought fresh resources from Italian bankers to finance the defence of the marches. What was clear is that the leaders of the army destroyed at Bannockburn, not just the king but also Aymer Valence, Hereford and Henry Beaumont, had been replaced in power by Lancaster and Warwick who had refused to serve in the campaign. There was a clear link between the battle and the shape of English politics. One chronicler recorded that none of those who had supported the Ordinances but who then broke them by serving at Bannockburn 'escaped capture or death, except Pembroke'.[15] Lancaster's political ascendancy depended, in part, on his ability to manage the war more effectively. There was considerable debate. Parliament met to consider 'the conquest of the Scots' in January, while further councils were held by the clergy and magnates of the north in January and May. Preparations were also laid for an army to be raised in July 1315.[16] Foot were ordered and in late June a summons was issued to nearly 300 knights to serve in this force with their men. According to the *Vita Edwardi Secundi*, a force of 500 cavalry was assembled.[17] Command of the force was given to Valence who was chosen, despite his poor relations with Lancaster, presumably because of his experience.

The muster of this relatively small force coincided with renewed Scottish attacks in the marches. Durham was once again plundered in late June, probably to provide the supplies for an ambitious move further west.[18] Carlisle was a key target. The castle and city was a block on Scottish movements in the west and 'frequently intercepted their raids and many times hindered their flight'.[19] Robert raised a host and, having ravaged the surrounding lands, laid siege to Carlisle on 22 July. The siege showed the limitations of Scottish warfare. Their stone-throwing engines caused little damage and attempts to place a *berefrai*

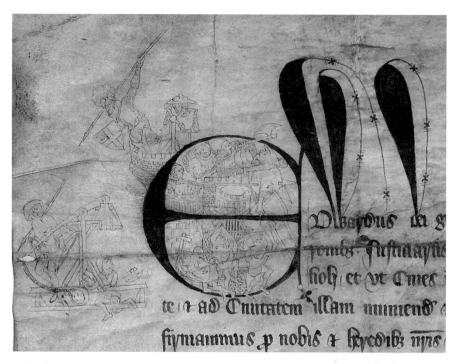

FIGURE 7.1 *From the illuminated letter of the royal charter to Carlisle, this shows the siege of the city in 1315. It depicts Andrew Harclay (in full armour) leading the defence and gives a good contemporary impression of Scots and northern English military dress. (By permission of Carlisle City Council)*

or siege tower against the walls failed dismally when it stuck in the mud. Efforts at mining, at scaling the walls with ladders and at the kind of surprise attack used at Edinburgh the previous year all failed against a determined defence led by the local knight, Andrew Harclay. After eleven days, probably aware of the approach of Valence's force, Robert withdrew, abandoning his engines. English chronicles celebrated a successful pursuit of the enemy, in which several Scots were killed or captured.[20] Though they exaggerate the result, it is clear that, despite Bannockburn, Bruce would not risk battle on terms which were so clearly disadvantageous.

King Robert's siege of Carlisle was not simply designed as a further attack on the northern marches of England. It was part of a widening of the war which the Bruces had embarked upon in spring 1315. After attending the council which confirmed him as Robert's heir, Edward Bruce set sail from Ayr with an army of several thousand men and landed on the coast of Antrim in Ireland on 26 May.[21] The aims of Edward's expedition have excited much debate and were probably flexible. Most simply, a major attack on Edward II's lordship of Ireland was a natural extension of the war. Robert had led galleys to Ulster in 1313 and, further back, in 1306 Ireland had been an element in the revival of Bruce fortunes.[22] The maritime region which included the Hebrides, the Irish coasts and Galloway had been a recognised and important theatre in the Scottish wars and remained a frontline in the conflict, where Robert's position was not secure. Edward II had long tried to strike at Bruce's influence round the Clyde and in the Isles and, though results had been disappointing, fresh efforts were underway in late 1314. Once again, John of Lorn was given ships and men to wage war on Bruce. This time, however, he won a major success. In early 1315 John captured Man from Bruce's garrison. From the island John planned a further naval campaign, and as in the previous year he was given powers to receive Islesmen into King Edward's peace.[23]

Robert must have been keen to counter this challenge. In March he was at Dumbarton, the Scottish crown's window on the west, accompanied by Edward Bruce and other leading magnates. Later in 1315 he would sail to Tarbert and receive the homage of leading Islesmen. At Dumbarton, plans may have been laid for a campaign into Ulster during the summer.[24] In such a campaign, a crucial role would have been played by Bruce's adherents in the Isles, in particular from Clan Donald and the MacRuairi family. As well as providing effective soldiers for Edward Bruce's army, these kindreds could exploit their own connections within Ireland. Clan Donald, in particular, had links with the leading Irish lords of Ulster, above all, Donal O'Neill of Tir Eoghain.[25] It would be as an ally of O'Neill and in conflict with his enemy, Richard Burgh earl of Ulster, that the Bruces would intervene in Ireland. Robert clearly recognised that his marriage to Earl Richard's daughter would not cut across established identities and provide him with allies in Ireland with the English community. As a result it was to Gaelic Irish leaders that Robert and Edward Bruce would appeal, using the language of common descent and shared enmity to the English.[26] At its ultimate

FIGURE 7.2 *The castle at Carrickfergus was the key to securing control of the earldom of Ulter. Edward Bruce and his allies laboured for two years to take the stronghold from its English garrison. (Copyright EHS Built Heritage)*

extent, this approach witnessed Edward Bruce claiming the kingship of Ireland for himself. The pursuit of his own realm and title was recognised by near contemporaries as Edward's main motive for going to Ireland. Raised in an aristocratic environment in which the ambition for a royal title had been fostered, Edward may well have sought his own crown. The voyage to Ulster was not just a foray like the campaign into northern England the previous year. Nor was it a diversion. King Robert would support his brother in person and with experienced leaders. The army which accompanied Edward included major captains like Thomas Randolph, John Menteith, Robert Boyd and Philip Mowbray along with other nobles, several from the west coast.[27]

Like events in northern England, the opening campaigns of the Irish war revealed the ascendancy of the Bruces. Soon after landing, Edward defeated the English tenants of the earl of Ulster and laid siege to Carrickfergus Castle. In June Bruce met with the leading Irish of Ulster who submitted to him and recognised him as king.[28] Bruce soon had a lesson in the uncertainties of Irish politics. Moving south from Ulster into Meath, Edward's men had to fight their way through an ambush laid by two of the lords who had earlier recognised his authority. However, in late June, once through the hills, Bruce stormed Dundalk, one of the English towns which supplied ships for the Scottish war.[29] By this stage, King Edward's government was finally reacting to the threat. The king's justiciar, Edmund Butler, gathered an army, while the earl of Ulster raised a force from his English and Irish dependants. Faced by this host, Edward Bruce, aided by Donal O'Neill, fell back northwards as far as Coleraine.[30] His refusal to give battle gradually wore down his opponents. Butler withdrew his men, while Earl Richard's army began to disperse. When Richard began to retreat towards his earldom, Bruce pursued and, catching the enemy at Connor, defeated them with a sudden charge. While the earl escaped, his cousin and lieutenant, William Burgh, was taken captive.[31]

Edward had scored a striking success but his long-term prospects were less certain. Against the resources of the English lordship, the numbers of Scots were small and their Irish allies had their own objectives. Randolph returned to Scotland to raise more troops in autumn 1315 and Edward besieged Carrickfergus without result.[32] A winter campaign solved none of these problems. Bruce demonstrated his army's ability to fight off English forces and devastate their estates. He marched through Meath again, defeating Roger Mortimer at Kells, and causing panic in Dublin, but was not able to mount a serious attack on the city or even take a well-defended castle at Rathangan. He won only very isolated recognition from English tenants in Ulster and Meath and faced a further display of hostility from an Irish lord in his camp.[33] Once again, his advance beyond Ulster allowed the justiciar to muster an army against him. In January 1316 Edward was confronted by this superior force near Ardscull south of Kildare. Bruce's host suffered significant losses but held the field, aided by divisions among the English nobles. Edward fell back into the bogs of Laois, while the English broke up. Though the Scots resumed their march through Leinster before returning north in February, Edward had had a lucky escape. The campaign had shown the skill of the Scots in a war of plundering forays but did not suggest Edward Bruce had the means to establish any extensive authority.[34]

Bannockburn had clearly provided the Bruces with the opportunity to extend the war beyond Scotland into King Edward's dominions. The submission of Tynedale, the siege of Carlisle and the war in Ireland all indicate an intention to claim lordship or control in lands beyond Scotland. However, the results of Bannockburn were not simply about the direct course and scale of the war. They were also about the impact of individual deaths among the nobility of the Plantagenet dominions. Most notable of these was Gilbert Clare earl of Gloucester. The young earl fell in battle without an heir. His lands came into royal custody while the rights of his sisters and their husbands were established.[35] The partition of Gilbert's estates would be a major issue in coming years but the treatment of these holdings was not just a matter of concern for the family. The Clares were major magnates in Wales and Ireland, areas where the role of a magnate was to provide justice and leadership to his tenants. In Ireland the earl might have provided a figure able to work with his father-in-law, Richard earl of Ulster, and other lords against Edward Bruce.[36]

However, it was in Gloucester's Welsh lordship of Glamorgan that the effects of his death were felt most rapidly.[37] Within a month of Bannockburn, the king appointed his own men to run the lordship. His actions immediately aroused the fears of the leading Welsh tenants of upland Glamorgan led by a local official, Llywelyn Bren. Experience had taught both crown and marcher lords to respond to such grievances and Edward II rapidly replaced his appointees with a retainer of Earl Gilbert, Bartholemew Badlesmere. Such sensitivity was part of a general anxiety about the state of Wales, fuelled by events in Ireland. During summer 1315 officials in the principality were ordered to guard castles and coasts, and abuses by these officers were examined. In addition, hostages were taken from leading Welsh squires. These efforts were clearly taken to prevent support for any landing by the Scots in Wales.[38] In Glamorgan too, Edward was nervous about the loyalties of the Welsh, appointing men to ensure the security of the lordship. However, at the same time the king wished to enjoy a hefty return from Glamorgan while he held it and it was the actions of his officials in seeking revenues which led to a rebellion breaking out in January 1316. Led by Llywelyn Bren and other local Welsh landowners, the rebels besieged Caerphilly Castle and burned Neath and numerous manors. The response was led by Humphrey earl of Hereford, the Mortimers and other marchers who forced the rebels back into the uplands. A royal force of 150 horse and 2,000 foot under William Montagu was sent to complete the suppression and Llywelyn surrendered to Hereford on 18 March.[39] The rising had been a protest against local misrule, not a fresh uprising against English lordship. However, in the circumstances of early 1316, with a Scottish army in Ireland and Scottish ships off Anglesey, fears that grievances felt by influential Welsh gentry like Llywelyn Bren could escalate into a wider rebellion were real and would continue.[40]

PESTILENCE, FAMINE AND WAR (SUMMER 1316–AUTUMN 1318)

For England north of the Humber the Scottish attacks in the years after Bannockburn marked the most sustained period of warfare between the Norman Conquest and the great Civil War. Even in Ireland, where the population were inured to raids and skirmishes, Edward Bruce's campaigns were seen as visiting special horrors on Gael and English alike.[41] The impact of war, direct and indirect, was exacerbated by three years of famine which struck England, Ireland and, probably, Scotland. The autumn of 1314 brought heavy rains which did not abate through 1315, leading to flooding and the failure of the harvest. The result was a shortage of food and a famine, which probably fell hardest in areas of overpopulation like southern England, but which was made worse further north by the widespread raiding of livestock by both Scots and local lords.[42] The author of the *Vita* even reported that thousands died of hunger and disease and that 'in Northumbria dogs, horses and other unclean things were consumed as food'. At the same time, the sheep on which many depended were struck by sickness, which reduced the value and quantity of their wool.[43] For the poor these conditions meant misery and death, but they also had an impact on the rival crowns and their efforts to pursue their ends. The attacks of the Scots in northern England may have had the search for provisions as one of their objectives and Edward Bruce's risky foray into Leinster in the winter of 1315–16 could similarly have been an attempt to feed his forces from the manors of English lords. In February 1316 part of the Berwick garrison made a raid up the Tweed towards Melrose because they were starving, only to be heavily defeated by a local force led by James Douglas and William Soules.[44]

On a larger scale, famine hindered the efforts of the English government to mount a major campaign to defend the north. Lancaster, who had been made captain of English forces in the north in August 1315, was probably the main sponsor of this venture.[45] An expedition planned for autumn 1315 was abandoned and in January 1316, in a parliament at Lincoln, a fresh effort was made to summon an army to meet in July at Newcastle. The king was granted a levy of a foot-soldier from every vill in England for the army as well as a financial subsidy. In the meantime, efforts were made to secure a truce.[46] Once more, these plans were derailed. Llywelyn Bren's rising proved expensive to suppress and a rising in Bristol, again over local issues but connected to the Scottish campaign, ended with the siege of the city in July.[47] The raising of men, money and supplies for the Scottish war imposed burdens on the population and strains on the government. Against this background, the campaign was postponed until October.[48] For people who had witnessed Edward II's repeated levies for campaigns before 1314, this renewed old grievances which, in turn, opened up the tensions at the heart of government, especially between the king and Thomas of Lancaster. The king's reluctance to observe the Ordinances which prescribed royal behaviour and his sudden abandonment of his progress northwards to join the army, led to the campaign being cancelled in October. It also led to an open breach with Lancaster. The earl's ascendancy since Bannockburn had produced little success. His character and the king's patronage meant he was now faced by a renewed royal party, including favourites like the Despensers and Beaumonts but also Valence and Hereford. As part of his loss of influence, in November Lancaster was replaced in command of the north by Edmund earl of Arundel, who was to be assisted in his role by Henry Beaumont.[49]

The cancellation of the English expedition allowed King Robert to give a new impetus to his brother's war in Ireland. Here too, though the English government had maintained a fleet off Ulster, supporting Carrickfergus and hindering contacts between Edward Bruce and Scotland, more ambitious plans foundered. An army of 200 men-at-arms and 2,000 foot which was to be sent from Gascony never materialised.[50] In the absence of a fresh relief effort, Carrickfergus finally surrendered to Edward Bruce in September 1316. However, despite this, the Scots suffered continued opposition from the English of Ulster.[51] Faced by this and without the means to extend his rule further, Edward returned to Scotland. The visit may have been linked to Robert's grant of Man to Randolph, but its prime purpose was to seek reinforcements.[52] At Christmas 1316 King Robert led an army to Ireland, in what

Irish annalists described as an effort 'to expell the Galls [foreigners] from Ireland'.[53] Whether this army did contain many Islesmen, as one account suggests, is not certain, but it clearly allowed the Bruces to take the initiative. In mid-February, at the head of a large host of Scots and Ulster Irish, Robert and Edward entered Meath. As in 1315, the approach of the enemy led the burgesses of Dublin to burn their suburbs. They also arrested Earl Richard Burgh, suspecting him of being sympathetic to his son-in-law. As the earl had been driven from his province by the Scots, he had no such sympathies and the act reveals the near-panic among the Dubliners.[54]

In reality Robert could not afford a winter siege in hostile territory. He bypassed Dublin and marched south, entering the rich farmlands of Kilkenny, the now vacant lordship of Gilbert Clare. The English lords and the justiciar, Edmund Butler, now styled earl of Carrick, gathered in Kilkenny town to oppose Robert.[55] Unlike 1315, it seems that they lacked the numbers to take the Bruces on. Instead, Butler and the new earl of Kildare, John FitzThomas, shadowed Robert as he led his host west into Munster. The king probably hoped to make contact with the O'Briens and other Irish nobles in the southwest and perhaps assault Limerick, but the pressure exerted by Butler and the arrival of new forces under Roger Mortimer persuaded Robert to turn northwards. His men were suffering from hunger and by early May were near Trim in Meath.[56] They straggled back into Ulster and by late May Robert was on his way back to Scotland. As a military venture, the campaign of early 1317 was probably as bold as any undertaken by Robert Bruce. By marching through Leinster and Munster he had shown the inability of the English justiciar and nobles to stop his depredations and encouraged Irish lords to make similar forays. Despite this, he had not solved the basic problems facing the Bruces in Ireland. They lacked the means to take Dublin or Limerick or to establish any base of influence beyond Ulster. They also failed to win the firm support of any Irish magnates except O'Neill. Though others, like Felim O'Connor and Brian Ban O'Brien, allied with the Bruces, they had done so to seek the aid of the Scots in their own regional struggles, rather than assist Edward's own ambitions. Robert left Ireland with his brother's position only marginally enhanced.[57]

The campaigns of the Scots in Ireland in 1315 and 1317 undoubtedly shook the confidence of Edward II's officials and English communities. Robert had taken his war hundreds of miles into the English king's dominions, claiming lordship and leadership over Edward's subjects. The effects of this were not merely confined to Ireland. In summer 1316 contingents of troops raised from north Wales were sent home in case they were needed to defend their land against Scottish attack. The leader of this force was Gruffydd Llwyd, a dependable Welsh adherent of the crown. However, probably in late 1316, Gruffydd was arrested. Though never charged, he was suspected of being in contact with Edward Bruce. Letters were sent from Bruce to Welsh leaders offering to assist them in expelling the English, as they had been expelled from Scotland.

Gruffydd Llwyd replied, declaring his support should Bruce bring an army to Wales. His motives for abandoning his normal loyalty to the English crown may not have been simply desire for liberation. As with Llywelyn Bren's revolt, Gruffydd's sudden antipathy towards English rule may have been driven by a more immediate hostility towards the local administration headed by the marcher lord, Roger Mortimer of Chirk.[58] After a spell in custody, the 'loyal Welshman' was released and renewed his links of service to Edward II. As in Ireland, the Bruces had an attraction as the opponents of the Plantagenet administration, but this appeal, though frightening for the English, could not be used to stir up large-scale uprisings in other lands.

King Robert's five-month absence from Scotland with an army in early 1317 must have been seen as an opportunity as well as a threat by English leaders. Efforts were made to finance the war and provide for effective leadership. The new lieutenant, Arundel, was allowed money to pay for garrisons in the north, a move intended to provide a paid core to his local forces. In addition, when in October 1316 the vacant bishopric of Durham was filled, the new bishop was Louis Beaumont. Louis, who was accused of illiteracy, was brother to Henry Beaumont, and was appointed to provide active leadership for his diocese and lordships which stood in the front line and included Norham Castle on the Tweed, described as 'the most perilous place in Great Britain'.[59] In late April 1317 Arundel, with a sizeable company, including Henry Beaumont and the exiled earl of Atholl, advanced over the Cheviots into Jedworth Forest. His aim may have been to take and refortify places in Teviotdale. James Douglas, who would later be granted Jedburgh and its forest, met the enemy with a smaller force. After falling back before them, Douglas ambushed an advanced contingent of enemy *schavaldours*, or raiders, at Lintalee in the forest and then killed a leading knight, Thomas Richmond, in a further skirmish. Discouraged, Arundel retreated.[60] The earl had planned his advance to occur in conjunction with an attack from the sea on Fife and the north-east coast by a fleet of five ships. Sailing into the Forth, the English landed near Inverkeithing and the armed sailors began 'to ryve'. The sheriff and perhaps the earl of Fife mustered a small force but hesitated to attack until Bishop William Sinclair of Dunkeld arrived with armour under his robes. According to Barbour, uttering the words 'Quha luffis his lord or his cuntre turne smertly agane with me', the bishop, whose property was at risk, led the Fife men in a charge which drove off the raiders. The English sailed away and the effort to exploit Robert's absence petered out.[61]

Though the efforts of the English in war lacked success, during the winter of 1316–17 they scored a diplomatic victory. Edward dispatched an embassy to the papal curia, partly to get himself released from the Ordinances, but also to seek Bruce's excommunication and the placing of Scotland under an interdict, the suspension of all the functions of the church. Such penalties were deserved, according to the *Vita Edwardi Secundi*, because of Bruce's seizure of Scotland and his attacks on Edward's realm. When these ceased, the English king promised 'to cross the sea against the pagans'.[62] Pope John XXII, who was seeking support for a crusade to recover the Holy Land, was clearly impressed by the English envoys. Though he refused to place sanctions on the Scots until he had heard both sides, in the summer he sent two cardinals to England to try to make peace between Edward II and the Scots and between the king and Lancaster. The actions of the cardinals would make it clear that they regarded Bruce as the problem and they intended to impose a truce which ceased hostilities. They were empowered to excommunicate Bruce and others if they proved obstructive.

In August the cardinals headed north but their progress was abruptly halted when they and their escorts, Louis bishop of Durham and Henry Beaumont, were waylaid by a local knight, Gilbert Middleton.[63] The capture was a scandal which exposed the disorder of Northumberland. The local population faced such threats regularly and, as well as paying off the Scottish king and his men, they had to buy the protection of knights like Middleton. Other captains had committed similar crimes. Jack le Irish kidnapped the rich widow of Robert Clifford after the latter's death at Bannockburn, and John Lilburn tried to kill a royal official in an act of vengeance. These men were not simply bandits; Middleton, le Irish and Lilburn were all royal retainers, well-connected soldiers who had fought in Scotland and now pursued their trade on home ground.[64] The attack on the cardinals was probably not an act of robbery but formed an episode in local disputes involving the Beaumonts. While the cardinals were released, the Beaumonts were imprisoned and Middleton and his men rebelled openly, ravaging church lands and attacking minor castles until his capture in December. The episode shows the effect of war in the English borders and wider anxieties. The hands of both Bruce and Lancaster have been seen in the rebellion, but this probably says more about prevailing fears than the actual events.[65] These are reflected in the *Vita*, where suspicions were voiced of a link between Thomas of Lancaster and Robert Bruce against Edward II in the context of 1317.[66]

Such a connection is highly unlikely at this stage, but Robert must have been aware of the crisis which followed Middleton's arrest. It presented him with an opportunity to take Berwick. Robert was also aware of the cardinals' mission. In August he had met with papal messengers but refused to meet with the cardinals until his royal title was recognised. As well as indicating his key goal, Robert's response may have been intended to delay any plan to impose a papal truce. Before this could happen, in late September Robert laid siege to Berwick, remaining outside the town until the end of November. His efforts failed and must have placed major strains on his people. However, he did not withdraw fully. In mid-December Bruce was near Auldcambus in Berwickshire with an army and siege engines for a renewed attack. It was here that a foolhardy friar found the king and tried to proclaim the Pope's truce.[67] This had been published in London on 27 November, but Robert rejected the bulls containing the truce as they refused him a royal title. He added that he 'would have Berwick', making clear that he was not ready to cease his military efforts at this crucial juncture.[68]

Any fresh attack on Berwick must have failed. In February the king was at Arbroath and Clackmannan with Randolph, Walter Stewart and others.[69] However, his ambitions had merely been delayed. Where formal sieges proved to be a weakness, Bruce's adherents remained skilled at using treachery and surprise. They were aided by events in Berwick. In February there had been a dispute between the castle garrison and the burgesses, who had been given charge of the town walls.[70] This caused the government some anxiety and, while Edward II appointed envoys to negotiate his own truce with the enemy, the Scots had made contact with one of Berwick's inhabitants, Peter Spalding. Spalding, who was an English townsman and a sergeant on the walls, was offered money and land to let a party of Scots into Berwick through the section of the defences manned by his men.[71] Barbour claims that he contacted Robert Keith, who was a kinsman by marriage. Keith informed the king, who sent him back with a small force raised from Lothian. One night at about the beginning of April, a small party scaled the wall and gained entry. They probably opened a gate to allow a force led by James Douglas and, perhaps, the earl of Dunbar into the town.[72] As at Bannockburn, however, the search for plunder limited the immediate success. The Scots dispersed, allowing some of the garrison to escape and others to rally at the castle. After a fight, the Scots secured the town but the castle remained untaken. Barbour says that Robert rushed there with an army gathered from Lothian and the marches to besiege the castle. According to *Scalachronica*, it took eleven weeks before the garrison surrendered 'for want of relief'.[73] The English burgesses, who had settled in Berwick after its bloody capture by Edward I, were expelled 'almost naked and despoiled'.[74]

For Robert and his leading lords, the capture of Berwick was a victory almost as great as that of Bannockburn. One chronicle reports that 'James [Douglas] entered the town with such lightness and joy in his heart that he claimed he had come into the city more cheerfully and affectionately than even paradise'.[75] After perhaps as many as six attempts, Berwick had fallen. The last burgh holding out against Bruce and the centre of the Edwardian administration in Scotland since 1296 had been taken. Symbolically the capture of town and then castle marked the completion of King Robert's realm and kingship. Robert was determined that Berwick would be re-established as a major royal centre. Rather than demolish the castle and town walls as he had done elsewhere, Robert left them standing. He garrisoned the castle and sought to repopulate the burgh with Scots. Robert clearly wished to restore Berwick as a key trading port, and to do this he needed to defend it. If, as Barbour says, the king appointed his son-in-law, Walter Stewart, as keeper of Berwick, it was a further mark of the importance of the burgh and its recovery.[76] However, in early 1319 it seems that Philip Mowbray was keeper of Berwick town and Douglas held the castle, two men of lesser status but greater experience.[77]

However, in practice, the capture of Berwick, a triumph though it was, brought as many problems as benefits. By according it such importance and preserving its fortifications, Robert was breaking his own rules. Like the rescue of Stirling in 1314, the recovery of Berwick in 1318 gave the English a clear target in the war against Bruce. Robert had staked much on taking Berwick, and holding it would be a risk. The actual capture of the burgh also represented a risk. Bruce had defied the papal truce in the most flagrant way possible. He and his people now faced the consequences. Not long after Berwick Castle had surrendered, sentences of excommunication were passed on Robert and on Douglas and Randolph, though they were not published until November.[78] English chronicles suggest that because of these sentences, 'great hope has . . . grown up amongst us'. *Vita Edwardi* tells of a priest who was ordered by Bruce 'the tyrant' to celebrate mass, being prevented by the intervention of a dove which flew down and 'carried off the Host, plucked from the priest's hand'.[79]

Whether these sanctions caused Robert major problems initially is unclear. The capture of Berwick was only the first of a run of successes. Already under siege, the castle of Wark on Tweed, where the host had mustered before Bannockburn, surrendered soon after, as did Harbottle further south. Mitford was captured 'by guile' and, according to the chronicle compiled at Lanercost near Carlisle, the Scots 'subdued nearly the whole of Northumberland as far as . . . Newcastle'.[80] Though Bruce's influence was probably more patchy than this suggests, Northumberland had been removed as any effective block on Scottish attacks. To demonstrate this, even before the surrender of Berwick Castle an army crossed the Tyne and Tees and entered Yorkshire. In two forces, the Scots plundered the North Riding and the Vale of York, reaching Wharfedale and Airedale before turning west and marching down the Ribble. They then seem to have returned to Scotland through the west march, driving off a great number of cattle. The campaign was probably designed to ensure that there would be no attempt to aid Berwick Castle. In addition, earlier fears that the Scots were seeking to exploit the disruption caused during the winter by Middleton and his allies may have resurfaced. There was, however, nothing to indicate any link between the Scots and Lancaster. Earl Thomas's lands suffered along with those of other landowners, though the common folk, as always, came off worst.[81]

The continued dominance of Scottish forces in northern England was, however, balanced by events in Ireland. Since Robert's departure in May 1317 his brother had been largely inactive beyond Ulster. The only tangible advance had come with the recapture of Man, which probably occurred in autumn 1317.[82] However, against this the Scots had suffered a defeat at sea in 1317 in which their leading sea captain, Thomas Dun, was captured and executed.[83] Edward Bruce's defensive stance probably reflects his lack of Scottish troops and sufficient supplies. However, it is also apparent that the English felt unable to challenge him in Ulster. It was Edward who broke the stalemate. In

October 1318 he moved south into Meath, perhaps hoping to exploit the absence of its leading lord, Roger Mortimer. Although later accounts suggest he acted without reinforcements, his army contained two leading Islesmen, perhaps Ruairi of Garmoran and Angus Og of Islay, and Philip Mowbray and John Soules. These nobles may have led new contingents to join Edward, and with this enlarged army Bruce set forth, also accompanied by some Irish and rebel English allies. On 14 October Edward was confronted at Fochart near Dundalk by an army of English from Louth and Meath under John Bermingham. Barbour, Gray and Irish annalists all suggest that Edward attacked before a fresh army, perhaps even led by his brother, could arrive. The attack turned into a disaster. Edward apparently let gaps grow between his three battles, allowing the English to meet them separately. In a short but savage fight the Scottish army was destroyed. Edward Bruce was slain by a townsman from Drogheda. All the other leaders were killed, except Philip Mowbray who fought clear. Edward's corpse was dismembered and its head carried to the English king.[84]

THE CRISIS OF ROBERT'S REIGN (DECEMBER 1318–AUGUST 1320)

The tradition which seeks to portray Edward Bruce as a rash and ambitious lord who created difficulties for his brother cannot obscure the real problems that his death at Fochart caused King Robert. The king's immediate response to news of the defeat was to summon a parliament. This met at Scone in early December and its statutes reveal the legacy of Fochart.[85] Central to this was the question of the succession to the throne. Edward's death had removed the possibility of an adult heir in the near future, and the vulnerability of the dynasty was emphasised by the earlier death of Robert's daughter, Marjory, and by the failure of the king and Queen Elizabeth to produce a son. In 'full parliament', a second act of succession, or tailzie, was issued by the king with the consent of the community of the realm. The new heir was to be Robert Stewart, Marjory's infant son. Though Thomas Randolph and then James Douglas were named as guardian should a child inherit the throne, Scotland was facing the uncertainty of a minority in a time of war.[86]

For an excommunicated usurper, such worries could be dangerous. Statutes were passed at Scone against the spreading of rumours and the making of conspiracies designed to sow discord between king and people, and to prevent noble feuding which resulted from 'disagreements and grievances' arising after the death of Alexander III.[87] These were coded references to the open rivalries and conflict over the throne which had only ended in 1314. Robert clearly feared the reopening of questions about his legitimate right to the kingship might be generated by debates over the succession and by the condemnation of the pope. Buoyed by success in war, Robert had generally been successful in winning lords to his cause. Thomas Randolph and John Menteith had only come to his peace in 1309 but were quickly elevated to leading roles in his realm. The earl of Ross and his son, Hugh, were similarly absorbed into the king's establishment, despite possible points of difference with Randolph as earl of Moray. Even among those who had fought long against Bruce until Bannockburn, there were examples of active service and reward. Philip Mowbray had played a leading role in Robert's campaigns since 1314. He had served in northern England and Ireland and was probably keeper of Berwick in early 1319, a key position.[88] John and William Soules had also been active in the war. John was killed at Fochart, while William had been involved in the borders and in 1319 would be restored to his family's office of butler of Scotland.[89]

However, Robert could not hope to remove lingering antagonisms in only a few years. For men like Brechin, Ingeram Umfraville, William Soules and Philip Mowbray's kinsman Roger, acceptance of Bruce as king rested on shallow roots. Personal grievances over patronage could easily lead to animosity over the degree of authority accorded to relatively minor nobles like Thomas Randolph and James Douglas. This could fuel a general disenchantment with the regime. Signs that the war could turn against Robert would encourage rumour and conspiracy within Scotland among those who had made peace only since Bannockburn, while the king would hardly be immune from anxiety about his position. At some point before March 1316, Robert had arrested Piers Lubaud, charging him with treason. Lubaud was the Gascon who had entered Bruce's allegiance after being Edward II's sheriff of Edinburgh. According to *Scalachronica*, Robert 'suspected him of treason . . . because he was too open' and had been 'always English at heart and was waiting for the best chance to betray him'. Whether such fears were justified, Robert had Lubaud hanged and drawn as a traitor because he could not trust a knight who had so openly changed sides. For men like Brechin, Umfraville and the Mowbrays, it was a stark warning.[90] The Scone parliament's concern with the equipment and discipline of the army and with the obligation to serve in the host may also reflect worries about the strains being placed on the kingdom by the war. The demands of continued campaigns in England and the losses of experienced soldiers at Fochart added to Robert's fears about the security of his kingship and dynasty in late 1318.[91]

These anxieties must have been increased by the knowledge that news of Fochart would encourage the enemy to maintain the fight. In Ireland the victory was celebrated by the English with the display of Edward Bruce's quartered body and the dispatch of his head to England. The end of direct involvement with the Scots was also celebrated by at least one Irish annalist.[92] Similarly, fears of the loss of Ireland and of rebellion in Wales, fomented by the Bruces, were ended by the battle. In reality, such fears had led to only limited action by Edward II, but in England too, Fochart was greeted as a major success by contemporary chroniclers. The *Vita Edwardi Secundi* cited the victory, along with Bruce's excommunication, as a sign of improving fortunes for England, a mood encouraged further by a good harvest and the end of dearth in 1318.[93] There were also the apparent signs of increased political harmony. These dated back to the disasters of the early summer. Like the collapse of Edwardian Scotland in late 1313 and early 1314, the loss of Berwick and the Northumbrian castles followed by the campaign into Yorkshire acted as a spur for a cessation of open tensions. Moderate supporters of King Edward sought an agreement of domestic issues which was reached in July.[94] Though this only papered over the cracks, it allowed preparations to be made for a campaign against Bruce. The goal of this effort may have been Norham, reportedly under siege in the summer. From early August until October plans were laid for an expedition, but in November the campaign was postponed, perhaps partly because the Scots had withdrawn from Norham.[95]

News of Fochart may have been one element in encouraging the English king and his barons to renew plans for a major campaign against the Scots. Edward himself remained at York through the winter and issued summons for cavalry and foot from the northern shires to be ready for the army which, in March, was set to muster at Newcastle on 10 June 1319.[96] In April Edward's new favourite, Hugh Despenser, was sent north with a small force empowered to prepare for the campaign and punish rebels. Papal permission was secured for a tax on the English clergy to finance the war. In May the king brought into his company an individual with a personal interest in the throne of Scotland. Edward Balliol was the son of the deposed King John of Scotland. Since his father's death in late 1313, Edward had spent most time in France but in late 1318 he returned to England.[97] Balliol's presence suggests that the English king saw a value in hinting that the question of the Scottish throne could be reopened. In another indication that Robert was seen to be vulnerable, an embassy was sent to Scotland with an offer of peace. According to the *Vita*, Bruce was offered merely life and limb in return for peace. Inevitably Robert rejected this proposal, replying that 'the kingdom of Scotland was his and belonged to him by hereditary right and by right of battle'. The *Vita* makes clear the offer was solely an effort to avoid Christian blood being spilled before the coming campaign.[98] However, it also served to remind Scots that Robert was risking their lands and lives in defence of his rights, which not all of them accepted with enthusiasm.

Plans for the English campaign continued. In June, when orders went out for English and Welsh foot, the date of muster was moved back to late July and it was finally in late August that the army gathered at Newcastle. Unlike the Bannockburn campaign, this army had almost universal support from the magnates. Even Lancaster appeared at the head of an impressive retinue and it has been estimated that the army numbered about 500 heavy cavalry, 1,000 lightly mounted hobelars and perhaps 8,000 foot.[99] This army was smaller than the host raised in 1314 and would suffer from desertion, but it was a significant force. It was supported by ships from English ports and by an extensive baggage train. The host left Newcastle at the end of August. Though the *Vita* implies that the decision to besiege Berwick was only taken when the army arrived before the town, it is more likely that, as Barbour, *Lanercost* and the *Anonimalle Chronicle* say, the burgh and castle were the main target of the campaign.[100] Strategically and symbolically, the recapture of Berwick would have been a significant success. The army crossed the Tweed and on 7 September 'with trumpets blowing' laid siege 'on the landward side' of Berwick, while the ships from the Cinque Ports blockaded the harbour. The next day a major assault was launched by land, which was met on the walls by the Scots who 'shouted at our people foully and hideously'. This came close to success before being beaten off.[101] Five days later a second attack was made, this time using engines brought up from Bamburgh and an assault from ships in the harbour, including a great vessel drawn up against the walls. Though this too failed, one English chronicle stated that Edward and his army felt they 'were on the point of having conquered the town easily'.[102]

It is uncertain whether the English king and magnates hoped that their siege of Berwick would draw the Scots into risking a battle to save the town, as it would do in 1333. Before the siege, Robert had promised to relieve Berwick if it was besieged and the threat to the town clearly posed a problem for him.[103] He could abandon his men and the burgh, damaging his prestige and position, or gamble on a battle which could prove a reverse of Bannockburn. Robert chose to do neither. Instead, while the English advanced through Northumberland, he sent Thomas Randolph and James Douglas into England. The two lords probably crossed into England via Liddesdale, and moving through Tynedale to the Tees they entered Yorkshire. By 4 September the Scottish force was, once again, ravaging the North Riding.[104] The archbishop of York, William Melton, raised a force of local levies and, leaving his city garrisoned, marched north to confront the enemy. However, this force lacked the knights and men-at-arms who could provide leadership and who were at Berwick. Without them, the men of York were unable to match the skill and mobility of the Scots. On 12 September Douglas and Randolph were at Myton-on-Swale when they became aware of the advancing levies. Disguising their movements by burning hay, the Scots fell upon the enemy as 'they marched all scattered . . . in no kind of array'. Despite efforts to form up in a schiltrom, the clergy and levies of York broke quickly and fled. The mayor of York and many others were killed in the pursuit, which was known as the 'Chapter of Myton' for the numbers of clergy in the archbishop's host. After their victory, the Scots spread over western Yorkshire, causing panic in York, before moving west into the hills.[105]

Word that Randolph and Douglas were a hundred miles to the south and had defeated an English force in Yorkshire reached Berwick on about 15 September. The news sparked a debate which was not just about military issues. King Edward possibly hoped to send a force south while maintaining the siege. However, the royal favourite, Hugh Despenser, later accused the earl of Lancaster of being in league with the Scots, a charge which may have stemmed from the earl's determination to depart and guard his Yorkshire estates.[106] On 17 September the English army raised the siege and headed back

towards Newcastle. The king reached Newcastle and dispersed his army on
20 September. Though Edward planned to remain at York with a force of 600
men-at-arms, he had, once again, been humiliated in war. Blame for the
failure of the campaign and for the escape of Randolph and Douglas through
the west march fell on Lancaster. However, as the *Vita* says, such charges represent hostile rumour, not real conspiracy.[107] They were signs of the ongoing
suspicions and antagonisms which would intensify during the coming
year. Such problems encouraged Edward to seek a truce with the Scots. In
December a two-year cessation of warfare was agreed.[108]

English chroniclers may have regarded this as a humiliation, in which the
Scots had ended their attacks because they did not need any more plunder.[109]
In reality, however, Robert was probably also keen to end the fighting temporarily. Fochart had shown the potential cost of any defeat for Bruce's position and, in late 1319, Robert continued to experience papal hostility. Pope
John summoned four Scottish bishops to come to the curia and answer
charges. The summons was a fresh reminder of the king's excommunication,

FIGURE 7.3 *The west front of the great abbey at Arbroath. This was the traditional
setting for the council which sent the letter of the barons to Pope John XXII in 1320.
Though the strength of its language and ideas have given this 'Declaration of Arbroath'
a timeless appeal, it was a product of the military and diplomatic crisis Bruce faced.
(Crown Copyright. Historic Scotland)*

which released his subjects from their obligation to serve him.[110] Bruce's response came in the form of a series of letters to the pope which proclaimed his rights and cause, sent in early May 1320. Of these, two, from the king and the clergy, do not survive. The third, known as the Declaration of Arbroath, was from the barons and freeholders of Scotland and proclaimed their adherence to Robert, the justice of his and their cause, and their willingness to continue the fight regardless of censure or sanction. Such sentiments form the most developed and articulate exposition of the Scottish Cause in an ongoing ideological and diplomatic struggle against claims of English royal sovereignty. They capture the key elements of the case presented by Scots for their rights as a separate people and realm and are justly famous.[111]

However, they were produced not as an outpouring of collective commitment to Bruce by his nobles and people, but by the king's chancery clerks to mitigate the effects of papal hostility at a critical point. The real atmosphere in Scotland during 1320 was characterised by continuing insecurities as much as determined loyalties. Among those whose seals had been appended to the letter in May were several whose allegiance to King Robert was far from total. During the summer Bruce was informed, perhaps by the Scottish exile Murdoch Menteith, that there was a conspiracy against him.[112] The aims of this conspiracy are not clearly stated but its leaders were all Scots who had opposed Robert before Bannockburn, many of whom had strong ties to the fallen house of Comyn. The apparent leader of the group was William Soules of Liddesdale, while implicated in the conspiracy were Ingeram Umfraville, David Brechin and Roger Mowbray. These nobles had fought hard against Bruce between 1306 and 1314. Their allegiance to Robert was a result of capture or defeat and was clearly a matter of necessity, like Bruce's own homage to John Balliol in the 1290s.[113]

The uncertain course of the war, the question of the succession and the pope's censure may have tempted such men to revert to previous loyalties. This process may have been encouraged by the presence of Edward Balliol in England, as a possible alternative king. The death, sometime in late 1319, of Philip Mowbray, a former opponent who was clearly trusted by Robert, may have removed a vital contact with other such lords.[114] Alerted to a possible threat from this quarter, Robert struck first. During the summer Soules, Roger Mowbray, David Brechin and several others were arrested and accused of conspiracy.[115] The past records of those accused, the acquittal of several of them and the absence of clear charges may suggest that the king was not reacting to an imminent threat but rounding up those suspected of treason, perhaps specifically in making contact with Edward II and Balliol. As with Piers Lubaud, Robert could not afford to wait for a conspiracy to develop and took action against men whose loyalty he had never fully secured. It was a sign that, though Bannockburn had compelled all Scottish landowners to pay homage to Bruce, it had not ended doubts about the king and his cause. This had brought Scotland not a secure future but war and the suspension of the sacraments.

SCOTS AND REBELS (AUGUST 1320–MAY 1323)

In early August at Scone, King Robert held a parliament to try the lords he had arrested. Mowbray had died in custody but was still condemned, and Brechin, 'the flower of knighthood', and three others were executed, hanged and drawn at Perth. Soules was condemned to imprisonment in Dumbarton, where he died by April 1321. Five others were acquitted. In subsequent months, others led by Ingeram Umfraville and Alexander Mowbray fled from Scotland, probably fearing arrest.[116] Though the exiled earls of Atholl and Angus were given powers to receive those Scots 'troubled' by papal sanctions into English allegiance, it seems unlikely that Edward II and his adherents had backed a challenge to Bruce during the summer.[117] When Robert moved against his enemies in June or July, Edward II was in France doing homage to King Philip V for Gascony. In the months which followed, though Edward still proclaimed his rival's excommunication and crimes, both kings seem to have been keen to maintain the truce.[118] Both remained uncertain about their authority over their realms, but it would be Edward who would face the more direct challenge in 1321.

Once again, the spark for this led back to that individual but highly significant event on the field of Bannockburn, the death of Earl Gilbert of Gloucester. The division of his estates between his sisters and their husbands had created insecurity among his Welsh tenants leading to rebellion. It would also lead to a much wider conflict arising from the partition of those lands. The beneficiaries were all favourites of the king, Hugh Despenser, Hugh Audley and Roger Damory, whose marriage was a reward for his bravery at Bannockburn. The division of the estates gave the principal share to Hugh Despenser, who received an even third of the English lands but the whole of the great lordship of Glamorgan.[119] For a noble whose stated aim was that 'Despenser shall be rich and may attain his ends', this was not enough. Using Edward's blind favour as a weapon, Despenser pursued his in-laws and other neighbours to enlarge his holdings, especially in the Welsh marches. His actions won him the hatred of his Welsh tenants and the hostility of the other marcher lords, especially Humphrey earl of Hereford and the Mortimers.[120] Recognising that the king would not restrain Despenser, these magnates were forced to look for allies to compel Edward to change his friends. The obvious ally was Earl Thomas of Lancaster.

Though he was reluctant to raise a revolt, in early 1321 Hereford was in talks with Lancaster and in March an uprising was planned in Wales. Edward and Despenser had prepared for the rebellion, but when it broke out in early May, they were swept away.[121] An army of marcher lords, led by Hereford, the Mortimers and Roger Clifford, son of Robert, overran Despenser's Welsh estates without resistance from Hugh's officials or his Welsh tenants. The king, who had been moving towards Wales, returned to London and agreed to hold a parliament in July. Buoyed by their success, the marcher lords travelled north

FIGURE 7.4 *The king's favourite. Hugh Despenser from the glass of Tewkesbury Abbey. A veteran of Bannockburn, Hugh's greed and his complete dominance of King Edward made him hated by many of that king's subjects in England and Wales. (Crown Copyright. NMR)*

to meet Lancaster.[122] However, the flaws in their position were already becoming clear. Though they claimed to be acting in defence of the crown's rights, the rebels had launched an attack on the king's authority. Whatever the justice of their complaints about Despenser and Edward II's misrule through evil counsel, the barons were open to charges of rebellion. A group of leading northern barons also met with Lancaster, but they were reluctant to pledge full support for the earl and the marchers. Moreover, the king's opponents were not a fixed party, but a shaky coalition united by hatred of the Despensers. Among the leaders were former favourites of the king like Damory, Audley and Bartholemew Badlesmere, who had been supplanted by Despenser, while Lancaster was a difficult figure, uninspiring and liable to indulge in his own feuds. As in the opposition to Gaveston, differing personal goals weakened their ability to secure their ends.[123]

Their basic problem was the lack of any means to control the king. At parliament in July, Edward's enemies turned up with armed retinues. According to the *Vita*, when the king resisted their demands the barons threatened to 'renounce their homage and set up another ruler to do justice . . . and make the guilty and arrogant bow their necks'. Persuaded by the ever-moderate Aymer Valence, Edward agreed to allow charges to be laid against Hugh Despenser and his father. Hugh was 'disinherited, as an evil and false counsellor of the lord king, as a deceiver and conspirator . . . and an enemy of the king and kingdom'.[124] The two Despensers were forced into exile. However, as with Gaveston, the punishment of his friends was the spur to royal action. Edward regarded the events of early 1321 as an unacceptable attack on his authority and immediately began to prepare his revenge. The exile of Despenser removed the main unifying factor for his opponents. In October Edward was able to forfeit Bartholemew Badlesmere and take his Kentish castles by storm. Lancaster, who had a private dispute with Badlesmere, would not aid this ally.[125]

Earl Thomas was experiencing the problems of opposition. He found it hard to get men to commit to open resistance against the king, while Edward secured the support of London, highly valuable in terms of men and money.[126] Faced with royal hostility and wavering support, Lancaster seems to have taken the risky step of approaching the Scottish king in late 1321. Given the existing rumours of the earl's treacherous contact with the enemy, this was a dangerous plan. Though he tried to keep the talks secret from the northern knights, one letter suggests that the marcher lords were ready to deal with Bruce and his men. Letters which King Edward's men later said were found on the earl of Hereford's body indicate that an alliance had been formed between the rebels or 'contrariants' and the Scots.[127] This would involve an army led by Randolph, Douglas, Walter Stewart and, unless 'prevented by illness', King Robert coming to aid Lancaster and Hereford in England, Wales or Ireland in 'their quarrel', while the earls promised to take part in no attack on Scotland with the English king. For Bruce, the tacit acceptance of his kingship by English magnates and the invitation to intervene in the Plantagenet dominions were a tempting reward. Though the Scots were to come 'without claiming lordship or conquest in the said lands', the invitation was a coup.[128] For the rebels it was the deepest treason. The truce with the Scots ended in early January and, to mark this, they entered the Durham palatinate, causing widespread destruction without pressing into Yorkshire. The leaders of the force were Randolph, Douglas and Stewart, suggesting a connection with their talks to Lancaster, and the *Lanercost Chronicle* reports that when the northern knights approached the earl to lead them against the Scots 'he feigned excuse; and no wonder!'[129]

Lancaster was caught between allies whose support would discredit him and the hostility of his own king. While the Scots burned Bishop Beaumont's lands, Edward II moved against the marcher lords. Initially the rebels held the royalists at bay. Led by Hereford and the Mortimers, they had raised a large army of English and Welsh tenants and checked the king's attempts to cross the Severn at Gloucester, Worcester and Bridgnorth in late December and early January.[130] However, soon afterwards the marchers' position was undermined. Though Despenser was hated by his Welsh tenants, King Edward enjoyed a considerable degree of support in the principality of Wales, especially against the unpopular Mortimers. Led by Gruffydd Llwyd, an army of Welsh mustered in the north and rapidly took the castles of Lancaster and Roger Mortimer of Chirk in the marches.[131] This threat to their rear, and the failure of Lancaster to send help, caused the marcher position to collapse. The Mortimers sued for pardon and were sent to prison, while Hereford led his retinue north to join Lancaster.[132]

Here, though, the rebels' position was also unpromising. In February 1322 Earl Thomas tried but failed to capture the royalist outpost at Tickhill and his own men began to desert. Meanwhile, King Edward gathered a large army and made clear his determination to destroy the rebels. Replying to the request of the leading knight in the west march, Andrew Harclay, for aid against the Scots, the *Vita* claims that Edward answered that, if faced by the rebels on one side and the Scots on the other, 'I would attack those traitors and leave Robert Bruce alone'. The Scots he said were in 'no way bound to me', and were thus natural enemies. If true, these words marked the extent to which Bruce's military successes had led the English to move away from previous claims that the Scots were rebel subjects themselves.[133] While he raised armies against his own people, Edward left the defence of the north to Harclay, once again failing to protect his realm. However, the king acted with energy. In early March he led a fresh army north and meeting Lancaster's force at Burton-on-Trent, outflanked it and continued his march. Faced by a large army led by the king, the rebels' position unravelled. Lancaster's castles at Kenilworth, Tutbury and finally Pontefract surrendered without a fight and Earl Thomas fell back with Hereford and a dwindling army.[134] Several sources suggest that the earls were seeking to reach their Scottish allies 'who had promised help against the king', but one account suggests that they were heading for Lancaster's new stronghold at Dunstanburgh in Northumberland.[135] They did not reach refuge. On 16 March at Boroughbridge in north Yorkshire, they found Andrew Harclay with an army raised from the English marches on the opposite bank of the River Ouse. Hereford attacked across the bridge, but against a 'wedge of men at arms' (also described as a 'schiltrom in the Scottish fashion') and archery his men were driven off. The earl, veteran of Bannockburn and victim of politics since then, was killed, stabbed from below through the planks of the bridge. The two sides agreed a truce, but the rebel force disintegrated overnight. The next day Harclay received reinforcements and moved on the rebels, who gave up. King Edward had his cousin, Lancaster, taken to his own castle of Pontefract. On 22 March he was beheaded in direct revenge for the death of Gaveston.[136]

The king's victory over his enemies showed the residual strength of the English crown, however unpopular or untalented was the man who wore it. The support from Welsh squires and the size of the army mustered against

Lancaster show the pull of royal authority after years of failure and crisis. The brief war also showed the disunity of the king's enemies and the absence of any strong appeal beyond private lordship. The aftermath of the war showed that, as always, Edward had learned nothing from events. The Despensers were back, their power now unchallenged. The king's enemies were treated with 'excessive cruelty'. *Lanercost* named eight barons and fifteen knights being executed after Boroughbridge, while others remained in prison or fled into exile.[137]

In these circumstances, Edward and his councillors turned back to Scotland. Only three days after Lancaster's execution, the king issued a summons for service in a major expedition against the Scots in the summer.[138] Driven by his victory against the rebels and awareness of the links between Lancaster and Bruce, Edward was clearly determined on a major demonstration of his power. In late March and early April nearly 40,000 English foot, 10,000 Welsh and 6,000 foot and 1,000 hobelars from Ireland were ordered to gather at Newcastle in June. In the meantime, the defence of the north was placed in the hands of Andrew Harclay, newly created as earl of Carlisle, who was to muster his own force to guard the west march.[139] When parliament met at York in early May, as well as cementing the king's victory and striking down the Ordinances as illegal restrictions on royal authority, it also granted Edward the right to call for a footman from each vill. These were to muster on 24 July, the new date for the campaign. In mid-July this date was put back again to 1 August, but in late July the army began to gather.[140] Though well short of the numbers called, the army which assembled at Newcastle was the biggest of Edward's reign and was described by one chronicler as 'heavy and stately'.[141] An Irish contingent was enroute and did not arrive until late August, but the principality and marches of Wales provided over 6,000 foot and 20,000 infantry mustered from the English shires. About 1,250 mounted men-at-arms served for pay and 500 or so were raised by feudal levy, suggesting a total of armoured cavalry smaller than that at Bannockburn, but still very large. As well as the Despensers, Henry Beaumont and the earls of Pembroke, Arundel, Richmond and Atholl all accompanied the king.[142] It was a host on a par with Edward I's great armies of 1296 and 1298, and his son clearly hoped it would allow a transformation of the course of the war, as recent events had apparently turned the tide of English politics.

However, Edward's calling together of such a force wilfully disregarded the nature of the war since 1314. The events of the summer and autumn of 1322 would prove to be not a reversal of Bannockburn, but a further humiliation for the English king, this time noted in continental chronicles. As in 1314, the slow build-up to the campaign allowed Robert and his men to seize the initiative. In early June Edward expressed fears about a Scottish attack and within weeks they were realised. Robert led an army past Carlisle and round the coast of Cumberland to Furness. The king then pressed on to Lancaster, where Randolph and Douglas joined him. They ravaged Lancashire to the Ribble and beyond before returning to Carlisle, destroying the crops, and re-entering Scotland as Edward's army mustered at Newcastle.[143] The Scots had, once again, shown their ability to reach quickly and deeply into England and with-draw with impunity. Their mobility and purpose contrasted totally with the English king's host. On 10 August Edward left Newcastle, passing through Alnwick before turning west up the Tweed and then north, following the route taken in 1314. The king and his army reached Musselburgh on 19 August and then entered Edinburgh. Here, if not before, Edward had to confront the prob-lems which had faced his father in 1298 and 1303.[144] He had elected not to besiege Berwick again but to take warfare back into the centre of Scotland. However, aside from Berwick, there was no obvious target to take or to draw out Bruce. Unlike 1314, having returned from the south, Robert made no attempt to offer battle. According to Barbour, he had all the cattle from Lothian driven into the hills and gathered his army at Culross across the Firth of Forth, secure from attack but well placed to respond should Edward advance further.[145] Edward did not. The efforts of his officials to assemble supplies and to collect ships to carry them had failed to produce enough food or the means to get it to the army. Only twenty-one ships gathered at Newcastle, and their attempts to supply the king at Edinburgh were hampered by bad weather in which at least one ship was wrecked at Leith, while Scottish and Flemish vessels prowled the North and Irish seas preying on English ships.[146] After a week, Edward turned back. As the army reached Melrose, his advance guard of hobelars was ambushed and cut up by James Douglas, leaving the English to take revenge on the religious houses at Melrose and nearby Dryburgh. Afraid of further attacks, the soldiers refused to 'budge from the army in search of food' and preferred to suffer hunger until they were back at Newcastle.[147]

Here, Edward dispersed his starving footmen and 'retreated with the magnates . . . to York'. However, the campaign was not over. In late September Robert crossed the Solway with an army from both sides of the Forth 'and from the Isles and other high lands'. With this host he crossed the hills into Yorkshire in pursuit of Edward and his remaining force, eluding the army which Harclay had raised in the west to block the Scots' advance. Crossing the Vale of York, Robert and his army came up behind Edward's force near Old Byland on 14 October. The English king's rearguard under John earl of Richmond formed up where the road to Rievaulx Abbey crossed the hills. Despite the steep slope against them, the Scots advanced led by Douglas and the men from Argyll, the Isles and the Highlands in the army. These soldiers reached the summit, took Richmond and several prominent knights prisoner and broke the rest of the enemy in rout. When news reached Edward at Rievaulx, the king, 'chicken-hearted and luckless in war', fled, abandoning his baggage to the Scots for a second time. The English were pursued to York and then Robert took his army into the East Riding, plundering country hitherto untouched by war, and extracting blackmail as far as Beverley and Bridlington. Though far inside England, the

Scots were able to withdraw unhindered with their spoils and prisoners by early November.[148]

The events of summer and autumn 1322 were a powerful demonstration of the ascendancy enjoyed by Bruce in his war against Edward of England. The failure of the massive invasion and the subsequent humiliating flight of the king well within his own realm reportedly convinced Andrew Harclay that Edward 'neither knew how to rule his realm nor was able to defend it against the Scots'. On 3 January Harclay met King Robert at Lochmaben and agreed to observe peace with the Scots and that Scotland was held in 'full right' and distinct from England. Though Robert offered to pay £40,000 to the English king if Edward accepted the agreement as the basis for peace, there was little likelihood of securing such consent.[149] Despite his defeats, Edward would not consider abandoning his claims to Scotland. Instead *Lanercost*, which had close knowledge of events, reported that when Edward heard of the agreement he proclaimed Harclay as a traitor. Though 'the poor folk, middle class and farmers' wished peace, Harclay was not popular with local knights, who resented his rapid rise and grasping character. A group of these, led by Anthony Lucy, surprised Harclay in Carlisle and had him executed on 2 March.[150]

Harclay's crime was to acknowledge Bruce's kingship. While his own king saw this as treason, even Edward recognised the advantages of securing a long cessation of warfare in the north. In April Randolph and Bishop Lamberton went south to Newcastle for talks with Hugh Despenser and Aymer Valence, and at the end of May a thirteen-year truce was agreed at Bishopsthorpe in Yorkshire. The terms were not unfavourable to Edward. The Scots would withdraw from Northumberland and all castles in the eastern marches, save Dunstanburgh, would be demolished. No recognition was accorded to Bruce and no mention was made of Scotland's status. Despite this and despite the defeats of recent years, the truce met with opposition from Henry Beaumont and others with claims to Scottish lands. The truce was also unpopular with more obvious reason in Scotland, where many must have profited from recent warfare.[151] Though the years of warfare between Robert Bruce and Edward II would be ended by the truce, conflict over Scottish crown and realm would last far longer.

Notes

1. *The Bruce*, ed. Barbour, 515; *C.D.S.*, iii, no. 1636. For the precarious state of Berwick, see *C.D.S.*, iii, nos 384, 422, 427, 430.
2. *C.D.S.*, iii, nos 373–4, 383, 385, 407, 721, 1636; *R.R.S.*, v, nos 70, 424, 428. Prenderguest, a local man, was being thanked for continued loyalty in early 1315, but later was said to have surrendered Jedburgh after Bannockburn (*C.D.S.*, iii, nos 419, 1636).
3. *R.R.S.*, v, no. 41; *A.P.S.*, i, 464.
4. *R.R.S.*, v, no. 42. In October 1314 Atholl was given three manors in Norfolk by Edward II to support him until he recovered his Scottish lands. The earl also

sought to recover his own English lands forfeited when he entered Bruce's allegiance in 1312 (*C.D.S.*, iii, nos 396, 414, 424).

5. *C.D.S.*, iii, nos 294, 391, 415, 587.

6. *Chron. Lanercost*, 211; *The Bruce*, ed. Bruce, 517; *C.D.S.*, iii, nos 371–2, 393. It is conceivable that the release of Ralph Monthermer without ransom may also have been an exchange, perhaps for his son-in-law Duncan earl of Fife.

7. *C.D.S.*, iii, no. 402; *Rot. Scot.*, i, 134.

8. *The Bruce*, ed. Duncan, 517. Barbour dates the wedding soon after Marjory's return. A second marriage was arranged between Andrew Murray and Christina Bruce, perhaps around this time.

9. *R.R.S.*, v, no. 58. The king remained at Ayr until early May.

10. *Chron. Lanercost*, 210; McNamee, *The Wars of the Bruces*, 72–3.

11. *R.R.S.*, v, no. 40 and n.

12. *Chron. Lanercost*, 212; *Rotuli Parliamentorum*, i, 293.

13. For this disorder, see A. King, '*Schavaldours*, Robbers and Bandits: war and disorder in Northumberland in the reign of Edward II', in M. Prestwich et al., *Thirteenth Century England*, IX (Woodbridge, 2003), 115–29.

14. *Vita Edwardi*, 98–101; Maddicott, *Thomas of Lancaster*, 164–8; Phillips, *Aymer de Valence*, 82–4; Tuck, *Crown and Nobility*, 70–1. *Vita Edwardi*, however, says that discussion of Scottish affairs was postponed until January.

15. *Chronica Monasterii de Melsa*, ed. E. A. Bond, 2 vols (Rolls series, 1866–7), ii, 331–2; Maddicott, *Thomas of Lancaster*, 165–6.

16. *Rot. Scot.*, i, 133–4; *Vita Edwardi*, 102–5; Maddicott, *Thomas of Lancaster*, 167–9.

17. *Rot. Scot.*, i, 130, 141–6; *Vita Edwardi*, 104–5.

18. *Chron. Lanercost*, 213; *Rot. Scot*, i, 147.

19. *Vita Edwardi*, 104–7.

20. *Chron. Lanercost*, 213–14; *Vita Edwardi*, 106–7; Maddicott, *Thomas of Lancaster*, 169–70; McNamee, *Wars of the Bruces*, 80–1.

21. *Chart. St Mary's Dublin*, ii, 344. For an excellent recent discussion of the course of Edward Bruce's campaigns in Ireland, see S. Duffy, *Robert the Bruce's Irish Wars* (Stroud, 2005), 9–44.

22. *Chart. St Mary's Dublin*, ii, 342.

23. *C.D.S.*, iii, no. 421; *Rot. Scot*, i, 132; McNamee, *Wars of the Bruces*, 169. Edward II granted lands in Argyll and held by John Menteith to a Gallovidian exile, suggesting plans to make a landing there in February 1315 (*C.D.S.*, iii, no. 423).

24. *R.R.S.*, v, nos 50, 51, 55, pp. 136–7. Those also present included Thomas Randolph, John Menteith and Walter Stewart, who had direct interests in the west and in the Irish expedition.

25. Duffy, 'Bruce Brothers', 60–3; R. Frame, 'The Bruces in Ireland, 1315–18', in R. Frame, *Ireland and Britain, 1172–1450* (London, 1998), 71–98, 82–3.

26. Duffy, 'Bruce Brothers', 86–7.

27. *The Bruce*, ed. Barbour, 521, 543; *Chart. St Mary's Dublin*, ii, 347–8.

28. Duffy, *Irish Wars*, 10–13.

29. *Chart. St Mary's Dublin*, ii, 345, 385; Duffy, *Irish Wars*, 13–15.

30. *The Bruce*, ed. Duncan, 539–47; *Chart. St Mary's Dublin*, ii, 346; Frame, 'Bruces in Ireland', 89–91; Duffy, *Irish Wars*, 15–18.

31. *The Bruce*, ed. Duncan, 545–55; *Chart. St Mary's Dublin*, ii, 346.

32. Duffy, *Irish Wars*, 19–27.

33. *The Bruce*, ed. Duncan, 536–9; Frame, 'Bruces in Ireland', 93–5.

34. *Chart. St Mary's Dublin*, ii, 347; Frame, 'Bruces in Ireland', 94–5.

35. Altschul, *The Clares*, 165–70.

36. Altschul, *The Clares*, 241–99; R. Frame, *English Lordship in Ireland*, 53.

37. For events in Glamorgan in 1314–16, see R. A. Griffiths, 'The Revolt of Llywelyn Bren, 1316', in R. A. Griffiths, *Conquerors and Conquered in Medieval Wales* (Stroud, 2004), 84–91; J. B. Smith, 'The Rebellion of Llywelyn Bren', *Glamorgan County History*, iii, ed. T. B. Pugh (Cardiff, 1971), 72–86.
38. Smith, 'Edward II and Wales', 145, 148–9.
39. Smith, 'Llywelyn Bren', 78–82.
40. *C.D.S.*, iii, no. 451.
41. *Chart. St Mary's Dublin*, ii, 349–50, 358; *Annals of Connacht*, 253; Duffy, *Irish Wars*, 26; McNamee, *Wars of the Bruces*, 167–8.
42. H. S. Lucas, 'The Great European Famine of 1315, 1316 and 1317', *Speculum*, v (1930), 343–77; Maddicott, *Thomas of Lancaster*, 163.
43. *Vita Edwardi*, 120–3; McNamee, *Wars of the Bruces*, 105–15.
44. *The Bruce*, ed. Duncan, 566–71; *C.D.S.*, iii, no. 470.
45. *Rot. Scot.*, i, 148.
46. Maddicott, *Thomas of Lancaster*, 182.
47. *Vita Edwardi*, 122–9; Maddicott, *Thomas of Lancaster*, 183–5.
48. *Rot. Scot.*, i, 155–7, 163–4.
49. *Vita Edwardi*, 130–1; *Rot. Scot.*, i, 166–7; Maddicott, *Thomas of Lancaster*, 187–8; Phillips, *Valence*, 103–6.
50. McNamee, *Wars of the Bruces*, 181.
51. *The Bruce*, ed. Duncan, 562–3; *Chart. St Mary's Dublin*, ii, 297; G. O. Sayles, 'The siege of Carrickfergus Castle, 1315–6', *I.H.S.*, x (1956–7), 94–100; Duffy, *Irish Wars*, 29. In November 1316 a Scottish force suffered a defeat by two English landowners from Ulster (*Chart. St Mary's Dublin*, ii, 298).
52. *R.R.S.*, v, no. 101 and n.
53. *Annals of Connacht*, 249; *Chart. St Mary's Dublin*, ii, 298–9; *The Bruce*, ed. Duncan, 581–3.
54. *Chart. St Mary's Dublin*, ii, 298–9; Duffy, *Irish Wars*, 35–6.
55. *Chart. St Mary's Dublin*, ii, 300–1; Frame, 'Bruces in Ireland', 95–7; R. Frame, 'The campaign against the Scots in Munster, 1317', in Frame, *Ireland and Britain*, 99–112; Duffy, *Irish Wars*, 36–8.
56. Duffy, *Irish Wars*, 37–8.
57. Frame, 'Bruces in Ireland', 82–8.
58. J. B. Smith, 'Gruffydd Llwyd and the Celtic Alliance', *Bulletin of the Board of Celtic Studies*, 26 (1976), 463–78; Smith, 'Edward II and Wales', 153–7.
59. *Scalachronica*, ed. King, 80–1; A. King, ' "Pur salvation du roiaume": Military Service and obligation in fourteenth-century Northumberland', in *Fourteenth-Century England II*, ed. C. Given-Wilson (Woodbridge, 2002), 13–31, 18; M. Prestwich, 'Gilbert Middleton and the attack on the Cardinals, 1317', in T. Reuter (ed.), *Warriors and Churchmen in the High Middle Ages* (London, 1992), 179–94. For Beaumont, see H. Schwyzer, 'Northern Bishops and the Anglo-Scottish War in the Reign of Edward II', in M. Prestwich, R. Britnell and R. Frame (eds) *Thirteenth Century England*, vii, (Woodbridge, 1999), 243–54, 249–52.
60. *The Bruce*, ed. Duncan, 599–603; Stevenson, *Illustrations of Scottish History*, 3; *Scalachronica*, ed. King, 77; *Rot. Scot.*, i, 170–1.
61. *The Bruce*, ed. Duncan, 606–13.
62. *Vita Edwardi*, 135–7; S. Layfield, 'The Pope, Scots, and their "self-styled" King: John XXII's Anglo-Scottish Policy, 1316–1334', in King and Penman, *Anglo-Scottish Relations*, forthcoming.
63. *Vita Edwardi*, 142–3; Prestwich, 'Gilbert Middleton', 179.
64. King, 'War and disorder', 117, 120–3; A. King, 'Jack le Irish and the abduction

of Lady Clifford, November 1315: The heiress and the Irishman', *Northern History*, 38 (2001), 187–95; McNamee, *Wars of the Bruces*, 155–7.

65. Prestwich, 'Gilbert Middleton', 183–6; Maddicott, *Thomas of Lancaster*, 205–7.
66. *Vita Edwardi*, 138–9.
67. *R.R.S.*, v, pp. 141–3.
68. *Foedera*, ii, 351; *R.R.S.*, v, p. 143.
69. *R.R.S.*, v, nos 129–34.
70. *C.D.S.*, iii, nos 588–9, 591–2; Stevenson, *Illustrations*, 5.
71. *Scalachronica*, ed. King, 79; *The Bruce*, ed. Duncan, 617–18; *Chron. Lanercost*, 219–20; Stevenson, 5.
72. *The Bruce*, ed. Duncan, 620; *Chron. Lanercost*, 220.
73. *Scalachronica*, ed. King, 79; *The Bruce*, ed. Duncan, 621–7; *Chron. Lanercost*, 219–20.
74. The townsmen were also punished for their carelessness by Edward II (*C.D.S.*, iii, nos 593–4).
75. *The Bruce*, ed. Duncan, 620; Stevenson, *Illustrations*, 5.
76. *The Bruce*, ed. Duncan, 627–9.
77. *The Bruce*, ed. Duncan, 627; *Scalachronica*, ed. King, 81; *R.R.S.*, v, p. 146.
78. *C.P.L.*, ii, 127–30, 191–2, 199.
79. *Vita Edwardi*, 155.
80. *Chron. Lanercost*, 220; *Scalachronica*, ed. King, 79.
81. *Chron. Lanercost*, 221; McNamee, *Wars of the Bruces*, 85–90; I. Kershaw, 'The Scots in the West Riding, 1318–9', *Northern History*, 17 (1981), 231–9.
82. *R.R.S.*, v, no. 101; *C.D.S.*, iii, no. 562; *Rot. Scot.*, i, 172.
83. *C.D.S.*, iii, no. 562.
84. *Chart. St Mary's Dublin*, ii, 359–60; *Annals of Connacht*, 253; *Chron. Lanercost*, 225–6; *The Bruce*, ed. Duncan, 663–77; Duffy, *Irish Wars*, 39, 42.
85. *R.R.S.*, v, no. 139.
86. *R.R.S.*, v, no. 301n; *A.P.S.*, i, 465–6.
87. *R.R.S.*, v, no. 139 (xx), p. 412.
88. *R.R.S.*, v, p. 146, no. 428; *The Bruce*, ed. Duncan, 521, 535, 541, 551, 673–5; McNamee, *Wars of the Bruces*, 138, 143.
89. *The Bruce*, ed. Duncan, 606n, 673; *R.R.S.*, v, nos 167, 437; M. Penman, 'A fell coniuration agayn Robert the douchty king: the Soules Conspiracy of 1318–20', in *Innes Review*, 50 (1999), 25–57, 36–7.
90. *Scalachronica*, ed. King, 73; *R.R.S.*, v, no. 84.
91. *R.R.S.*, v, no. 139 (xxvii).
92. *Annals of Connacht*, 253.
93. *Vita Edwardi*, 154–7.
94. *Vita Edwardi*, 156–7; Maddicott, *Thomas of Lancaster*, 213–39; Phillips, *Aymer de Valence*, 136–83.
95. *Vita Edwardi*, 150–3; Maddicott, *Thomas of Lancaster*, 232.
96. *Rot. Scot.*, i, 190–2; M. Powicke, 'Edward II and Military Obligation', *Speculum*, xxxi (1956), 556–62.
97. *Rot. Scot.*, i, 194; Maddicott, *Thomas of Lancaster*, 240; *C.C.R.*, *1318–23*, 140; *C.D.S.*, iii, no. 701; Penman, 'Soules Conspiracy', 39.
98. *Vita Edwardi*, 160–1.
99. *C.D.S.*, iii, no. 668; *The Bruce*, ed. Duncan, 630n; Maddicott, *Thomas of Lancaster*, 244; Phillips, *Aymer de Valence*, 184.
100. *Vita Edwardi*, 162–3; *Chron. Lanercost*, 226; *The Bruce*, ed. Duncan, 629–31; *Anonimalle Chronicle*, 95–7.
101. *Vita Edwardi*, 162–3; *The Bruce*, ed. Duncan, 635–41; *Anonimalle Chronicle*, 97.

102. *Anonimalle Chronicle*, 97.
103. *The Bruce*, ed. Duncan, 627–9.
104. *Chron. Lanercost*, 226; *The Bruce*, ed. Duncan, 643; *Scalachronica*, ed. King, 86–7; McNamee, *Wars of the Bruces*, 88–91.
105. *Chron. Lanercost*, 226–7; *The Bruce*, ed. Duncan, 643–7; Schwyzer, 'Northern Bishops and the Anglo-Scottish War', 247–51.
106. Maddicott, *Thomas of Lancaster*, 247–9; Stevenson, *Illustrations*, 6–7.
107. *Vita Edwardi*, 162–9, 174–5; Maddicott, *Thomas of Lancaster*, 249–51.
108. For the text of this truce, see *R.R.S.*, v, no. 162. Douglas and Randolph led a further foray into England in early November when the west march was plundered and the Scots returned with 'a very large spoil of men and cattle' (*Chron. Lanercost*, 227–8).
109. *Vita Edwardi*, 174–7.
110. *C.P.L.*, ii, 127–30, 191–2, 199.
111. For the context and significance of the Declaration of Arbroath, see G. Simpson, 'The declaration of Arbroath revitalised', *S.H.R.*, 56 (1977), 11–33; A. A. M. Duncan, *The Nation of Scots and the Declaration of Arbroath* (London, 1970); E. Cowan, *For Freedom Alone: The Declaration of Arbroath, 1320* (East Linton, 2003); G. Barrow (ed.), *Declaration of Arbroath*.
112. *Scalachronica*, ed. King, 79; *The Bruce*, ed. Duncan, 699n.
113. The best account of the conspiracy is given in Penman, 'Soules Conspiracy'.
114. Mowbray was alive in early 1319 (and did not die at Fochart as claimed in some accounts) but his absence from the list of those who sealed the Declaration of Arbroath and those named in the events surrounding the conspiracy suggest he was already dead by May 1320.
115. *Chron. Fordun*, ii, 341; *Scalachronica*, ed. King, 79.
116. *Chron. Fordun*, ii, 341; *Scalachronica*, ed. King, 79; *The Bruce*, ed. Duncan, 701–5; *C.D.S.*, iii, nos 721, 723–4.
117. *C.D.S.*, iii, nos 709–11, 719–21, 724; Penman, 'Soules Conspiracy', 49–52.
118. *Vita Edwardi*, 178–9.
119. Altschul, *The Clares*, 165–71, 304–5; Underhill, *Elizabeth de Burgh*, 18–26.
120. *Vita Edwardi*, 182–5; Davies, *Lordship and Society*, 279–80; J. C. Davies, 'The Despenser war in Glamorgan', *T.R.H.S.*, 3rd series, 9 (1915), 21–64, 25–48.
121. Maddicott, *Thomas of Lancaster*, 261–7.
122. *Vita Edwardi*, 184–91; Davies, 'Despenser War', 53–7; Maddicott, *Thomas of Lancaster*, 267–73.
123. Maddicott, *Thomas of Lancaster*, 268–74.
124. *Vita Edwardi*, 192–5; Phillips, *Aymer de Valence*, 209–10.
125. *Vita Edwardi*, 196–9; Maddicott, *Thomas of Lancaster*, 293–4.
126. Maddicott, *Thomas of Lancaster*, 297–8; N. Fryde, *The Tyranny and Fall of Edward II* (Cambridge, 1979), 49–51.
127. Trokelowe, *Annales*, 118–20; *R.R.S.*, v, pp. 151–2.
128. Trokelowe, *Annales*, 118–20.
129. *Chron. Lanercost*, 230; McNamee, *Wars of the Bruces*, 96–8. There was no truce in early 1322.
130. *Vita Edwardi*, 200–3; Fryde, *Tyranny and Fall*, 54–5.
131. Smith, 'Edward II and Wales', 157–63.
132. *Vita Edwardi*, 202–5; Maddicott, *Thomas of Lancaster*, 294.
133. *Vita Edwardi*, 204–7; Maddicott, *Thomas of Lancaster*, 306–9.
134. *Chron. Lanercost*, 231; *Vita Edwardi*, 208–9.
135. *Chron. Lanercost*, 231–2; *Vita Edwardi*, 208–9; A. King, 'Thomas of Lancaster, Dunstanburgh Castle and the Lancastrian Castle Affinity in Northumberland, 1296–1322', *Archaeologia Aeliana*, 888 (2001), 223–34, 229–30.

136. *Chron. Lanercost*, 232–4; *Vita Edwardi*, 210–15; Trokelowe, *Annales*, 112–24; Maddicott, *Thomas of Lancaster*, 310–12.
137. *Chron. Lanercost*, 235–6.
138. *C.P.R., 1321–4*, 73–4.
139. *C.P.R., 1321–4*, 90–8; N. Fryde, 'Welsh troops in the Scottish Campaign of 1322', *B.B.C.S.*, 26 (1974–5), 82–9; Smith, 'Edward II and Wales', 161–3; Frame, *English Lordship in Ireland*, 135–7.
140. *C.P.R., 1321–4*, 123–30; *The Bruce*, ed. Duncan, 678; Fryde, *Tyranny and Fall*, 124–7.
141. Trokelowe, *Annales*, 124.
142. *C.P.R., 1321–4*, 184–90; Fryde, *Tyranny and Fall*, 128; Fryde, 'Welsh Troops', 83.
143. *Chron. Lanercost*, 237–8; McNamee, *Wars of the Bruces*, 98–9; Fryde, *Tyranny and Fall*, 123. There were fears of a Scottish invasion from early in May as well (*C.P.R., 1321–4*, 100, 130).
144. *C.P.R., 1321–4*, 193–8; *Scalachronica*, ed. King, 89; *The Bruce*, ed. Duncan, 678–9; Fryde, *Tyranny and Fall*, 129.
145. *The Bruce*, ed. Duncan, 679–81.
146. M. Prestwich, 'Military Logistics: The case of 1322', in M. Strickland (ed.), *Armies, Chivalry and Warfare in Medieval Britain and France* (Stamford, 1998), 276–88; Fryde, *Tyranny and Fall*, 130.
147. *Scalachronica*, ed. King, 89; *Chron. Lanercost*, 237–8; *The Bruce*, ed. Duncan, 681–3.
148. *Chron. Lanercost*, 239–40; *Scalachronica*, ed. King, 89; Stevenson, *Illustrations*, 7; *The Bruce*, ed. Duncan, 679–97; McNamee, *Wars of the Bruces*, 104–5. The Scots also besieged Norham during September 1322. The defence of the castle was not helped by a dispute between King Edward and the Beaumonts over the castle (*C.D.S.*, iii, nos 770, 772, 774, 777; Schwyzer, 'Northern Bishops and the Anglo-Scottish War', 252–3).
149. *Chron. Lanercost*, 240–2; Stevenson, *Illustrations*, 8; *R.R.S.*, v, no. 215; Stones, *Anglo-Scottish Relations*, no. 39.
150. *Chron. Lanercost*, 242–5; H. Summerson, *Medieval Carlisle*, 2 vols (Carlisle, 1993), i, 230–56.
151. *R.R.S.*, v, no. 232; *C.D.S.*, v, no. 687; McNamee, *Wars of the Bruces*, 236–8.

CHAPTER 8

The Legacy

VICTORY OR STALEMATE

The terms of the truce agreed at Bishopsthorpe in May 1323 seem to suggest that success on the battlefield at Bannockburn could not be turned into a lasting and decisive victory. Nine years after the battle, Robert Bruce agreed to a truce which did not include either the English king's abandonment of his claims to sovereignty over Scotland or any statement that Bruce enjoyed legitimate authority in his realm. Robert had sought this recognition consistently since 1314 and in this light his acceptance of a truce, which, unlike his deals with Lancaster and Harclay in 1321 and 1322, included no such terms must be seen as a climbdown. In return for a cessation of hostilities which, though lengthy, gave no lasting guarantees for either Robert or Scotland, it was Bruce who apparently made concessions. By agreeing that both sides would return the lands they occupied in the opposing realm, Robert was giving up the grip on Northumberland which had been the most concrete success achieved beyond Scotland.[1] The conflict may have widened dramatically in scale and scope, but after major warfare in Scotland, Ireland and northern England, and related political upheaval in Wales and England, Robert seems to have conceded that he was unable to secure peace and recognition for his kingdom and dynasty, let alone challenge the rule of King Edward in his own dominions.

However, to expect Bannockburn to precipitate an immediate and lasting settlement of the war in favour of the victor is to misunderstand the way battle and war fitted into wider political structures in the period. The rarity of battles like Bannockburn in medieval warfare has already been discussed, but it is also important to recognise that major clashes which could be could be regarded as decisive were also highly unusual. The battle of Bouvines in 1214, where King Philip II of France defeated the Emperor Otto, did break up a shaky political coalition and restored the status quo, while in internal clashes, like the battle of Evesham in 1265 or the fight at Boroughbridge, decisive results were much more common, linked to the greater readiness of participants in such civil wars to risk the field of battle.[2] However, just as few campaigns involving forces from different realms produced battles, so clashes between armies, even if they resulted in the complete disintegration of one side, did not tend to see

171

the end of war. The bloodbath at Courtrai, compared by several observers to Bannockburn, marked merely the beginning of a long, if sporadic, conflict between the French king and his Flemish opponents.[3] In his Scottish wars, Edward I's armies had won decisive victories at Dunbar in 1296 and Falkirk two years later. Neither led to a lasting collapse of Scottish resistance any more than the success won by Wallace at Stirling Bridge in the preceding year had caused Edward I to abandon his Scottish ambitions.[4]

The Scottish and French wars waged by Edward I's grandson, Edward III, scattered with famous and, apparently decisive, victories on the field of battle, confirm this pattern. At Dupplin Moor in 1332 and Halidon Hill a year later, Scottish armies were defeated with heavy losses, especially among the leading adherents of the Bruce dynasty. Though these battles allowed Edward and his allies to take the submissions of many Scots, within a few years the English king's lordship was in rapid decline.[5] In France too, neither the famous battle of Crécy in 1346 nor that of Poitiers ten years later ended the war. Though the French king was captured at Poitiers, encouraging Edward III to press for complete victory in the late 1350s, he ultimately settled for more limited, though still spectacular, gains in the peace of Brétigny.[6] However, in the coming years Edward proved unable to secure these gains and war with the French resumed. In a similar way, Robert Bruce secured his own peace treaty in 1328 with England, which recognised him as independent king of Scots. However, it too proved to be purely temporary. Within five years the English crown renounced its recognition of Bruce kingship and Scottish sovereignty and renewed the war.[7] This conflict, like the war in France, would rumble on for over a century. Military ascendancy, even if marked by spectacular success on the field of battle, did not easily translate into the political surrender of one realm to another in late-medieval warfare.

Instead, battlefield victory tended to be subsumed into the continuing patterns of military and political competition. Though clearly decisive in its outcome on the day, Bannockburn was, as the previous chapters have shown, just one event in a war which spanned over sixteen years. The core reason for this struggle remained fixed on Bruce's kingship in Scotland, but within the conflict Bannockburn marked the end of one phase and the beginning of other. Before 24 June 1314, the ground on which the war had been fought was overwhelmingly Scottish. After that date, the focus of fighting shifted primarily to Edward II's dominions. The outcome of the battle made this shift more dramatic and clear cut, but it could be said that the defeat suffered by the English king's host had largely confirmed and accelerated existing military patterns. After all, since 1307 Bruce had been whittling away at Plantagenet-held Scotland, extracting the submissions of nobles and local communities and demonstrating the inability of the enemy to protect its adherents. Victory at Bannockburn completed this process in Scotland. It also gave the Bruces the confidence and momentum to extend the war into England and Ireland in late 1314 and early 1315. The increased scale, frequency and ambition of the campaigns in northern England between 1314 and 1322 can be traced directly back to Bannockburn. Similarly, the dispatch of an army to Ulster in 1315, though presaged by Bruce contacts with that province since 1306, suggests that, in the wake of their victory on the field, Robert and Edward Bruce were ready to open new fronts and consider new goals beyond their Scottish power base.

However, once this more ambitious strategy had been launched, the direct military impact of Bannockburn can probably be considered a diminishing factor. Both in northern England and Ireland, the Scots had to maintain their military ascendancy by continued campaigning, often against the odds. The marches which Edward Bruce and his brother made through Ireland were their only means of projecting their power. The dangers of this approach were demonstrated by the fatal campaign and battle of Fochart in late 1318, which displayed the limited resources at the Bruces' disposal in their Irish war compared to those of their opponents. In northern Britain too, the apparent advantage enjoyed by the Scots overlay a continued weakness in manpower and even certain military skills. In 1317, 1319 and 1322 English invasions were launched into Robert's realm which the Scottish king and his men felt unable to meet head on. Despite Bannockburn, and in contrast to the strategy pursued in Ireland, the Scots refused to offer battle in defence of territory. While ready to engage with Yorkshire levies at Myton and with a poorly led and retreating force at Byland, Bruce's forces clearly chose to avoid facing an English army in battle in 1319 and 1322. They relied instead on scorched earth to deny the enemy the means to remain in Scotland, on the harrassment of foraging parties and on diversionary attacks into northern England. This last method, spectacularly employed to raise Edward II's siege of Berwick in 1319, was related to the series of large-scale campaigns launched into England from 1314. All these attacks penetrated well beyond the normal reach of Scottish incursions, inflicting damage and spreading fear into Yorkshire and Lancashire. Under the leadership of talented captains like James Douglas and Thomas Randolph and probably composed of experienced soldiers, the Scots' successes weakened the resources of northern England and added to Edward's record of failure in the war. The rout of the English king by his rival at Byland was the clearest expression of the Scots' mastery in the war. Though having defeated his own rebellious subjects, and after raising thousands of men for the war against Bruce, Edward had to flee from a Scottish force hundreds of miles inside his own realm. Yet, despite their success, the invasions launched between 1314 and 1322 were, like the Irish campaigns, bold ventures which involved risks of defeat far from home. Though the campaigns can be compared with later English *chevauchées* in France, unlike these mounted forays across enemy territory the Scots were not facing a cowed opponent intent on refusing battle. Instead, despite Bannockburn, there is nothing to suggest that Edward II or his commanders would have turned down a fresh chance to meet the Scots in the field. The skills of Randolph and Douglas involved their ability to elude English armies as much as their prowess in battle. The mixed records of Scottish sieges at Carlisle, Carrickfergus and Berwick show that the advantages enjoyed by Bruce's forces were limited to certain aspects of warfare. As before Bannockburn, Robert's skill was in recognising these limitations and in continuing to exploit the flaws in the position of his enemy.

Equally, Bruce's key advantage remained the ineptitude of the English leadership and the divisions in the English polity. The character of the war continued to be shaped not simply by the strategies pursued by the Bruce brothers, but by the fragmented nature of the English war effort. The rivalry between the king and Lancaster prevented or hampered the prosecution of the war in late 1314, in the summer of 1316, during the siege of Berwick in 1319 and in 1321, when civil war broke out. The civil war even opened the possibility that Bruce might be able to secure his political goals by intervening in English politics. It would, ultimately, be divisions of this kind, following the deposition and death of Edward II, which would lead the new regime to recognise Bruce's kingship in Scotland in 1328.[8] Even when such rivalries were suspended or removed, as in the 1322 campaign, the king and his lieutenants showed an unwillingness to adapt to the lessons of the Scottish wars. The recruitment of a massive army, inadequate preparations to feed it in Scotland and an absence of any clear strategy for the campaign led almost inevitably to the failure of the expedition and encouraged Bruce to counterattack. Though new approaches to recruitment were tried after Bannockburn, with the aim of providing larger numbers of footmen, the need was not really for larger hosts of poorly trained levies.[9] Instead, the decision of Andrew Harclay to form up his men-at-arms on foot in a close body has been seen as the first attempt to adapt tactics in response to Scottish experience. However, it is striking that such lessons were learned by northern English knights, not the king. It would be another decade before a royal-led English army would follow this example.[10]

The limited and largely unsuccessful efforts at military reform undertaken by English governments after 1314 do, at least, indicate the continued commitment of all parties to waging war against Bruce.[11] The defeat suffered at Bannockburn had not reduced the determination of King Edward and his barons to recover Scotland from this enemy. The scale of the defeat and the humiliations which followed it may even have led both the king and Lancaster to regard the war as a key test of their rule. Despite accusations to the contrary, it was only when in rebellion and faced with a traitor's death that Lancaster sought to deal with Bruce. Lancaster's treason seems only to have encouraged Edward II to follow the defeat of the rebels with a major Scottish campaign, and elsewhere there was no sign of a peace party among the English nobility until Harclay travelled to Lochmaben in early 1323. Though landowners, burgesses and local communities in the far north were prepared to buy off Bruce and, in the English border dales, men did homage to the Scottish king, such capitulations hardly affected the resources at the disposal of Edward II.

Though the costs of the war continued to cause problems for the crown, Bannockburn and the subsequent depredations of Scottish forces in northern England did not significantly reduce the ability of the Plantagenet realm to wage war, nor did it cause Edward to consider conceding the rights he had inherited in Scotland. Faced by this resilience, or intransigence, Bruce lacked the means to compel his enemy to recognise his rights. Moreover, while Edward refused to lay aside his claims to Scotland, neither Pope John nor Edward's brothers-in-law the kings of France would show much sympathy with Bruce's cause. Bannockburn did not deliver Bruce a final victory over the English king.

BANNOCKBURN AND SCOTLAND

To seek a decisive military resolution to those issues in conflict between Edward II and Robert Bruce in the outcome of Bannockburn is to miss the significance of the battle. Instead, the legacy of the fight is to be found in its role in shifting the focus of the war which would produce long-term conse- quences for the British Isles. Not surprisingly, this significance is clearest with regard to Scotland. In terms of the kingdom's government, politics and society, Bannockburn was a decisive event. The victory won by Robert on the field led within weeks to the fall of the last remaining English-held castles, except Berwick, the submission or exile of those Scots who had refused to accept Bruce as king and the effective end of Edwardian lordship in Scotland for a generation. After nearly two decades of intense warfare waged on Scottish soil for the allegiance of the kingdom's lords and people, Bannockburn brought a period of relative peace and security to the land. Despite the poor weather which brought famine to neighbouring regions, Barbour claimed that after Bannockburn 'the contré haboundyt weill of corne and fe [cattle] and of alkyn other ryches'.[12] Though Fife was raided in 1317 and the borders with England remained subject to attack up to 1322, the disruption and damage caused to Scotland by the ongoing war was much reduced. Even Edward II's large-scale attacks in 1319 and 1322 did little to shake this situation, being brief in duration and limited to the south-east in their impact.[13]

The eight years of war after Bannockburn and then the next decade in which Scotland remained free from major warfare allowed the kingdom to recover from the damage done by the conflict waged from 1296 to 1314. Instead, in the years after the battle the war became a source of considerable profit to the Scots. As we have seen, even before Bannockburn Bruce had derived the resources he needed to maintain his forces by launching attacks into England in search of plunder and blackmail. The attacks directed across the border from late 1314 produced even greater returns. Direct plunder, but even more, the payments of English communities to avoid Scottish attacks, gave Bruce and his subjects perhaps as much as £20,000 in the years up to 1323.[14] However, of probably greater importance to the Scots was the absence of these costs and damages from their own lands. The records of royal government from the 1320s show the extent to which Scotland had recovered from the conflict. These suggest that the burghs, often at the centre of warfare before 1314, were now able to render considerable sums to the crown in rents and customs duties. Even Berwick, which remained in a war zone until 1323, recovered much of its economic importance in the 1320s.[15] The wider recovery of the kingdom was suggested by the success of the crown in extracting grants of taxation from the community. In 1326 Robert pleaded his own impoverishment due to the war and asked for an annual financial subsidy from parliament. Though allowance was made in this for lands wasted by war, the readiness of the Scottish community to make an unprecedented annual payment to the king indicates a degree of prosperity. Two years later they undertook, in addition, to pay off the sum of £20,000 owed for the peace with England, making the payments in three instalments.[16] While this evidence comes from the end of Robert's reign, the peace which produced this prosperity can be traced back to the aftermath of Bannockburn.

To both Scottish and English chroniclers, the results of the battle proved Bruce's rights to be king of Scotland. The chronicle of *Lanercost* reported that, after Bannockburn, 'Robert de Brus was commonly called King of Scotland by all men, because he had acquired Scotland by force of arms'.[17] The test of battle was regarded by contemporaries and later writers as divine judgement. While the English blamed their own side's arrogance and pride, Scots saw victory as proof of the justice of King Robert's cause. Robert was himself keen to give thanks for God's favour. Though he did not found a religious house on the site of his triumph, like King Philip of France at Saint Victoire or Joao of Portugal at Batalha, Bruce also showed his gratitude.[18] Just over three years after Bannockburn, on 5 July 1318, Robert promised to make an annual grant of £66 to the shrine of St Andrew 'in commemoration of the signal victory given to the Scots at Bannockburn by the blessed Andrew, protector of the kingdom'. His bequest was made at the dedication of the new cathedral of St Andrews, which he attended along with 'seven bishops, fifteen abbots and nearly all the nobles of the kingdom'. The completion of the cathedral was employed as a ceremony of national thanksgiving and the king's grant was followed by grants from other figures 'for the same reason'.[19] The occasion symbolised the role of the battle in turning Bruce from a usurper into a legitimate king; the divine support for his cause which he had claimed in 1309 was now proved.

Bannockburn also had a direct impact on Bruce's hopes of founding a dynasty. The capture of Humphrey earl of Hereford in the battle allowed Robert to secure the release of his queen, Elizabeth Burgh, and his daughter, Marjory, in exchange for the earl.[20] The return of these ladies was to prove vital for the future of the Scottish monarchy. Though Edward Bruce was initially recognised as his brother's heir, after his death at Fochart in 1318 the succession would depend on the offspring of Queen Elizabeth and Lady Marjory.

Marjory's hastily arranged marriage to Walter Stewart in 1315 and the birth of a son to the couple the next year would provide Bruce with his only male heir in the six years after 1318. This child, named Robert after his grandfather, would spend the next half-century in the line of succession. His presence, though often creating tensions, also provided a degree of security for the royal line and the realm and resulted, in 1371, in his accession to the throne, the founder of a Stewart royal dynasty.[21] This new line, which would be proud of its descent from Robert Bruce and acted as the defenders of his legacy, stemmed from the release of the royal ladies in 1314. This was also true of Robert's direct successor. The release of Queen Elizabeth allowed Bruce to hope for his own son to extend his line. In 1324 a son was finally born to King Robert. Named David, his birth was remembered as a matter of jubilation for Scots. Though by this time Robert himself may have been ailing, and he would die in 1329 leaving David to succeed him as a child, the possession of a son was greeted as a guarantee for the future of the dynasty and kingdom.[22] Without Bannockburn, the release of Marjory and Elizabeth would have been unlikely and the long-term hopes of the Bruce Cause far more uncertain.

Beyond the dynasty, Bannockburn had a central importance in shifting the character of Scottish political society. Before the battle, though Robert's military successes had won over a growing proportion of the kingdom to his allegiance, he remained an intensely partisan figure. Up to 1313 and 1314 many Scots, especially in the south, continued to oppose Bruce in war. Bannockburn ended this civil war and destroyed the power of his Scottish enemies. Some of those opponents, like the young John Comyn, were killed in the battle, others were captured, while more fled to England, like David earl of Atholl. However, the majority of this group chose to regard the battle as a decisive victory. They recognised that the ultimatum issued by Robert in late 1313, threatening the forfeiture of all landowners who failed to pay him homage, would now be fulfilled. Lords like Patrick earl of Dunbar and Ingeram Umfraville led the way, before Robert passed the statute at Cambuskenneth pronouncing the disinheritance of his remaining enemies. The statute demonstrated that the open conflict of allegiance in Scotland was over.[23] Tensions certainly continued and former opponents like David Brechin and William Soules may have resented Bruce's handling of issues of patronage.[24] The king's direct dealings with Duncan earl of Fife, who had returned to Scotland after Bannockburn, suggest Robert was ready to exert pressure on lords to strengthen his own position.[25] The arrest and trial of former enemies like Brechin and Soules in 1320 shows the continued flaws in the unity of the realm, but any threat to Robert's kingship was now one of hidden conspiracy, not open defiance.[26]

The evidence of internal friction, while confined, was not insignificant. It should not, though, distract overly from the general picture. Alongside new defections and disaffection can be set examples of returning exiles like Murdoch Menteith, who may have brought Bruce news of contacts between Scottish lords and Edward Balliol. Also significant was the decision of Margaret, daughter of

FIGURE 8.1 *The abbey of Cambuskenneth lay in a bend of the River Forth within sight of Stirling Castle and the field of Bannockburn. This proximity made it an obvious setting for Bruce's victory parliament of November 1314 which deprived those killed or exiled by the battle of their Scottish lands. (Crown Copyright. Historic Scotland)*

Bruce's convinced opponent, Alexander Abernethy, to return to Scotland 'to recover her hereditary lands' in 1325.[27] Her choice showed recognition of Bruce's growing security in office and confirmed that, after Bannockburn, Robert was unchallenged ruler of Scotland. The course of the war to 1323, especially when allied to papal censure from 1318 to 1320, could cause anxieties, but did not lead the vast majority of his subjects to question the legitimacy of the Bruce claim to the throne established in war. The victory outside Stirling ushered in not just peace, but a period of political stability unknown since the 1280s. Central to this was the acceptance of the Bruce dynasty as the rightful defenders of Scotland as a sovereign realm. Robert encouraged this process by the promotion of his most trusted and valued adherents. Nobles like Thomas Randolph, James Douglas and Walter Stewart were rewarded for their efforts in Bruce's wars by influence, land and status.[28] They were the tip of an iceberg of patronage which saw a large proportion of the nobles who recognised Robert have their rights confirmed or enlarged. Such favour was not limited to those who had fought for Bruce since 1309 or before. Even late recruits like Alexander Seton, whose defection at Bannockburn may have been hugely influential, could reap benefits from the king. Seton rose to be keeper of Berwick and steward of the household of the young Prince David, both marks of great royal trust.[29] For a wide group of nobles, recognition of Bruce and their enjoyment of his patronage bound them to King Robert's cause. The families of Robert's loyalists, like the Douglases, Hays, Keiths, Murrays and many others, would be reluctant to risk lands and status by abandoning their loyalty to the Bruce dynasty in future.[30] Such loyalty was not solely motivated by material concerns. Service in a largely successful war, at Bannockburn above all, surely generated an ideological attachment to King Robert. The period of stable landholding which followed the battle cemented allegiances created in warfare.

Within Scotland, the importance of Bannockburn was in its strengthening of the Bruce dynasty, both immediately and in the decades to come. The creation of a relatively stable and peaceful environment in the kingdom after 1314, the part the battle played in allowing the formation of a Bruce dynasty, and the role of the victory in strengthening attachment to King Robert and his rights all had a lasting significance. These all proved to be vital factors when a renewed assault was launched against the Bruce dynasty by both the English crown and the heirs of Robert's Scottish enemies during the 1330s. The ability of a new generation of Bruce adherents to defend the cause of Robert's son, David II, owed something to the legacy of the earlier battle, which survived the battlefield defeats of 1332 and 1333.[31] The later war was won by the efforts of this later generation, most successful of whom was Andrew Murray, another Scot freed after Bannockburn. Murray's military successes, in which he risked battle against his Scottish opponents but not against Edward III of England, owed much to Robert Bruce's normal approach to warfare, abandoned for the day of Bannockburn. However, in the appeal of Murray and his comrades to Scots, these leaders benefited from a residual support for 'Davy', which stemmed from memories of the Bannockburn war.[32]

BANNOCKBURN AND THE BRUCE WARS

The most striking military result of Bannockburn came in the decision of Robert and Edward Bruce to carry the war into the lands of their enemy in Ireland and England. While, as we have seen, the efforts made by the Scots in these lands did not force Edward II to recognise Robert's kingship, the period of Scottish predominance begun by Bannockburn was not devoid of consequences for the peoples of Ireland and the English north. This situation is apparent with regard to the lordship of Ireland. On the surface, Bruce ambitions in Ireland came to naught. The campaigns of Edward Bruce on the island from 1315 to 1318 did not cause the collapse of Plantagenet authority. Bruce's assumption of the high kingship appeared as an unrealistic and doomed exploit with no lasting significance. His brief occupation of eastern Ulster did not survive the disaster at Fochart and the Scots' marches through Meath, Leinster and Munster brought no lasting shifts in allegiance. By 1322 Edward II could, once again, call on his English and Irish lieges in the lordship to provide men and supplies for the Scottish war.[33]

However, if the Bruce brothers failed in their direct goals, the presence of Scottish forces in Ireland did have an impact. The importance of these armies of several thousand experienced soldiers, the victories they won at Connor, Skerries and Ardscull and their marches across English Ireland were a new element in Irish politics. Their significance came in relation to the existing wars and local conflicts, especially in Gaelic Ireland and the borderlands. As we have seen, before 1315 these already pitted English lords against Irish leaders, as well as Irish against Irish in dynastic disputes which drew in English nobles like William Burgh and Richard Clare. These conflicts, especially that between Donal O'Neill and Richard earl of Ulster, had played a role in drawing the Scots to Ireland and Edward Bruce was probably encouraged to seek the support of other Irish leaders as the basis of high kingship. The letter sent to the Pope on behalf of the Irish princes and in support of Edward in 1317 related the complaints of the Irish nation and presented Scottish support as a Gaelic alliance.[34] Such claims were employed by the Bruces in 1306–7, but as a platform for lasting power in Ireland appeals to Irish unity were of limited value. Instead of recruiting powerful Irish allies and leading an uprising against the English, as they had done in Scotland, the Bruce brothers found themselves drawn into the regional and dynastic conflicts which characterised Gaelic Ireland. As a result, when the Scots forged alliance with Irish leaders, like Felim O'Connor and Brian Ban O'Brien, they pushed the family rivals of these lords into active support of the English administration.[35] Rather than raising armies of Irish allies, Edward and Robert found themselves bogged down in existing wars.

Against their Irish friends, the Scots united rival Irish leaders and the English in opposition. By championing the Irish nation, the Bruces had limited their appeal to the English community. Though a few English did homage to Edward Bruce, they were either Ulster tenants, motivated by the need to retain their lands, or malcontents who hoped to benefit from a change in regime.[36] The vast majority of the English nobility and community stood firm in the face of the new threat. Though, up to Fochart, their military performance against the Scots was poor, failing to exploit advantages of numbers and position, the king's officers and other English lords did not waver in their loyalty. In 1315 and 1317 they kept the field and prevented the Scots from making significant advances, while operating against Bruce's Irish allies.[37] The victory of William Burgh at Athenry in 1316 saw the death of Felim O'Connor and the end of Bruce influence in Connacht. The leadership of Edmund Butler, Roger Mortimer and others was persistent and, ultimately, the advantages of the English in Ireland proved decisive in the defeat of Edward Bruce at Fochart.[38]

However, just as the failure of Edward Bruce's war was due to the character of Irish politics, so the effects of these campaigns was to bring about, or accelerate, shifts in this character. Instead of a uniform pattern of change, these shifts altered the regional relationships and situations which defined Ireland. Though fragmented and varied, such changes could have long-term significance. Most directly altered by the Scottish campaigns was Ulster. Before 1315 Earl Richard Burgh's dominance of the province was largely secure. His defeat at Connor by the Scots led to Edward Bruce occupying the heart of his earldom in Antrim and Down for over three years. Earl Richard was driven into exile, an object of suspicion to his compatriots. After the defeat of Bruce in 1318, the earl had to wait two more years to recover custody of his province, and though the earldom remained peaceful until Richard's death in 1326, the long-term position may well have shifted.[39] Beyond eastern Ulster, the earl's power had depended on the services he could demand from Irish magnates. Though the most troublesome of these, Donal O'Neill, had suffered defeat in the wake of Fochart, the authority of the earl in western Ulster may never have recovered fully from Connor.[40] Strains also existed among the English tenants of the earls after the Bruce occupation. Earl Richard's death was followed by the minority of his grandson, William, which may have further undermined Burgh authority. The new earl's efforts to exert control over his own kinsmen led to his murder in 1333 by Walter Burgh, son of his grandfather's key adherent William.[41]

This run of misfortunes dealt a fatal blow to the ability of the earls of Ulster to manage and contain the Irish of the north-west. The Bruce invasion had begun this process which would result in the contraction of English lordship in a wide part of northern Ireland. This process included Connacht, where the retreat of the earls left their junior kinsmen, William and Walter Burgh, as leading figures. Though English rather than Irish, these local lords would prove much less responsive to the king's officials, signalling a further geographical reduction in the crown's reach.[42] More worrying for the English community were signs of increased Irish aggression in different regions. These were not unconnected with the presence of Scottish armies in Ireland. The advance of the Bruces through Leinster in 1316 and 1317 prompted local Irish kindreds like the O'Mores and O'Byrnes to step up their own raids on English lands and communities. Though they experienced several local defeats, the Leinster Irish acted in concert with the Bruces and extended their trail of destruction through the province. Their success was marked by contracting English interests in the southern midlands, close to the centres of the lordship.[43] In such struggles, the role of the Scots acted as an accelerant to existing conflicts. Elsewhere, conflict continued on its own terms. In Thomond, the war waged by Richard Clare to establish his lordship over the O'Briens continued despite the opposition of the head of the kindred, Murtough, to the Bruces in 1317. In May 1318 Clare was defeated and killed by Murtough at Dysert O'Dea. His death was followed by the rapid collapse of English influence north of the Shannon.[44] Though unconnected to Bruce ambitions, the aggression shown by the Irish in the battle may have been influenced by the Scots' demonstration of English military vulnerability the previous year. In a number of regions, the years during and after the Bruce expeditions witnessed major changes to patterns of local lordship which had been established, if not necessarily stable, over several decades.

These changes worked to limit the range and effectiveness of the English king's government and to undermine the security of the English community in Ireland. The physical damage done to the property and persons of English landowners in the heartlands of the lordship during the Scottish campaigns of 1316 and 1317 may have been repaired fairly rapidly. The psychological effect of the Scottish campaigns and the associated upsurge in attacks by Irish leaders proved to be more long-term in its implications. The Bruce expeditions contributed to the increased anxieties of the English about their Irish neighbours, which were displayed repeatedly through the next two centuries. The warfare launched with grand hopes by the Scots after Bannockburn may not have secured a second Bruce kingdom, but it left a deep impression on the peoples of Ireland.

The harrying of northern England by King Robert's men had a similar impact. Though its direct results were limited, it was still a formative experience for the communities north of the Humber. These attacks had begun before 1314, but it was Bannockburn which gave Bruce the security and ambition to escalate his forays into England. Before the battle, Scottish raids were brief advances into the English border dales for money and livestock. The campaigns launched every year from late 1314 until 1319 and again in 1322 took the war further and further into England. In 1314 and 1315 the valleys of the Tees and Eden were harried. In 1316 the Scots plundered into Yorkshire and Lancashire as far as Wharfedale and the Ribble. In 1319 and 1322 Bruce's armies reached the Vale of York and almost to the banks of the Humber.[45] Scottish armies rode with impunity through the north, demonstrating their ability to outmanoeuvre or defeat English forces and to damage property. In the face of such attacks, local communities frequently chose to buy off the Scots, paying large sums in return for avoiding attacks. It has been estimated that Durham alone paid £4,000 for such truces, while the shires further north and west contributed about £12,000 to the Scots and Yorkshire perhaps £5,000.[46] Through direct attack and the threat of devastation, Robert was able to impoverish the north and bring disruption to a large region of his enemy's kingdom.

Apart from providing Bruce and his adherents with the money and supplies to wage war, the impact of this military ascendancy cannot be measured in terms of direct political gains. Though it would be after another skilled and successful campaign in the north in 1327 that the English government would finally agree to a peace treaty which recognised Robert's kingship, the series of campaigns which followed Bannockburn did not result in a capitulation by

Edward II. Both the king and his rival, Lancaster, spent heavily on the defence of the north from 1314, maintaining garrisons and retaining captains and companies of soldiers in Northumberland and neighbouring shires and paying for military expeditions like those of Arundel in 1317 and of the king in 1319 and 1322.[47] His priorities are further suggested by the elevation of Louis Beaumont to the see of Durham. The king's support for Beaumont, who was reputedly uneducated, stemmed from his belief that as bishop, Louis would provide effective support for his brother, Henry, in the defence of the north-east. To Edward's disgust, these hopes proved to be empty.[48] Despite the ineffectiveness of these measures against the Scots and his own personal humiliation in 1322, Edward II was not induced to make concessions on the issue of his lordship of Scotland by Bruce's attacks on his realm. Instead the king encouraged his northern subjects to make truces with the enemy, conceding his inability to protect them. Though they could hardly be immune from the loss of face and revenues caused by these attacks, neither Edward nor Lancaster allowed the protection of the north to alter their main priorities. In 1321 and 1322 Lancaster, who was probably the greatest magnate in the north, failed to provide either leadership or protection for the nobles of the region who clearly sought his aid. Just as his concentration was on the growing struggle with the king, so Edward apparently told the northerners to protect themselves against the Scots while he dealt with Lancaster.[49] The impression is given that for the king and his greatest subject, the harrying of the north was not sufficient reason for them to alter their political behaviour. When the leading commander from the English borders, Andrew Harclay, took the decision to make his own settlement with Bruce, he suffered death at the hands of his king.[50] Edward's action shows a clear lack of sympathy with any idea that the recent fate of his northern lands should have any bearing on the crown's rights in Scotland.

However, Harclay's fatal decision in early 1323 suggests that, as in Ireland, the effects of sustained war in the aftermath of Bannockburn should be sought within the lands which experienced increased conflict. *Lanercost* states that 'the poor folk, middle class and farmers in the northern parts' were happy to see Robert recognised as king if 'they themselves might live in peace'.[51] This sympathy did not prevent King Edward from securing the support of a group of local knights to arrest Harclay as a traitor, but indicates the war weariness of the English north after a dozen years of attacks. At its most extreme, this led border communities, in Tynedale and north Northumberland for example, to pay homage to Robert. This was a major step up from purchasing truces from the Scots and indicates the disintegration of allegiance to the English crown. Even though Bruce was clearly prepared to bargain away such claims to fealty in the negotiations of early 1323, the submissions of English borderers does show the political impact of sustained pressure.[52] The scale of this pressure had other, less directly political, effects. Most obviously the Scottish attacks inflicted considerable damage on the wealth of the region. The paths taken by the Scots in their expeditions have been traced by subsequent exemptions from, or reductions in, the payments owed by local communities in taxation. In north Northumberland and in Durham, much further south, incomes from land show a fall of a third to three-quarters from their values before 1311. Evidence also shows lands being abandoned and damage to the mills and granges which were vital to local economies.[53] However, though this pattern is striking, it is harder to draw conclusions about its longer-term impact. Though values of land in the far north never fully recovered, rents did revive initially and the general downturn may have involved other factors than war.

The real significance of the Scottish attacks after Bannockburn was their role in transforming the lands north of the Tees into a military borderland. Though this process had begun with the onset of Anglo-Scottish warfare in 1296, the decade from 1314 was the key period in the shift in the character of the English marches. Bannockburn made the north of England a war zone. The leading landowners of the region, lay and ecclesiastical, were ordered by the crown to defend their estates rather than attend parliament, the first signs of a military role being developed for the north. The tenants-in-chief of the crown were already required to garrison royal castles and defend their locality in time of war. After 1314 the value of this was tested regularly for the first time. It proved to be inadequate. Instead Edward II opted to pay for garrisons in both royal and private castles, as he had done in Scotland. He also retained local lords and captains, paying for their service with annuities and with access to royal favour. Knights like Thomas Gray, Robert Raymes and Gilbert Middleton became the king's servants, as well as developing careers in the war. By 1324 the effect of this local recruitment was indicated by the high number of knights and men-at-arms recorded in Northumberland.[54] Scottish attacks and the English crown's response resulted in the rapid militarisation of the north after 1314. The needs and pressures of war altered the normal structures of local society. The plundering of the Scots was matched by the activities of captains like Jack le Irish and Gilbert Middleton, whose private enterprises added to the disorder of Northumberland. Le Irish's kidnapping of Maud Clifford and Middleton's rebellion were extreme manifestations of disruptiveness which was frequently condoned by King Edward. The careers of these robbers, or *schavaldours*, as contemporary sources called them, marked a long-term change which saw the dominance of the marches by military captains, employed by the crown in the Scottish war.[55] The permanent state of war which prevailed in the borders from the 1330s saw a similar process develop in southern Scotland but, while in the Scottish borders the years from 1314 were ones of unusually secure allegiance and general peace, for the English north they provided a formative period of intense conflict and disruption.[56]

It is harder to see Bannockburn as having a lasting effect on politics in the heartlands of the Plantagenet dominions in midland and southern England. The ability of Edward to ignore the north and the patchy interest shown in the conflict by English chroniclers, reflect a sense of distance from the Scottish war felt by the king and his leading subjects. Bannockburn was just one further humiliation for Edward in a run of defeats and failures which, in many ways, reached a climax in 1322 at Old Byland. The king's political problems began long before the disaster of 1314 and the direct impact of the defeat quickly became obscured in continuing displays of ineptitude and disunity by Edward and his opponents. Bannockburn did have an immediate political fallout in England. For Thomas of Lancaster, the result of the battle was an opportunity. It would have been typically small-minded if he had shared the view of certain chroniclers that the defeat was a judgement on those, like Pembroke, Hereford and Clifford, who had deserted the Ordainers to join the expedition. Other rumours suggest that the king would have moved against Lancaster had the war gone well.[57] The earl had clearly regarded the campaign as contravening the Ordinances and its outcome forced Edward to agree to accept these restrictions and to give Lancaster a leading role in the government. In the event, this apparent reconciliation would prove to be just one more milestone in the breakdown of relations between the king and his enemies.[58] The next eight years witnessed a series of stand-offs, attempted settlements and half-hearted displays of unity. Some of these related to the Scottish war, but, as we have seen, this was the main priority for neither Edward nor Lancaster. Though this history of division and inept leadership was a major factor in Bruce's success, Edward's ultimate victory against Lancaster in early 1322 did not lead to a reversal of fortune in Scotland. Neither, subsequently, did the cessation of hostilities with Robert from 1323 guarantee the English king freedom from problems in his own realm. Though Edward had conceded nothing in the 1323 truce, the failure to erase memories of his previous humiliations at Bruce's hands remained a judgement on his kingship.[59] In 1326–7 he was deposed from office by his own subjects, led by his own queen, Isabella, and her lover, the exiled rebel Roger Mortimer of Wigmore. Among the rebels were many northerners led by Henry Beaumont, unhappy with the truce of 1323. The loss of Scotland was named among Edward's failings in the charges against him, but it was the mixed harshness and incompetence of his rule in England which drove his subjects to drastic measures.[60]

THE RESHAPING OF THE BRITISH ISLES

The significance of Bannockburn was not limited to royal wars and the politics of the English and Scottish realms. It also represented a key turning point in the fortunes and attitudes of many of the aristocratic dynasties which had done much to define and connect the communities of the British Isles during the previous two and a half centuries. This effect could derive from the individual as much as the collective results of the battle. The death of Gilbert Clare earl of Gloucester was identified by English, Welsh and Irish chroniclers as the most striking loss on the field. Gilbert, described by a Gaelic Irish writer as 'he who of all the English was of most nobility and dignity and inherited the greatest estate', was the last of his line.[61] As we have seen, his death set in train a series of events centred on his lands in lordships but with much wider implications. The passage of the Clare inheritance first into royal custody and then its division between Earl Gilbert's three sisters and their husbands had consequences which were both local, affected whole lands and spanned the English king's dominions.[62] The effects went far beyond the concerns of a single noble family, its estates and tenants. In Wales, the death of Earl Gilbert broke the ties of lordship, protection and reward which were so important in linking the Welsh community into the framework of English rule. Concerns for the future prompted the rebellion of Llywelyn Bren in 1316, which sparked fears of renewed war in Wales. Though brief and local, the dangers of the rebellion and the importance of maintaining the structures by which Welsh leaders could find employment and advancement from English lords and officials were recognised by the crown. A similar but much more extensive failure of lordship in the 1390s would lie behind the great rebellion of Owain Glyn Dŵr, which would threaten to overturn English rule in Wales.[63]

The Clare inheritance also raised issues between English families. The husbands of Gilbert's sisters were all initially favourites of King Edward but, characteristically, the king alienated two of these men, Hugh Audley and Roger Damory, by his excessive support of the third, Hugh Despenser. Though arrogant and aggressive in England, it was in the Welsh marches, where traditions of aristocratic behaviour were more robust, that Despenser exploited this royal support to harass the other heirs to secure the whole lordship of Glamorgan and carve out a wider empire in south Wales. More than anything else, it was this struggle over the Clare inheritance which led to the other marcher lord, Hereford, the Mortimers and others taking up arms against Despenser and the king in 1321. It was this 'Despenser war' which led directly to the civil war of 1322, the death of Lancaster and the tyranny and fall of Edward II.[64] Though an accident of war, rather than a planned policy, the death of Gloucester at Bannockburn was a key turning point in the politics of Wales and England in the fourteenth century. It demonstrated the importance of aristocratic concerns in these politics and the direct, and potentially destabilising, effect of the close contact between the Welsh marches and principality and English politics.

Though less immediate in its impact, Gloucester's death also symbolised a shift in structures of lordship in Ireland. His lordship of Kilkenny was a profitable and largely peaceful estate. After his death, Kilkenny was changed from a private liberty into a royal county and the Clare lands were divided between the three heiresses. However, these sisters and their husbands would be preoccupied with events in England and Wales, which would lead to the forfeiture of all three between 1322 and 1327.[65] The surviving heiresses would recover their lands, but their disrupted tenure was another factor limiting their active involvement in Kilkenny. Unlike the Clares, who had at least visited their Irish lands on occasion, the new owners were absentees, prepared to sell off portions of the lordship. While it remained profitable, partition and absenteeism meant that Kilkenny was less effective as a focus for local English leadership.[66] In fourteenth-century Ireland there was an increased need for such leadership in the face of local warfare. If this was no longer provided by the heirs of the Clares, it would come from other sources closer at hand. Edmund Butler, justiciar of Ireland during the Bruce wars, had been rewarded for his efforts with an earldom. His son was made earl of Ormond and given Tipperary as a private liberty in 1328. During subsequent decades the Butlers provided regional leadership for the English of the southern midlands. While their hold on Tipperary came under pressure from local Irish kindreds, the Butlers extended their lands and lordship eastwards into Kilkenny. They cemented their influence in the latter county by purchasing the lands of absentee owners, creating a landed dominance to match their personal connections.[67] This death of Gilbert Clare was part of a more general process by which the leadership of English Ireland passed from great noble dynasties tied closely to England, to families whose interests were focused on Ireland. In the decade after Fochart, earldoms were created for the heads of four such lineages. Families like the Butlers were English in identity and held some English interests, but their aims and methods marked them as distinct in practice from the chief subjects of the king in England.[68]

Events at Bannockburn and their aftermath can be linked to the reshaping of the English-speaking nobility in the British Isles. This reshaping was directly connected to the outbreak and course of the Scottish wars. These wars were, from one perspective, a conflict between different parts of the Anglo-French aristocracy which had dominated most of the isles for over two centuries. Their outcome was the fragmentation of patterns of alliance and landholding which had previously spanned the various realms. Bannockburn was an important point in this process, not merely because of the security it gave Robert Bruce as king of Scots but also because of its sequel. In November 1314 Bruce issued the statute of Cambuskenneth. This act was the political verdict of Bannockburn. It fulfilled the ultimatum probably issued in October 1313 to all Scottish landowners who had not recognised Bruce as king.[69] Those who still refused to do homage to Robert for their Scottish lands now lost all rights to those lands. Bruce was exploiting the victory on the field to mark an end to the divided allegiances of the preceding decade, but his action had a wider significance. The unchallenged hold of Robert on Scotland and the continued refusal of Edward II to recognise his rights as king there created a lasting separation between the elites of England and Scotland. Those who refused to pay fealty to Bruce lost their Scottish lands. Those who recognised him were seen as traitors by King Edward and lost any fiefs they held in the Plantagenet dominions. These circumstances marked a new and, as it would prove, lasting block on patterns of dual loyalty which had been a normal and accepted part of landholding in the British Isles. In the thirteenth century, many earls, barons, knights and lesser men held lands in both England and Scotland, serving the kings of both realms.[70]

Such shared allegiances were unproblematic in a time of peace, but when war broke out in 1296 they rapidly became an issue. Scottish lords who opposed Edward I and his heirs were deprived of their lands in his territories, while they were restored, individually or collectively, when they submitted. The statute of Cambuskenneth, in practice, demanded that Scottish landowners accept that any lands in the Plantagenet dominions could only be recovered as part of a settlement in which Bruce claims to kingship were recognised by the English crown. Though it did not mark the final end of these shifts, the act proved to be the lasting model for Anglo-Scottish land-holding. The lords and families who lost their Scottish lands and claims in 1314 did not accept their losses quietly. Men like Henry Beaumont, David Strathbogie earl of Atholl and Robert Umfraville earl of Angus formed a powerful pressure group in England.[71] The peace agreed with King Robert in 1328 was supposed to see the restoration of the disinherited on both sides. However, Bruce was not prepared to see such committed enemies of his dynasty become leading landowners in Scotland and no major restoration of land occurred during the brief years of peace.[72] The importance of the disinherited in Anglo-Scottish relations can hardly be exaggerated. It was the claimants to Scottish lands and titles, led by Beaumont, Strathbogie and the disinherited royal candidate Edward Balliol, who were responsible for the renewal of war in 1332. The Bruce party's hard-won victory in this war served to confirm the exclusion of the disinherited and the separation of the elites of the two realms.[73]

These separate structures of land and loyalty in Scotland and the Plantagenet dominions produced a hard political frontier instead of the permeable boundary which had existed between the royal lordships in the thirteenth century. Though natural in a modern context, in the Middle Ages such demands for the exclusive allegiance of subjects were unusual. Though aristocratic interests were most directly involved in these questions of conflicting loyalties, the implications of separation extended throughout Scottish and English societies, shaping identities and activities. In the borderland, where the rival realms touched, the hardening of allegiances cut through links of family, trade and landholding.[74] In the Scottish kingdom as a whole, the statute of Cambuskenneth marked a significant stage in the consolidation of a political society which was politically independent and structurally distinct from the Plantagenet dominions and ideologically opposed to the English king's lordship. This was the most striking product of an era of shifting political identities and practices in the northern and western British Isles. The role of Bannockburn in these changes was not negligible. In initiating a period of security for Scotland under Bruce, a period of unparalleled internal warfare in northern England and escalating conflicts within Ireland, Bannockburn contributed to the alteration of the political and ideological map of the isles. As a symbol of Scotland's status as a fully sovereign and separate realm and community and of the limits to the power of the

English crown, Bannockburn captures an era of conflict and competing national identities.

NOTES

1. *R.R.S.*, v, no. 232.
2. Duby, *Legend of Bouvines*; Carpenter, *Battles of Lewes and Evesham.*
3. Verbruggen, *The battle of the Golden Spurs*, 240–50.
4. Watson, *Under the Hammer*, 67–70.
5. Nicholson, *Edward III and the Scots* (Oxford, 1966), 75–173.
6. Rogers, *War, Cruel and Sharp*, 415–22; J. Sumption, *The Hundred Years War: Trial by Fire* (London, 1999), 195–585.
7. Nicholson, *Edward III and the Scots*, 42–56, 105–12.
8. Nicholson, *Edward III and the Scots*, 15–56.
9. Powicke, 'Edward II and Military Obligation', 101–17. Some efforts were made to improve the equipment of English foot and to provide for light horsemen or hobelars (ibid., 102–4).
10. T. F. Tout, 'The tactics of Boroughbridge and Morlaix', *E.H.R.*, 19 (1904), 711–15; DeVries, *Infantry Warfare*, 86–99; A. Ayton, *Knights and Warhorses: Military Service and the English Aristocracy under Edward III* (Woodbridge, 1994), 9–19.
11. Powicke, 'Military Obligation', 101–17.
12. *The Bruce*, ed. Duncan, 517. Barbour's words are echoed by *Gesta Annalia* (*Chron. Fordun*, ii, 340).
13. *The Bruce*, ed. Duncan, 599–613, 678; Stevenson, *Illustrations of Scottish History*, 3; *Scalachronica*, ed. King, 77; *Chron. Lanercost*, 238–9.
14. For the profitability of these attacks to the Scots and their cost to the northern English communities, see McNamee, *Wars of the Bruces*, 74–115; J. Scammell, 'Robert I and the North of England' *E.H.R.*, 73 (1958), 385–403.
15. *E.R.*, i, 59–83, 173–4; Barrow, *Robert Bruce*, 302.
16. *A.P.S.*, i, 475–6; *E.R.*, i, 102–11.
17. *Chron. Lanercost*, 210; *Scotichronicon*, ed. Watt, vi, 352–5; *Vita Edwardi*, 95.
18. Duby, *Legend of Bouvines*, 141–2; S. Guimares de Andrade, *Batalha Monastery* (Lisbon, 1999).
19. *Scotichronicon*, ed. Watt, vi, 412–14, 485–6; *R.R.S.*, v, no. 500.
20. *Chron. Lanercost*, 211; *The Bruce*, ed. Bruce, 517.
21. *Scotichronicon*, ed. Watt, vi, 385; Boardman, *The Early Stewart Kings: Robert II and Robert III* (East Linton, 1996), 3–4.
22. *Scotichronicon*, ed. Watt, vii, 12–15; M. Penman, *David II* (East Linton, 2004), 7, 19, 27.
23. *R.R.S.*, v, no. 44.
24. In 1315 David Brechin's daughter and heiress was married to David Barclay. The match may have united a very reluctant supporter of the king with an early adherent, but it could have been an alliance promoted by Robert to benefit his cause and perhaps resented by Brechin (NAS, GD45/16/3038).
25. *R.R.S.*, v, no. 72.
26. Penman, 'Soules Conspiracy', 54–7.
27. *C.D.S.*, iii, no. 830; *R.M.S.*, i, nos 141, 247; appendix 2, no. 356; M. H. Brown, '*Scoti Anglicati*: Scots in Plantagenet Allegiance during the Fourteenth Century', in King and Penman, *England and Scotland in the Fourteenth Century*, forthcoming.
28. *R.R.S.*, v, nos 391–2; Barrow, *Robert Bruce*, 196, 277, 280–2, 284; Brown, *Black Douglases*, 24–5.

29. *E.R.*, i, 139, 311.
30. Barrow, *Robert* Bruce, 258; Penman, *David II*, 37–75.
31. For the opening stages of this war, see R. Nicholson, *Edward III and the Scots*, 75–138; Penman, *David II*, 37–53.
32. Wyntoun, *Chronicle*, vi, 39; Penman, *David II*, 54–75; Brown, *Wars of Scotland*, 239–42.
33. Frame, 'Bruces in Ireland', 88–9; Frame, *English Lordship in Ireland*, 132–7.
34. *Scotichronicon*, ed. Watt, vi, 384–403; J. R. S. Phillips, 'The Irish Remonstrance of 1317: an international perspective', *I.H.S.*, 27 (1990), 86–99; Lydon, *Lordship of Ireland*, 118–19.
35. Frame, 'Bruces in Ireland', 83–4, 86–8; Otway-Ruthven, *Medieval Ireland*, 226–7.
36. B. Smith, *Colonisation and Conquest*, 105–11; Frame, *English Lordship in Ireland*, 132–5.
37. Frame, 'Bruces in Ireland', 91–7; R. Frame, 'The Campaign against the Scots in Munster, 1317', in Frame, *Ireland and Britain*, 99–112.
38. *Annals of Connacht*, 244–7; Otway-Ruthven, *Medieval Ireland*, 227.
39. Frame, *English Lordship in Ireland*, 133–5, 137; R. Frame, 'Power and Society in the Lordship of Ireland, 1272–1377', in Frame, *Ireland and Britain*, 191–220, 195–7.
40. K. Simms, 'Tir Eoghain, The Kingdom of the Great O'Neill', in C. Dillon and H. A. Jeffries (eds), *Tyrone: History and Society* (Dublin, 2000), 27–62; K. Simms, 'Tir Eoghain north of the Mountain', in G. O'Brien and W. Nolan, *Derry and Londonderry: History and Society* (Dublin, 1999), 149–74.
41. Frame, *English Lordship in Ireland*, 144–6, 222–3.
42. Frame, 'Power and Society', 197–8, 205–6.
43. E. O'Byrne, *War, Politics and the Irish of Leinster* (Dublin, 2003), 67–9, 83–6.
44. K. Simms, 'The battle of Dysert O'Dea and the Gaelic Resurgence in Thomond', in *Dal gCais*, v (1979), 59–66.
45. McNamee, *Wars of the Bruces*, 72–115; Scammell, 'Robert I and the North of England'.
46. McNamee, *Wars of the Bruces*, 139–40.
47. King, 'Military service and obligation'; McNamee, *Wars of the Bruces*, 123–8.
48. Prestwich, 'Gilbert Middleton'.
49. *Chron. Lanercost*, 230; *Vita Edwardi*, 204–5.
50. Fryde, *Tyranny and Fall*, 156–8.
51. *Chron. Lanercost*, 242; McNamee, *Wars of the Bruces*, 104–5.
52. *Chron. Lanercost*, 212, 220.
53. Scammell, 'Robert I and the North of England', 390–1; J. A. Tuck, 'War and society in the Medieval North', *Northern History*, 21 (1985), 33–52, 36–7; R. Lomas, *North-East England in the Middle Ages* (Edinburgh, 1992), 54–65; McNamee, *Wars of the Bruces*, 72–122.
54. King, 'Military service and obligation', 21–4, 31.
55. King, 'War and disorder', 117, 120–3.
56. M. Brown, 'War, Allegiance and Community in the Anglo-Scottish Marches: Teviotdale in the Fourteenth Century', *Northern History*, 41 (2004), 219–38; M. Brown, 'Development of Scottish Border Lordship, 1332–58', *Historical Research*, 70 (1997), 1–22.
57. *Vita Edwardi*, 98–9; Knighton, i, 410; *Chron. Melsa*, ii, 331–2.
58. Maddicott, *Thomas of Lancaster*, 160–213.
59. Fryde, *Tyranny and Fall*, 158–9.
60. Fryde, *Tyranny and Fall*, 149–206.
61. *Annals of Connacht*, 229–31; *Chart. St Mary's Dublin*, ii, 344; *Brut y Tywysogion*, 123; *Vita Edwardi*, 90–3.

62. Altschul, *The Clares*, 165–71.
63. Griffiths, 'The Revolt of Llywelyn Bren, 1316', 84–91; Smith, 'Llywelyn Bren', 72–86; R. R. Davies, *The Revolt of Owain Glyn Dŵr* (Oxford, 1995), 65–93.
64. Davies, *Lordship and Society*, 279–80; Davies, 'The Despenser war', 25–48.
65. Altschul, *The Clares*, 165–74
66. Frame, *English Lordship*, 52, 62–5.
67. C. A. Empey, 'The Butler Lordship', *Journal of the Butler Society*, i (1970–1), 174–87.
68. Frame, 'Power and Society', 198–205; Frame, *English Lordship in Ireland*, 13–16, 52–74.
69. *R.R.S.*, v, no. 44.
70. K. Stringer, 'Identities in Thirteenth-Century England: Frontier Society in the Far North', in C. Bjorn, A. Grant and K. Stringer, *Social and Political Identities in Western History* (Copenhagen, 1994), 28–66; K. Stringer, 'Scottish Foundations: Thirteenth-Century Perspectives', in A. Grant and K. Stringer (eds), *Uniting the Kingdom? The Making of British History* (London, 1995), 85–96.
71. A. Ross, 'Men for all Seasons? The Strathbogie Earls of Atholl and the Wars of Independence, c.1290–1335, 2'; Nicholson, *Edward III and the Scots*, 64–78.
72. A. Ross and S. Cameron, 'The Treaty of Edinburgh and the Disinherited (1328–1332)', *History*, 84 (1999), 237–56.
73. Brown, 'Scoti Anglicati', forthcoming.
74. R. Frame, 'Overlordship and Reaction, c.1200–c.1450', in Grant and Stringer *Uniting the Kingdom?*, 65–84; A. Grant, 'Scottish Foundations: Late Medieval Contributions', 97–110.

Bibliography

PRIMARY SOURCES

1) Chronicles and narrative sources

The Acts of the Parliaments of Scotland, ed. T. Thomson and C. Innes, 12 vols (Edinburgh, 1814–75).

The Anonimalle Chronicle 1307 to 1334 , ed. W. Childs and J. R. Taylor (Leeds, 1991).

Annales Gandenses, ed. H. Johnstone (Oxford, 1951).

'Annales Londoniensis', in *Chronicles of the Reigns of Edward I and Edward II*. ed. W. Stubbs, 2 vols (Rolls series, 1882–3).

The Annals of Connacht, ed. A. M. Freeman (Dublin, 1944).

Barbour's Bruce, ed. M. P. McDiarmid and J. A. C. Stevenson, 3 vols (Scottish Texts Society, 1980–4).

Barbour, John, *The Bruce*, ed. A. A. M. Duncan (Edinburgh, 1997).

Bower, Walter, *Scotichronicon*, ed. D. E. R. Watt, 9 vols (Aberdeen, 1987–98).

Brut y Tywysogyon or the Chronicle of the Princes. Peniarth MS 20 version, ed. and trans. T. Jones (Cardiff, 1952).

Chartularies of St Mary's Abbey, Dublin and the Annals of Ireland, 1162–1370, ed. J. T. Gilbert, 2 vols (Rolls series, 1884–6).

Chronicle of the Kings of Mann and the Isles, ed. G. Broderick and B. Stowell (Edinburgh, 1973).

The Chronicle of Lanercost, trans. H. Maxwell (Edinburgh, 1913).

Chronica Monasterii de Melsa, ed. E. A. Bond, 2 vols (Rolls series, 1866–7).

The Chronicle of Walter of Guisborough, ed. H. T. Rothwell, Camden Society (London, 1957).

Chronicles of the Reigns of Edward I and Edward II, ed. W. Stubbs, 2 vols (Rolls Series, 1882–3).

Chronicon de Lanercost, ed. J. Stevenson (Edinburgh, 1839).

Fordun, John de, Chronica Gentis Scottorum, *ed. W. F. Skene, 2 vols (Edinburgh, 1871–2).*

Flores Historiarum, ed. H. Luard, 3 vols (Rolls series, 1890).

Les Grandes Chroniques de France, ed. J. Viard (Société de l'histoire de France, 1935).

Illustrations of Scottish History, ed. J. Stevenson (Glasgow, 1834).

Paris, Geoffroy de, *Chronique Rimée*, ed. N. de Wailly and L. Delisle (Receuil des historiens de la Gaule et de la France).

Scalachronica, ed. A. King, Surtees Society (Woodbridge, 2005).

Thomas Wright's Political Songs of England, ed. P. Coss (Cambridge, 1996).

Johannes de Trokelowe and Henrici de Blandeford, Chronica et Annales, ed. H. T. Riley (Rolls series, 1866).

Vita Edwardi Secundi, ed. W. Childs (Oxford, 2005).

Wyntoun, Andrew de, *The Original Chronicle*, ed. F. Amours, 6 vols (Scottish Text Society, 1908).

2) Record sources

Calendar of Charter Rolls, vol. iii, *1300–1326* (London, 1908).

Calendar of Close Rolls (London, 1892–1945).

Calendar of Documents Relating to Scotland, 4 vols, ed. J. Bain (1881–8).

Calendar of Documents Relating to Scotland, vol. v, ed. G. G. Simpson and J. D. Galbraith (1988).

Calendar of Papal Letters, ii, *1305–42* (London, 1895).

Calendar of Patent Rolls (London, 1894–1942).

Coupar Angus Charters, 2 vols, Scottish History Society (Edinburgh, 1947).

Documents Relating to the History of Scotland, ed. F. Palgrave (London, 1837).

English Historical Documents, iii, ed. H. T. Rothwell (London, 1975).

Foedera, Conventiones, Litterae et Acta Publica, ed. T. Rymer, revised edition (London, 1816–69).

Historic Manuscripts Commission: Reports of the Commission on Historical Manuscripts (London, 1870–).

National Archives of Scotland, GD45 Dalhousie Muniments.

Facsimiles of the National Manuscripts of Scotland, vol. ii (Edinburgh, 1870).

Regesta Regum Scottorum, vol. v, The Acts of Robert I (Edinburgh, 1988).

Registrum Episcopatus Aberdonensis, 2 vols (Aberdeen, 1845).

Registrum Magni Sigilli Regum Scottorum, ed. J. M. Thompson et al., 11 vols (Edinburgh, 1882–1914).

Rotuli Parliamentorum, 1272–1326 (London, 1767).

Rotuli Scotiae in Turri Londonensis et in Domo Capitulari Westmonasteriensi asservati, ed. D. Macpherson, 2 vols, ed. J. Strachey (London, 1814).

Stevenson, J. (ed.), *Documents illustrative of the History of Scotland*, 2 vols (Edinburgh, 1870).

Stones, E. L. G., *Anglo-Scottish Relations 1174–1328* (Oxford, 1965).

Stones, E. L. G. and Simpson, G. G., *Edward I and the throne of Scotland*, 2 vols (Oxford, 1978).

Secondary works

Altschul, M., *A Baronial Family in England: The Clares* (Baltimore, 1965).

Armstrong, P., *Stirling Bridge and Falkirk* (Oxford, 2001).

Armstrong, P., *Bannockburn 1314* (Oxford, 2002).

Ayton, A., *Knights and Warhorses: Military Service and the English Aristocracy under Edward III* (Woodbridge, 1994).

Barnes P. and Barrow, G. W. S. 'The movements of Robert Bruce between September 1307 and May 1308', *S.H.R.*, 69 (1970), 46–59.

Barr, N., *Flodden* (Stroud, 2001).

Barron, E., *The Scottish Wars of Independence* (reprinted New York, 1998).

Barrow, G. W. S. 'The Scottish Clergy in the Wars of Independence', *S.H.R.*, 41 (1962), 1–22.

Barrow, G. W. S., 'Lothian in the War of Independence', *S. H.R.*, 55 (1976), 151–71.

Barrow, G. W. S., 'The army of Alexander III's Scotland', in N. Reid, *Scotland in the Reign of Alexander III, 1249–86* (Edinburgh, 1986), 132–47.

Barrow, G. W. S., *Robert Bruce and the Community of the Realm of Scotland* (Edinburgh, 1988).

Barrow, G. W. S., *The Declaration of Arbroath: History, Significance, Setting* (Edinburgh, 2003).

Bean, J. M. W., 'The Percies' Acquisition of Alnwick', *Archaeologia Aeliana*, 4th series, 32 (1954), 309–19.

Bean, J. M. W., 'The Percies and their estates in Scotland', *Archaeologia Aeliana*, 4th series, 35 (1957), 91–9.

Boardman, S., *The Early Stewart Kings: Robert II and Robert III* (East Linton, 1996).

Brown, M., 'The Development of Scottish Border Lordship, 1332–58', *Historical Research*, 70 (1997), 1–22.

Brown, M., *The Black Douglases* (East Linton, 1998).

Brown, M., *The Wars of Scotland, 1214–1371* (Edinburgh, 2004).

Brown, M., 'War, Allegiance and Community in the Anglo-Scottish Marches: Teviotdale in the Fourteenth Century', *Northern History*, 41 (2004), 219–38.

Brown, M., '*Scoti Anglicati*: Scots in Plantagenet Allegiance during the Fourteenth Century', in A. King and M. Penman (eds), *England and Scotland in the Fourteenth Century*, 94–115.

Brown, R. A., Colvin, H. M. and Taylor, A. J., *The History of the King's Works*, vol. 1, The Middle Ages (London, 1963).

Cameron, S., 'Keeping the Customer Satisfied: Barbour's *Bruce* and a Phantom Division at Bannockburn', in E. J. Cowan and D. Gifford (eds), *The Polar Twins* (Edinburgh, 1999), 61–74.

Carpenter, D., *The Battles of Lewes and Evesham* (Keele, 1987).

Carr, A. D., 'An aristocracy in decline: The native Welsh lords after the Edwardian Conquest', *W.H.R.*, v (1970), 103–29.

Christison, P., *Bannockburn: A Soldier's Appreciation of the Battle* (Edinburgh, 1960).

Connolly, S. J. (ed.), *The Oxford Companion to Irish History* (Oxford, 1998).

Costa Gomes, R., *The Making of a Court Society: Kings and Nobles in Late Medieval Portugal* (Cambridge, 2003).

Coutts, A., 'The Knights Templars in Scotland', *Records of the Scottish Church History Society*, 7 (1938), 126–40.

Cowan, E., *For Freedom Alone: The Declaration of Arbroath, 1320* (East Linton, 2003).

Curry, A., *The Battle of Agincourt: Sources and Interpretations* (Woodbridge, 2000).

Duby, G., *The Legend of Bouvines*, trans. C. Tihanyi (Berkeley, 1990), 141–66.

Duncan, A. A. M., *The Nation of Scots and the Declaration of Arbroath* (London, 1970).

Duncan, A. A. M., *Scotland: The Making of the Kingdom* (Edinburgh, 1975).

Duncan, A. A. M., 'The War of the Scots, 1306–1323', *Transactions of the Royal Historical Society*, 6th series, ii (1992), 125–51.

Duncan, A. A. M., 'The Declarations of the Clergy', in G. Barrow, *The Declaration of Arbroath: History, Significance, Setting* (Edinburgh, 2003), 32–49.

Davies, J. C., 'The Despenser war in Glamorgan', *T.R.H.S.*, 3rd ser. 9 (1915), 21–64.

Davies, J., *The Baronial Opposition to Edward II* (London, 1918).

Davies, R. R., *Lordship and Society in the March of Wales, 1282–1400* (Oxford, 1978).

Davies, R. R., *The Age of Conquest, 1063–1415* (Oxford, 1987).

Davies, R. R., *Domination and Conquest: The Experience of Ireland, Scotland and Wales, 1100–1300* (Cambridge, 1990).

Davies, R. R., *The First English Empire: Power and Identities in the British Isles, 1093–1343* (Oxford, 2000).

DeVries, K., *Infantry Warfare in the early Fourteenth Century* (Woodbridge, 1996).

Duffy, S., 'The Bruce Brothers and the Irish Sea World, 1306–29', *Cambridge Medieval Celtic Studies*, no. 21 (1991), 55–86.

Duffy, S. (ed.), *Robert the Bruce's Irish Wars: The Invasions of Ireland, 1306–29* (Stroud, 2003).

Edwards, G., 'Sir Gruffydd Llwyd', *E.H.R.*, 30 (1915), 589–601.

Edwards, J., 'The Templars in Scotland in the Thirteenth Century', *S.H.R.*, 5 (1908), 13–25.

Empey, C. A., 'The Butler Lordship', *Journal of the Butler Society*, i (1970–1), 174–87.

Frame, R., 'Power and Society in the Lordship of Ireland, 1272–1377', *Past and Present*, 76 (1977), 3–33.

Frame, R., *English Lordship in Ireland, 1318–61* (Oxford, 1982).

Frame, R., *The Political Development of the British Isles, 1100–1400* (Oxford, 1990).

Frame, R., 'Overlordship and Reaction, c.1200–c.1450', in Grant and Stringer, *Uniting the Kingdom?*, 65–84.

Frame, R., 'The Defence of the English Lordship, 1250–1450', in T. Bartlett and K. Jeffery (eds), *A Military History of Ireland* (Cambridge, 1996), 76–98.

Frame, R., *Ireland and Britain* (London, 1998).

Frame, R., 'The Campaign against the Scots in Munster, 1317', in Frame, *Ireland and Britain*, 99–112.

Frame, R., 'The Bruces in Ireland, 1315–8', in Frame, *Ireland and Britain*, 71–98.

Frame, R., 'Power and Society in the Lordship of Ireland, 1272–1377', in Frame, *Ireland and Britain*, 191–220.

Fryde, N., 'Welsh troops in the Scottish Campaign of 1322', *B.B.C.S.*, 26 (1974–5), 82–9.

Fryde, N., *The Tyranny and Fall of Edward II* (Cambridge, 1979).

Gillingham, J., 'William the Bastard at War', in C. Harper-Bill, C. Holdsworth and J. Nelson (eds), *Studies in Medieval History presented to R. Allen Brown* (Woodbridge, 1989), 141–58.

Gillingham, J., 'Richard I and the Science of War in the Middle Ages', in J. Gillingham and J. C. Holt (eds), *War and Government in the Middle Ages* (Woodbridge, 1984), 78–91.

Goodman, A., *The Wars of the Roses: Military Activity and English Society, 1452–97* (London, 1981).

Gransden, A., *Historical Writing in England, ii, c.1307 to the Early Sixteenth Century* (London, 1982).

Grant, A., 'Aspects of national consciousness in medieval Scotland', in C. Bjorn, A. Grant and K. Stringer (eds), *Nations, Nationalism and Patriotism in the European Past* (Copenhagen, 1994), 68–95.

Grant, A. and Stringer, K. (eds), *Uniting the Kingdom? The Making of British History* (London, 1995).

Grant, A., 'Scottish Foundations: Late Medieval Contributions', in Grant and Stringer, *Uniting the Kingdom?*, 97–110.

Griffiths, R. A., *The Principality of Wales in the Later Middle Ages: The Structure and Personnel of Government: South Wales, 1277–1536* (Cardiff, 1972).

Griffiths, R. A., 'The Revolt of Llywelyn Bren, 1316', in R. A. Griffiths, *Conquerors and Conquered in Medieval Wales* (Stroud, 2004), 84–91.

Guimares de Andrade, S., *Batalha Monastery* (Lisbon, 1999).

Hamilton, J. S., *Piers Gaveston Earl of Cornwall 1307–1312* (Detroit, 1988).

Haines, R. M., *King Edward II: Edward of Caernarfon, his life, his reign, and its aftermath, 1284–1330* (Montreal, 2003).

Harriss, G. L., *King, Parliament and Public Finance in Medieval England to 1369* (Oxford, 1975).

Haskell, M., 'Breaking the Stalemate: The Scottish Campaign of Edward I, 1303–4', in *Thirteenth Century England*, vii, eds M. Prestwich, R. Britnell and R. Frame (Woodbridge, 1999), 223–42.

Keegan, J., *The Face of Battle* (London, 1976).

Kershaw, I., 'The Scots in the West Riding, 1318–9', *Northern History*, 17 (1981), 231–9.

King, A., 'Lordship, Castles and Locality: Thomas of Lancaster, Dunstanburgh Castle and the Lancastrian Affinity in Northumberland, 1296–1322', *Archaeologia Aeliana*, 29 (2001), 223–34.

King, A., 'Jack le Irish and the abduction of Lady Clifford, November 1315: The heiress and the Irishman', *Northern History*, 38 (2001), 187–95.

King, A., ' "Pur salvation du roiaume": Military Service and obligation in fourteenth-century Northumberland', in *Fourteenth-Century England II*, ed. C. Given-Wilson (Woodbridge, 2002), 13–31.

King, A., '*Schavaldours*, Robbers and Bandits: war and disorder in Northumberland in the reign of Edward II', in M. Prestwich et al. (eds), *Thirteenth Century England*, ix (Woodbridge, 2003), 115–29.

King, A. and Penman, M. (eds), *Anglo-Scottish Relations 1296–1420* (Woodbridge, 2007).

Layfield, S., 'The Pope, Scots, and their "self-styled" King: John XXII's Anglo-Scottish Policy, 1316–1334', in King and Penman, *Anglo-Scottish Relations*, 157–71.

Little, A. G., 'The Authorship of the Lanercost Chronicle', *E.H.R.*, 31 (1916), 269–79.

Lomas, R., *North-East England in the Middle Ages* (Edinburgh, 1992).

Lomax, D. W., *The Reconquest of Spain* (London, 1978).

Lucas, H. S., 'The Great European Famine of 1315, 1316 and 1317', *Speculum*, v (1930), 343–77.

Lydon, J., 'An Irish Army in Scotland, 1296', *Irish Sword*, v (1961–2), 184–9.

Lydon, J., 'Irish Levies in the Scottish Wars, 1296–1302', *Irish Sword*, v (1963), 207–17.

Lydon, J., 'Edward II and the revenues of Ireland in 1311–12', *I.H.S.*, 14 (1964), 39–57.

Lydon, J., *The Lordship of Ireland in the Middle Ages* (Dublin, 1972).

Lydon, J., 'Edward I, Ireland and the War in Scotland, 1303–4', in J. Lydon (ed.), *England and Ireland in the Later Middle Ages* (Dublin, 1981), 43–59.

Lydon, J., 'Ireland and the English Crown', *I.H.S.*, 29 (1995), 281–94.

Lydon, J. (ed.), *Law and Disorder in Thirteenth-century Ireland* (Dublin, 1997).

Lydon, J., 'The Scottish soldier abroad: the Bruce invasion and the Galloglass', in S. Duffy (ed.), *Robert the Bruce's Irish Wars* (Stroud, 2002), 89–106.

MacDonald, A. J., *Border Bloodshed, Scotland, England and France at War* (East Linton, 2000).

MacDonald, A. J. 'Kings of the wild frontier? The earls of Dunbar and March, c.1070–1435', in S. Boardman and A. Ross, *The Exercise of Power in Medieval Scotland c.1200–1500* (Dublin, 2003).

McDonald, A., *The Kingdom of the Isles: Scotland's Western Seaboard, 1100–1336* (East Linton, 1997).

Macdougall, N., *James IV* (Edinburgh, 1989).

McFarlane, K. B., *The Nobility of Later Medieval England* (Oxford, 1973).

Mackenzie, G., *The Lives and Characters of the most eminent Writers of the Scottish Nation* (Edinburgh, 1708–22).

Mackenzie, W. M., *The Battle of Bannockburn* (Glasgow, 1913).

McKerral, A., 'West Highland mercenaries in Ireland', *S.H.R.*, 30 (1951), 1–29.

McNamee, C., *The Wars of the Bruces: Scotland, England and Ireland 1306–28* (East Linton, 1997).

Maddicott, J. R., *Thomas of Lancaster* (Oxford, 1970).

Malcolm, N., *Kosovo: A short history* (London, 1998).

Matthew, H. C. G. and Harrison, B. (eds), *The New Oxford Dictionary of National Biography* (Oxford, 2004).

Miller, T., *The Site of the Battle of Bannockburn* (London, 1931).

Morillo, S., 'Battle Seeking: The Contexts and Limits of Vegetian Strategy', in B. Bachrach (ed.), *Journal of Medieval Military History*, 1, 21–42.

Morris, J. E., *The Welsh Wars of Edward I* (Oxford, 1901).

Morris, J. E., *Bannockburn* (Cambridge, 1914).

Nicholls, K., *Gaelic and Gaelicised Ireland in the middle ages* (Dublin, 1972).

Nicholson, R., 'A sequel to Edward Bruce's invasion of Ireland', *S.H.R.*, 42 (1963), 30–40.

Nicholson, R., *Edward III and the Scots* (Oxford, 1966).

Nusbacher, A., *The Battle of Bannockburn, 1314* (Stroud, 2000).

O'Byrne, E., *War, Politics and the Irish of Leinster* (Dublin, 2003).

Oman, C., *A History of the Art of War in the Middle Ages*, 2 vols (London, 1928).

Otway-Ruthven, J., *A History of Medieval Ireland*, 2nd edn (New York, 1992).

Penman, M., 'A fell coniuration agayn Robert the douchty king: the Soules Conspiracy of 1318–20', in *Innes Review*, 50 (1999), 25–57.

Penman, *David II* (East Linton, 2004).

Phillips, G., *The Anglo-Scottish Wars, 1513–1550* (Woodbridge, 1999).

Phillips, J. R. S., *Aymer de Valence earl of Pembroke* (Oxford, 1972).

Phillips, J. R. S., 'The Irish Remonstrance of 1317: an international perspective', *I.H.S.*, 27 (1990), 86–99.

Powicke, M., 'Edward II and Military Obligation', *Speculum*, xxxi (1956), 556–62.

Powicke, M., *Military Obligation in Medieval England* (Oxford, 1962).

Prestwich, M., 'Victualling estimates for English garrisons in Scotland during the early fourteenth century', *E.H.R.*, 82 (1967), 536–43.

Prestwich, M., 'Isabella de Vescy and the Custody of Bamburgh Castle', *Bulletin of the Institute of Historical Research*, 44 (1971), 148–52.

Prestwich, M., *War, Politics and Finance under Edward I* (Oxford, 1972).

Prestwich, M., 'Cavalry Service in Early Fourteenth Century England', in J. Gillingham and J. Holt (eds), *War and Government in the Middle Ages* (Woodbridge, 1984), 147–58.

Prestwich, M., 'Colonial Scotland: the English in Scotland under Edward I', in R. Mason (ed.), *Scotland and England 1286–1815* (Edinburgh, 1987).

Prestwich, M., *Edward I* (London, 1988).

Prestwich, M., 'The Ordinances of 1311 and the Politics of the Early Fourteenth Century', in J. Taylor and W. Childs (eds), *Politics and Crisis in Fourteenth Century England* (Gloucester, 1990).

Prestwich, M., 'Gilbert Middleton and the attack on the Cardinals, 1317', in T. Reuter (ed.), *Warriors and Churchmen in the High Middle Ages* (London, 1992), 179–94.

Prestwich, M., 'Military Logistics: The case of 1322', in M. Strickland (ed.), *Armies, Chivalry and Warfare in Medieval Britain and France* (Stamford, 1998), 276–88.

Prestwich, M., *Plantagenet England, 1225–1360* (Oxford, 2005).

Reese, P., *Bannockburn* (Edinburgh, 2000).

Reid, W. S., 'Trade, Traders and Scottish Independence', *Speculum*, 29 (1954), 210–22.

Rogers, C. J., *War, Cruel and Sharp: English Strategy under Edward III, 1327–1360* (Woodbridge, 2000).

Rogers, C. J., 'The Vegetian Science of Warfare in the Middle Ages', in *Journal of Medieval Military History*, 1, 1–20.

Ross, A., 'Men for all Seasons? The Strathbogie Earls of Atholl and the Wars of Independence, c.1290–1335, 1', *Northern Scotland*, 20 (2000), 1–30.

Ross, A., 'Men for all seasons? The Strathbogie Earls of Atholl and the Wars of Independence, c.1290–1335, 2', *Northern Scotland*, 21 (2001), 1–15.

Ross, A. and Cameron, S., 'The Treaty of Edinburgh and the Disinherited (1328–1332)', *History*, 84 (1999), 237–56.

Sayles, G. O., 'The siege of Carrickfergus Castle, 1315–6', *I.H.S.*, x (1956–7), 94–100.

Scammell, J., 'Robert I and the North of England, *E.H.R.*, 73 (1958), 385–403.

Schwyzer, H., 'Northern Bishops and the Anglo-Scottish War in the Reign of Edward II', in. M. Prestwich, R. Britnell and R. Frame (eds), *Thirteenth Century England*, vii (Woodbridge, 1999), 243–54.

Scott, W. W. C. *Bannockburn Revealed* (Rothesay, 2000).

Seymour, W., *Battles in Britain*, 2 vols (London, 1975) .

Simms, K., 'The battle of Dysert O'Dea and the Gaelic Resurgence in Thomond', in *Dal gCais*, v (1979), 59–66.

Simms, K., *From Kings to Warlords: the changing political structure of Gaelic Ireland in the later Middle Ages* (Woodbridge, 1987).

Simms, K., 'Tir Eoghain north of the Mountain', in G. O'Brien and W. Nolan, *Derry and Londonderry: History and Society* (Dublin, 1999).

Simms, K., 'Tir Eoghain, The Kingdom of the Great O'Neill', in C. Dillon and H. A. Jeffries (eds), *Tyrone: History and Society* (Dublin, 2000), 27–62.

Simpkin, D., 'The English Army and the Scottish Campaign of 1310–1', in King and Penman, *Anglo-Scottish Relations*, 14–39.

Simpson, G., 'The declaration of Arbroath revitalised', *S.H.R.*, 56 (1977), 11–33.

Smail, R. C., *Crusading Warfare 1097–1193* (Cambridge, 1965).

Smith, B., *Colonisation and Conquest in Medieval Ireland: The English in Louth* (Cambridge, 1999).

Smith, J. B., 'The Middle March in the Thirteenth Century', *B.B.C.S.*, 24 (1970–2), 77–93.

Smith, J. B., 'The Rebellion of Llywelyn Bren', *Glamorgan County History*, iii, ed. T. B. Pugh (Cardiff, 1971).

Smith, J. B., 'Gruffydd Llwyd and the Celtic Alliance', *B.B.C.S.*, 26 (1976), 463–78.

Smith, J. B., 'Edward II and the allegiance of Wales', *W.H.R.*, 8 (1976–7), 139–71.

Smith, L. B., 'The Governance of Edwardian Wales', in T. Herbert and G. E. Jones, *Edward I and Wales* (Cardiff, 1988), 73–96.

Stevenson, A., 'The Flemish Dimension of the Auld Alliance', in G. Simpson (ed.), *Scotland and the Low Countries 1124–1994* (Aberdeen, 1996), 28–42.

Strayer, J. R., *Medieval Statecraft and the Perspectives of History* (Princeton, 1970).

Stringer, K., 'Identities in Thirteenth-Century England: Frontier Society in the Far North', in C. Bjorn, A. Grant and K. Stringer, *Social and Political Identities in Western History* (Copenhagen, 1994), 28–66.

Stringer, K., 'Scottish Foundations: Thirteenth-Century Perspectives', in Grant and Stringer, *Uniting the Kingdom?*, 85–96.

Summerson, H., *Medieval Carlisle*, 2 vols (Carlisle, 1993).

Sumption, J., *The Hundred Years War: Trial by Fire* (London, 1999).

Tout, T. F., 'The tactics of Boroughbridge and Morlaix', *E.H.R.*, 19 (1904), 711–15.

Tout, T. F., *The Place of the Reign of Edward II in English History* (Manchester, 1936).

Tuck, J. A., 'War and society in the Medieval North', *Northern Histroy*, 21 (1985), 33–52.

Tuck, J. A., 'The Emergence of a Northern Nobility, 1250–1400', *Northern History*, 22 (1986), 1–17.

Underhill, F., *For her good estate: The Life of Elizabeth de Burgh* (London, 1999).

Vale, M., *The Origins of the Hundred Years War: The Angevin Legacy 1250–1340* (Oxford, 1990).

Vathjunker, S., 'A study of the career of Sir James Douglas: the Historical record versus Barbour's *Bruce*' (unpublished Ph D thesis, University of Aberdeen, 1992).

Verbruggen, J. F., *The Battle of the Golden Spurs: Courtrai, 11 July 1302*, ed. K. DeVries (Woodbridge, 2002).

Watson, F., 'Settling the stalemate: Edward I's peace in Scotland, 1303–1305', in M. Prestwich, R. Britnell and R. Frame (eds), *Thirteenth-Century England*, vi (Woodbridge, 1997), 127–43.

Watson, F., *Under the Hammer: Edward I and Scotland, 1286–1307* (East Linton, 1997).

Watt, D. E. R., *A Biographical Dictionary of Scottish Graduates to 1410* (Oxford, 1977).

Webster, B., 'Scotland without a King, 1329–41', in A. Grant and K. Stringer, *Medieval Scotland: Crown, Lordship and Community* (Edinburgh, 1993), 222–38.

Young, A., *Robert the Bruce's Rivals: The Comyns, 1212–1314* (East Linton, 1997).

Index

200

TERMS AND CONDITIONS OF USE